Sexual Harassment as an Ethical Issue in Academic Life

Issues in Academic Ethics
Series Editor: Steven M. Cahn

Campus Rules and Moral Community: In Place of In Loco Parentis
  by David A. Hoekema, Calvin College
University–Business Partnerships: An Assessment
  by Norman E. Bowie, University of Minnesota, Twin Cities
A Professor's Duties: Ethical Issues in College Teaching
  by Peter J. Markie, University of Missouri–Columbia
Neutrality and the Academic Ethic
  by Robert L. Simon, Hamilton College
Ethics of Scientific Research
  by Kristin Shrader-Frechette, University of South Florida
Academic Freedom and Tenure: Ethical Issues
  by Richard T. De George, University of Kansas
Diversity and Community in the Academy: Affirmative Action in Faculty Appointments
  by Celia Wolf-Devine, Stonehill College
The Moral Dimensions of Academic Administration
  by Rudolph H. Weingartner, University of Pittsburgh
Free Speech on Campus
  by Martin P. Golding, Duke University
Sexual Harassment as an Ethical Issue in Academic Life
  by Leslie Pickering Francis, University of Utah

Sexual Harassment as an Ethical Issue in Academic Life

Leslie Pickering Francis

ROWMAN & LITTLEFIELD PUBLISHERS, INC.
Lanham • Boulder • New York • Oxford

ROWMAN & LITTLEFIELD PUBLISHERS, INC.

Published in the United States of America
by Rowman & Littlefield Publishers, Inc.
4720 Boston Way, Lanham, Maryland 20706
http://www.rowmanlittlefield.com

12 Hid's Copse Road
Cumnor Hill, Oxford OX2 9JJ, England

British Library Cataloguing in Publication Information Available

Library of Congress Cataloging-in-Publication Data
Francis, Leslie, 1946–
    Sexual harassment as an ethical issue in academic life / Leslie Pickering Francis.
      p. cm. — (Issues in academic ethics)
    Includes index and bibliographical references.
    ISBN 0-8476-8170-X (cloth : alk. paper) — ISBN 0-8476-8171-8 (pbk. : alk. paper)
    1. Sexual harassment in universities and colleges—Moral and ethical aspects—United
States. I. Title. II. Series.
    LC212.862.F72   2001
    378.1'98—dc21   00-027019

Printed in the United States of America

♾™ The paper used in this publication meets the minimum requirements of American
National Standard for Information Sciences—Permanence of Paper for Printed
Library Materials, ANSI/NISO Z39.48-1992.

to John

Contents

Preface   ix

Acknowledgments   xiii

Part One

1 Sexual Harassment: The Issues   3

2 The Roles of Education, Expression, and Freedom   19

3 Sexual Harassment in the Law   46

4 Sexual Harassment as a Moral Wrong:
Assaults, Threats, and Offers   67

5 The Wrongs of Sexual Harassment:
Seductive Behavior and Gender Harassment   86

6 Consensual Sex on Campus   99

7 Sexual Harassment Policies and Procedures   113

Part Two

8 Sexual Harassment of Working Women:
A Case of Sex Discrimination   129
Catharine A. MacKinnon

9 The Lecherous Professor   146
Billie Dziech and Linda Weiner

10   Sexual Harassment: Offers and Coercion   157
      Nancy Tuana

11   Sexual Harassment as Sex Discrimination:
      A Defective Paradigm   164
      Ellen Frankel Paul

12   A Feminist Definition of Sexual Harassment   175
      Anita M. Superson

13   Sexual Harassment and the University   183
      Robert L. Holmes

14   Feminist Accused of Sexual Harassment   191
      Jane Gallop

15   Reconciling Rapture, Representation, and
      Responsibility: An Argument against
      Per Se Bans on Attorney-Client Sex   209
      Linda Fitts Mischler

16   Exploited Consent   212
      David Archard

17   Illustrative Policies   219

Notes   249

Selected Bibliography   266

Index   273

About the Author   281

Preface

When I was a graduate student twenty-five years ago, sexual harassment didn't have a name. Yet conduct that makes women—and sometimes men—uncomfortable because of their sex and their sexuality was all around us then and is all around us now. The difference is that sexual harassment now has a name, thanks in no small part to Catharine MacKinnon's pathbreaking *The Sexual Harassment of Working Women,* from which a selection is reprinted in part II of this volume. With a name, we suddenly see sexual harassment everywhere: the label "sexual harassment" has been applied to many quite common forms of conduct in university settings: sexual banter, debates about politics and sex, and dating and mating. A principal goal of this volume is to encourage moral scrutiny of these common forms of conduct. I begin each chapter with a story; I hope these stories will seem familiar and readers will add similar stories of their own. I also hope these stories will be taken as they are intended: as describing ordinary features of academic life that may, or may not, be desirable—paradigm cases for moral research.

But sometimes "sexual harassment" names too much. An equal goal of the stories and selections in this volume is to question whether each of the varieties of conduct that have been called sexual harassment is morally problematic or is just a part of the give and take of academic life. Jane Gallop, for example, in a selection from *Feminist Accused of Sexual Harassment* reprinted in part II, argues that education is necessarily sexy and sexualized. Sexual content is integral to some, but not all, university courses. Just as it is important to identify and discourage conduct that is morally flawed, so it is important not to chill the dissent and diversity our universities celebrate.

Indeed, the central goal of this volume is to provide balanced accounts of what has been meant by sexual harassment, why and when it is morally problematic, and what should be done about it when it occurs. To further this goal, I begin with an overview of the landscape of sexual harassment as it has been mapped in the literature. Both my own discussions in part I and the selections in part II are aimed to allow the reader to understand and evaluate a wide variety of perspectives on sexual harassment. I also include an account of the legal coordinates within which this mapping has occurred, because the identification, discussion, and treatment of sexual harassment has been driven by the law of both employment and education. In part II, chapter 17, I include several sexual harassment policies that have been developed on campuses in this country, not to single out any particular policy as exemplary but to show a range of responses to harassment that can serve as a basis for discussion.

As an ethical issue in academic life, sexual harassment must be viewed in the context of the aims of the academy. I argue that on liberal views, the academy has two fundamental aims: the development and transmission of knowledge and the expansion of opportunity. Communitarian theory views universities as either preserving the canon or as nurturing a variety of different communities. Radicals may see the university as repressive or as the engine of critique. Depending on which of these aims are judged as paramount, different features of the landscape of sexual harassment will be emphasized. An emphasis on opportunity, for example, will focus on behavior that makes women uncomfortable in the academy and on university actions to prevent and remediate its effects when it occurs. In substantive chapters about the moral permissibility of conduct that has been labeled "sexual harassment," I trace out how these different views about the academy play a role in moral evaluation.

Several moral concerns are implicated in the discussion of sexual harassment. In assessing whether a type of behavior is problematic sexual harassment in the academy, it is critical to consider the extent to which these concerns come into play. Has the behavior failed to respect the victim's choices about his or her sexuality, an especially intimate matter, and thus failed to respect autonomy? Has the behavior wronged the victim's intimates by its failure to respect her (or him)? Has the behavior affected access to education or otherwise denied equality of opportunity? Has the behavior compromised campus community, by engendering fear or by chilling expression? All important, the answers to these questions may differ depending on the aims of the academy and unique features of particular educational settings. In the chapters in part I that are devoted to different types of behavior that may be viewed as harassment—sexual assault, coercion, and bribery; seductive behavior and gender harassment; and consensual sexual relationships—I develop the answers to these questions for a variety of academic settings.

The selections in part II present some of the best and most influential writing about sexual harassment from diverse perspectives. Again, my goal is to enable readers to understand and evaluate different positions about harassment. As I have already mentioned, Catharine MacKinnon's work has been highly influential in publicizing and shaping the understanding of sexual harassment; MacKinnon sees harassment as a form of domination. In the selection from *The Lecherous Professor,* Dziech and Weiner identify conduct that should serve as a warning about professorial sexual harassment, for both colleagues and students. They also discuss the responsibilities of the academy in responding to suspected harassment so that equality of educational opportunity can be achieved.

The selections from Tuana, Frankel Paul, Superson, and Holmes present significant approaches to the understanding and evaluation of sexual harassment. Tuana, a feminist, argues that sexual offers can be coercive and thus be harassment analogous to sexual threats. Frankel Paul, a libertarian, argues that sexual harassment is a wrong only when it damages individual victims and that as a result the appropriate remedy is compensation in tort. Superson, in direct conflict with Frankel Paul, contends that sexual harassment is a wrong against all women and that dealing with cases on an individualized basis will not solve the problems of dominance that harassment poses. Holmes agrees that sexual harassment is a more widespread wrong than is commonly believed, but identifies the wrong as invasion of privacy rather than as repression or loss of opportunity.

Finally, I hope this volume will encourage reflection about the professional obligations of academicians. The brief selection in part II from Linda Fitts Mischler's article on sexual relations between lawyers and their clients is intended to provide a taste of the comparisons that might be drawn to other professions, as is the discussion in chapter 4 of responsibilities for colleagues' conduct. David Archard's analysis of coerced consent raises another aspect of the cross-professional comparison: whether consensual sexual relationships on campus should be analogized to the issues of informed consent in areas such as medicine or law.

Academics tend to view themselves in highly individualistic terms: doing their own research, teaching classes in accord with their own expertise, mentoring their students, and generally being responsible for their own time and their own work. Jane Gallop, whose description of education is reprinted in part II, may exemplify this conception. Such freedom, virtually unprecedented in large employment settings, is critical to the kinds of innovation and exploration that academic settings provide. Its risk, however, is the need to think seriously about co-professional obligations within the academy. Other professionals bear responsibilities for the effects of their conduct on others, for fostering good conduct and discouraging unprofessional conduct by their colleagues, and for the quality of the communities within which they work. Academics should do no less.

Acknowledgments

I am grateful to my colleagues in the Department of Philosophy and the College of Law at the University of Utah for their helpful comments, to the College of Law for financial support from the Excellence in Research and Teaching fund, and to editors at Rowman & Littlefield for their help and their patience.

Part One

1

✛

Sexual Harassment:
The Issues

In the late 1960s, I was about to enter graduate school in philosophy at a large midwestern university. The week before the fall semester of my first year, I met another entering student. He asked me out for Saturday night. I found him attractive, so I accepted the invitation. We had a very good time at the movies. At the end of the evening, he said to me, "That was a great deal of fun. I'm sorry we won't be able to do it again."

"Why?" I asked, puzzled.

"Because we'll be fellow students on Monday," he replied.

"What?" I said.

"We'll be colleagues, students together," was the explanation.

His explanation took me aback at first. Then it began to seem utterly reasonable. We became and remained very good friends and colleagues throughout graduate school, although we haven't seen each other for years.

I've thought about this interchange many times since. What my friend said surely was unusual for twenty-five years ago. Was it wise or silly? Was it only the minimally morally decent thing to do? Was it simply a way to ward off an undesired social relationship? Was it a model to be emulated? Was it an act of supererogation? Was it far too scrupulous a decision, one that caused us both to miss out on a good deal of fun or perhaps a deeply meaningful relationship?

In the twenty-five years since this interchange, the discussion of sexual relationships within American colleges and universities has become remarkably contentious and complex. This book explores one aspect of these debates: sexual harassment as an ethical issue in higher education. There is general agreement that forcible sex is wrong, whether within or without the academy. There also is general agreement that sexist behavior can be particularly morally troubling within the academy if it effectively excludes groups of students from full participation in the educational process. But underneath these claims lie deep disagreements: about the role of the university in condoning or condemning sexual harassment, about understandings of sexual harassment, about why harassment is problematic, and even about the extent to which harassment is objectionable.

This introductory chapter has three goals. The first is to introduce the issues involved in conceptualizing sexual harassment by presenting an overview of the kinds of behavior that have been characterized as harassment and the ensuing controversies over these conceptualizations. The second is to present an overview of what is and what is not known about the epidemiology of sexual harassment. The final goal is to outline the structure of the volume. The fundamental claim advanced throughout is that sexual harassment in higher education must be understood in terms of the aims and functions of the academy itself.

CONCEPTUALIZING SEXUAL HARASSMENT

What is sexual harassment, the subject of this book? The term is used typically to express a conclusion or set of conclusions that the behavior at issue is properly judged objectionable on grounds that have something to do with sex. One of these conclusions is legal: that the behavior is sex discrimination, prohibited under state or federal civil rights statutes. Another is moral: that the behavior violates appropriate standards of respect for others when sexual difference or sexual behavior is involved. Still another is social: that the behavior crosses lines of expected conventions of civility in the development of sexual relationships.

Because such a wide variety of behaviors has been described as harassment, it is not helpful to begin a book on the ethical issues raised by harassment in higher education by developing a set of hard and fast criteria of what is or is not harassment. Instead, it is more fruitful to begin with a description of some of the principal kinds of behavior that have been perceived as harassment. In marking out the subject matter of the volume in this way, I do not assume that any of the described behaviors are, in fact, to be condemned. My plan is to open up for discussion whether, to what extent, and why a range of sexual or sexist behavior on campus might be regarded as harassing, and whether any of these concerns are justifiable.

A useful starting place is a list that the National Advisory Council on Women's Educational Programs compiled for its survey of harassment rates reported by college women.[1] The council described sexual harassment generally as "the use of authority to emphasize sexuality or sexual identity of a student in a manner which prevents or impairs that student's enjoyment of educational benefits, climates, and opportunities."[2] Under this rubric, the council identified and named five kinds of behavior as potentially problematic sexual harassment. These categories have been used in several subsequent studies of harassment and represent a fairly standard list. The categories are quite broad and are, in some cases, as the ensuing discussion will show, ill-defined in scope. I use them to outline the concept as it is understood generally in the literature, not to take a position on whether the categories are defined well enough to be the basis for meaningful measurement of the frequency of sexual harassment.

Gender Harassment

The advisory council's first category, "gender harassment," consists of "generalized sexist remarks and behavior." This category has been taken to include both sexual references and materials and sexist remarks and conduct. It also includes both behavior that is targeted to a general audience and behavior that singles out particular people. These are important distinctions and it is helpful to have terminology to mark them out. The inclusion of sexual material I call *sexuality*; behavior that is demeaning or discriminatory based on sex I call *sexism*. Either *sexuality* or *sexism* can be *generalized*; if it is aimed at particular people, it is *targeted*.

Several of the most highly publicized lawsuits alleging sexual harassment have involved generalized sexuality by way of introducing explicitly sexual references or material into the classroom, in allegedly inappropriate settings. For example, a well-known harassment complaint of this type involved a writing instructor at the University of New Hampshire who compared "focus" in writing to sexual intercourse.[3] A similar complaint involved a faculty member at the College of the Albemarle who presented synonyms for sexual slang as examples of paraphrase.[4] A faculty member at the Chicago Theological Seminary was disciplined for using an anecdote from the Talmud to illustrate the biblical account of intentional action. In the anecdote, a man falls off a roof into the arms of a woman and they have intercourse; this allegedly illustrated a nonintentional act.[5]

Whether the use of explicit sexual material in the classroom or in other academic contexts is inappropriate, however, is deeply contested. Significant issues of academic freedom are foremost here. As an example, consider the undergraduate course I teach in philosophy of law. The legal enforcement of morality is a major subject in the course, including whether it is permissible to ban the public exhibition of allegedly offensive material. I have considered the possibility that these discussions would be enhanced if I displayed materials at the center of controversy, such as Robert Mapplethorpe's explicit photography or the 2 Live Crew album *Nasty as They Wanna Be*. It could be helpful for the class to examine these works to assess the difficulties of drawing distinctions between material that is "merely offensive" and material that is "obscene," whether these distinctions are captured by current legal tests for obscenity, or whether these distinctions should matter to the law. Yet students might be offended and, some might argue, harassed by the inclusion of the sexually explicit material. Unimaginative, cowardly, or prudent, I haven't as yet put the issue to the test.

Sexist behavior that is not necessarily sexual also has been included within the category of gender harassment. Typical examples are speech that makes derogatory reference to one sex, such as comments in a criminal law class that women ask for rape or in a surgery rotation that women aren't suited to the pressures of the profession. Other examples are comments about the incapacities of women during menstrual periods, pregnancy, or menopause. Another was, in the eyes of at least one male student, the remark made by a woman teaching assistant in a human sexuality course at the University of Nebraska; while discussing how to put on a condom, she said that the timing was important because, like basketball players, men "dribble before they shoot."[6] Yet another example is a highly controversial memo recently sent over the Internet by four Cornell undergraduates that advanced "75 reasons why women shouldn't have free speech." In another much-publicized example, a history professor at California State University at Chico circulated a satirical memo suggesting that extra office space could be allocated for a water bed that women students could use to improve their grades.[7]

Behavior that makes the educational situation worse for one sex also has been characterized as gender harassment. Examples include recognizing males who volunteer to talk in class in preference to females, being more forthcoming with comments or supplementary materials for members of one sex than for the other, or calling on only female students the day rape is the topic.

Categorizing sexuality together with sexism as gender harassment is controversial, especially for writers who see dominance as a necessary component of sexual harassment. Catharine MacKinnon, for example, distinguishes between sexual and sexist speech. In her view, sexual speech is a sexual act, akin to rape as an act of dominance. Sexist speech, although part of the culture of dominance, is not such an act of immediate violation. In MacKinnon's words, sexist speech "works through its content" and should be treated as a form of defamation.[8] Because she believes that most sexist speech also is sexual, MacKinnon does not regard the category of sexist speech as very significant. An example supportive of this frequent identification of sexual and sexist speech is the Cornell memo, which characterized women in both belittling and sexual ways. Nonetheless, if there is a considerable amount of sexist speech without sexuality, the distinction could loom large. For at least as MacKinnon views it, sexual harassment is a manifestation of the sexual violation of women, warranting prohibition. Verbal sexism is a less invasive form of inequality that should, in her view, be treated as a civil wrong for which compensation is the appropriate remedy.

Like the Cornell memo, many instances of both sexuality and sexism go out to a general audience. These instances are targeted only in the sense that they affect all women coming in contact with them, rather than purposefully targeting specific women. For some commentators, this is targeting enough.[9] Other commentators view remarks that single out particular people as far more serious wrongs: questioning a female law student about her experience of rape, or explaining in a political science class that "If you want to see an example of a bimodal curve, just look at Mary's breasts."[10] Perhaps surprisingly, the National Advisory Council lists no separate category for such targeted remarks; the council seems to regard them just as another form of gender harassment. And in a sense, they are; in humiliating Mary with the comment about her breasts, the instructor also is belittling the other women present and quite likely embarrassing most of the people in the room. Yet remarks such as these also may have very direct crushing effects on the students to whom they refer, effects that may be regarded as particularly significant morally.

If the category of "gender harassment" spans the range just described, it is broad indeed, as it includes group and individually targeted behavior as well as sexual and sexist behavior. That gender harassment has been understood so broadly perhaps explains why it is the most diffuse category of harassment and the most difficult to assess in terms of frequency.

Seductive Behavior

A second major category developed in the Advisory Council study, "seductive behavior," means inappropriate sexual advances. Examples range from watching or "ogling," to social invitations or dates, to persistent letters or telephone calls, to following or even stalking the object of seductive interest.

In a sexual harassment case brought against a professor at Cornell University, charges included purchasing expensive clothing and jewelry for the women pursued.[11]

The adjective in the label for this category—"seductive"—is itself a source of controversy. Included here are activities that, many would argue, are simply ordinary social interchanges. In the view of these critics, invitations to lunch or to go out on dates are normal social pleasantries, not "seduction" in any sense of the term, even if they are rebuffed. A world without such pleasantries, it is said, would be puritanically gray. In the view of others, however, context is central; such invitations are harassment even if they are welcomed if they occur on the job or in the classroom, or between unequals such as a faculty member and a student in his class, or a supervisor and her subordinate. The same commentators might argue, however, that invitations are not harassment if they occur between students and are much harder to assess if they occur between near-equals, such as teaching assistants and undergraduates, or faculty and postdoctoral fellows.

In the view of still others, unwelcomeness is the critical issue in labeling seductive behavior as harassment: Preliminary skirmishes are not harassment, but an ongoing campaign in the face of rejection should be condemned. Indeed, whether seductive behavior must be "unwelcome" to constitute harassment and what "unwelcomeness" itself means is a second major area of controversy concerning this category. Are invitations or telephone calls by themselves harassment? Must the target of the invitations make it clear that they are undesired? What if signals are ambivalent? What if advances were initially welcomed and then the subject has a change of heart? From whose perspective is the understanding of unwelcomeness to be assessed—pursued or pursuer? Answers to these highly controversial questions likewise depend on the view of the university and its social functions. Defenders of the view that welcomed advances cannot be harassment argue that to conclude otherwise would be to exclude the development of ordinary social relationships from the academy. Others argue that at least some members of the academic community are bound by standards of professional ethics that prohibit certain kinds of relationships—sex between professors and students in their classes, for example—even if the relationships are apparently embraced by both parties.[12]

Sexual Bribery

The third category, "sexual bribery," is identified as the solicitation of sexual activity by a promise of rewards. In this category fall offers contingent on sex, from grades, to fellowships, to recommendations, to employment. The employment at issue might be academically related, but in some harassment cases such as one at Cornell, it has involved nonacademic but flattering opportunities—parts in a video or baby-sitting in the professor's home.

Outright, linked offers—what the courts call "quid pro quo"—are clear examples of this kind of harassment. More difficult cases involve apparently consensual relationships between subordinates and superiors, in which the superior is in a position to confer benefits on the subordinate yet there is no indication that the benefits are made contingent on continuation of the relationship. For example, is it sexual bribery for the director of a doctoral dissertation to be engaged in a long-term relationship with his student? (I use the gendered language here advisedly; in most fields, the doctoral supervisor is likely to be male and the outright prohibition of such relationships is likely to involve difficult choices for women students.) For as long as the relationship continues, the student is likely to receive benefits that are not generally available to other students—casual conversation, shared opinions of others in the field, the opportunity to observe a more experienced professional at work on a daily basis. These benefits surely are contingent on the continuation of the relationship, but it is sexual bribery for other benefits—reading and commenting on work in early stages, approval of the dissertation, or letters of reference—likewise to be so dependent. Additional complications here are that the relationship may antedate the supervision (or even the decision to pursue a graduate degree) and that the student may be limited in choices of alternate supervisors at her institution.

Sexual Coercion

The fourth of the council's categories, "sexual coercion," means threatening harm to obtain sex. Typical harms include bad grades, poor references, poor evaluations, academic discipline, and loss of benefits such as jobs or fellowships. This category is the mirror image of sexual bribery; whether it should be separated from bribery depends on whether there are conceptual or moral differences between threats and bribes.

Sexual Assault

The fifth category, "sexual assault," means "gross sexual imposition" or assault, including rape. Sexual assaults are crimes, whether they occur on or off campus. Major issues of definition and proof beset the identification and prosecution of sex crimes, however. Is the victim's apparent consent a defense to a rape charge? From what perspective must the consent be apparent? What are the standards of proof for sexual assaults? Is the victim's word enough, or must there be corroboration? What kind of evidence can be used to impeach the credibility of the victim? Should "date rape" be regarded as a species of "real rape," as a lesser offense, or as an unfortunate form of adolescent experimentation?

Ranging from generalized sexuality to sexual assault, the council's typology of harassment encompasses a wide array of sexual and sexist behavior on campus. Although I have tried to develop the typology neutrally, as descriptions of particular clusters of behavior, the designation of behavior as "harassment" is often not just a neutral categorization but a condemnation. The conceptualization of harassment remains a subject of continuing controversies. The next section provides a brief introduction to these controversies.

ONGOING CONTROVERSIES IN CONCEPTUALIZING SEXUAL HARASSMENT

Conceptual accounts of sexual harassment have been developed to serve many purposes, and conflicts among these purposes underlie debates about definition of the term. So do deep conflicts in political theory, such as the dispute between liberal and radical feminists over the nature of gender as a category of oppression. The reader should bear in mind five particular areas of debate throughout this book. First, is pervasiveness a requirement for harassment or will isolated episodes suffice? Second, is power central to the definition of harassment? Third, can women harass men or is the structure of harassment necessarily male against female? Fourth, can there be same-sex harassment, and in what ways do issues about gender identity relate to the sexual harassment debates? And fifth, should sexual harassment be understood as an objectively identifiable phenomenon, or are different epistemological perspectives integral to the characterization of harassment?

Pervasiveness

A major source of published definitions of harassment has been the law, and it should not be surprising that legal definitions put forth pervasiveness as an element of harassment. Because a legal judgment that harassment has occurred carries significant consequences—injunctive relief, damages, perhaps even fines or imprisonment—the law is concerned that what it condemns be both serious (or it is not worth using the force of the law) and provable (or it is unfair to impose sanctions). Pervasiveness is helpful on both counts. However, critics contend that the criteria for pervasiveness are unclear—how much is too much?—and that even a single event can be devastating to the woman who experiences it.

Although chapter 3 considers the current legal status of sexual harassment in the academy in some detail, it is helpful to have some legal basics in mind from the outset. Sexual harassment as a legal theory began as a type of employment discrimination. The initial cases alleged that the employee's conditions of employment were subject to sexual bribery or threats: what came to be known as a quid pro quo for gaining employment advantages or, more likely, warding off employment disadvantages. Such quid pro quo offers or threats seemed a clear form of sexual discrimination because they imposed a burden on the basis of sex. Subsequent cases recognized that a hostile employment environment could likewise impose burdens on grounds of sex, and it is here that the issue of pervasiveness emerged. Could an environment be regarded as sufficiently hostile to warrant condemnation on the basis of a single or limited number of events?

In regulations implementing Title VII of the Civil Rights Act, the employment discrimination title, the Equal Employment Opportunity Commission (EEOC) has developed a definition of sexual harassment that includes both quid pro quo and hostile environment harassment: "[u]nwelcome sexual advances, requests for sexual favors, and other verbal or physical conduct of a sexual nature . . . when (1) submission to such conduct is made either explicitly or implicitly a term or condition of an individual's employment, (2) submission to or rejection of such conduct by an individual is used as the basis for employment decisions affecting such individual [both (1) and (2) are quid pro quo harassment] or (3) such conduct has the purpose or effect of unreasonably interfering with an individual's work performance or creating an intimidating, hostile, or offensive working environment [(3) is hostile environment harassment]."[13] In defining both sexual and racial harassment, the EEOC takes the position that conduct must be significant enough to create a hostile working environment, as judged by a reasonable person.[14] EEOC regulations thus take positions on several of the controversies outlined here: Harassment must be pervasive, need not involve power, and is to be determined from an objective standpoint of reasonableness.

The regulations implementing Title IX of the Civil Rights Act, the education title, do not make separate provision for sexual harassment.[15] Courts generally have followed the Title VII employment discrimination regulations in litigation under Title IX, an identification that was rejected by the U.S. Supreme Court in a case seeking damages for harassment by a teacher, and that is not obvious if the conditions for equality of opportunity in employment are significantly different from those in education. These legal issues will be developed in chapter 3; chapter 4 will consider the question of whether in an educational context, pervasiveness is an important feature in the identification of wrongful harassment.

Power and Harassment

Feminist theorists who see gender oppression as a critical social variable regard a difference in power between harasser and harassee as crucial to the characterization of harassment. Catherine MacKinnon, who played a formative role in the creation of the theory of sexual harassment as employment discrimination (see pp. 129–46), builds power differences into her proposed definition of harassment: "the unwanted imposition of sexual requirements in the context of a relationship of unequal power."[16] Anita Superson recently has offered a feminist definition of harassment in terms of dominance: "any behavior (verbal or physical) caused by a person, A, in the dominant class directed at another, B, in the subjugated class, that expresses and perpetuates the attitude that B or members of B's sex is/are inferior because of their sex, thereby causing harm to either B and/or members of B's sex."[17] Jane Gallop (see pp. 191–208) recently has questioned whether the celebration of feminist sexuality can be harassment.

As Superson's definition indicates, accounts of harassment in terms of power see it as a structural issue rather than as solely a problem of relationships between people. Harassment involves a member of the dominant sex, race, or class, imposing unwanted sexuality on a member of the subjugated sex, race, or class. As such, it is a wrong not only against the particular victim but against the subject group.

An issue related to the question of power and harassment is race. Anita Hill is the most famous example of a sexual harassment case that also involved race, but there are many others. For example, Dr. Jean Jew, a member of the University of Iowa medical school faculty who won a protracted sexual harassment suit against the university, was subjected to both sexist and racist epithets ("Chinese pussy" was one).[18] On some theoretical paradigms, racial harassment is a different, more serious problem than sexual harassment; issues of power are transformed utterly when race comes into play. On other paradigms, race is an add-on factor, sex-plus as it were, deepening sexual harassment. On still other paradigms, race-sex harassment is a separate phenomenon from either form of harassment alone. Although this book is about sexual harassment, racial harassment cannot be ignored. Legal theories of racial and sexual harassment have borrowed from each other and sexual harassment is often also racist.

The link between power and harassment will be an important theme in the discussion below, particularly concerning consensual sexual relationships, but I do not want to begin this study by adopting a particular theoretical paradigm. The discussion below will thus begin with the inclusive assumption that harassment at a university may come from faculty, staff, students, or even clients or visitors, and may be directed against people in any of these categories, regardless of their relative power.

Female/Male Harassment

There are important moral and political issues, including the relevance of power, about whether male-female harassment is a different kind of problem from female-male or same-sex harassment. Dominance theorists say that because members of the dominant class are the more powerful, it is not possible, except in very unusual circumstances in which power relationships are altered, for them to be the victims of harassment. Women thus cannot harass men unless the men are marginalized by virtue of other power relationships: They are gay, or disabled, or perhaps very young. Superson, for example, grants that women may harm men by sexual advances and that lawsuits in tort might be appropriate responses for the harms, but she denies that the harm can rise to the status of harassment: "When a woman engages in the very same behavior harassing men engage in, the underlying message implicit in male-to-female harassment is missing."[19] MacKinnon sees gender relationships as fundamental relationships of dominance, with men always in the dominant position. She therefore believes that harassment cannot occur from women to men and considers it possible to have harassment by a more junior man against a more senior woman.

Arguing that harassment is a form of gender discrimination rather than dominance, MacKinnon's critics contend that harassment can occur wherever inappropriate sexuality or sexism creates discrimination. Discrimination, on this view, is a matter of how people treat each other. If a subordinate woman sexually pursues a superior man, for example, it is harassment, even if the superior has the power to dismiss the subordinate. Similarly, it is harassment for a woman student to make sexual advances to a male faculty member, even if the faculty member is securely tenured and will be grading the student.

Studies show that the majority of perceived harassment is indeed directed by men against women, with women reporting about two to three times more harassment than do men.[20] Nonetheless, several recent popular fictional accounts, including Michael Crichton's *Disclosure* and David Mamet's *Oleanna*, pit a male victim against a female perpetrator, making these situations a part of the public consciousness of harassment allegations.

Moreover, some studies indicate that males define harassment differently from females. Despite agreement that sexual bribery, threats, and assaults constitute harassment, there is a greater likelihood that women classify obscene speech, teasing, looks and gestures, or sexual overtures as harassment.[21] Another study, however, argues that when scenarios are described in detail, gender differences in the perception of harassment are minimal; it is life-experience differences that are significant: People in the workforce are more likely to perceive that behavior is harassment than are students.[22] There are important moral and political issues, including the relevance of power, about whether male-female harassment is a different kind of problem from female-male or same-sex harassment. At a minimum, because of their popular salience, these issues should not be excluded by definition from this volume.

Same-Sex Harassment

Power also plays a key role in discussions of whether harassment can occur between members of the same sex. Some commentators hold that same-sex behavior cannot be harassment because of the lack of structural power differences between members of the same sex. Others contend that same-sex harassment is possible when sexual orientation is the issue, because the marginalization of gays and lesbians in American society makes them more powerless, increasing their vulnerability to sexual harassment in a wide range of areas. The possibility of same-sex harassment between women is more complex, however, because on the one hand, lesbians are marginalized for their gender identity, but on the other hand, there is no male power dominance, although there might be other forms of power imbalance.

On the view that individualized sex discrimination is the core of harassment, same-sex behavior cannot constitute harassment because it is not discrimination by one sex against another. This is an area of considerable confusion, debate, and change.[23] Chapter 4 presents an ethical approach that can help in understanding when same-sex behavior is problematic harassment.

The Epistemology of Harassment

The fifth basic controversy about the concept of sexual harassment is the point of view from which harassment is to be identified. Some argue that harassment must be an objectively identified phenomenon, with the "reasonable person" as the standard. On this view, behavior such as a friendly greeting that a reasonable person would not find to be offensive is not harassment. Others argue that the "reasonable person" standard as it has been developed really represents the view of the "reasonable man"; the standard for harassment should instead be that of the "reasonable woman." Men and women, these critics contend, experience different kinds of behavior as offensive; a pat on the back may be a greeting to a man but a grope to a woman.[24] Stephanie Riger has argued that if there are significant differences between what men and women identify as harassment, constructing a "reasonable person" standard will simply suppress these differences. Still other commentators argue that because sexual harassment is a harm to the particular woman who is harassed, the standard should be subjective: Did this woman find this behavior offensive? Critics of a subjective standard claim that it imposes unfair burdens of understanding on those perceived as harassers.

Such epistemological controversy is not unique to the question of sexual harassment. Feminist theorists have argued that women occupy different epistemological standpoints from men.[25] Attacks on the standard of abstract reasonableness in other areas of civil law are well developed. For example, the law of informed consent to health care in many jurisdictions has shifted from the reasonable-physician standard to the reasonable-patient standard, and in one jurisdiction has flirted with a subjective standard. In rape law, standards for consent based on abstract "reasonableness" also are coming under fire. These epistemological issues will receive fuller scrutiny in the discussion of procedures recommended for harassment complaints in chapter 7.

THE EPIDEMIOLOGY OF SEXUAL HARASSMENT

What is known about the incidence of harassment? More specifically, who are most likely to be harassers and harassees? What is the comparative frequency of the various types of harassment identified in the National Advisory Council on Women's Educational Programs study and described earlier in this chapter? In what settings is harassment most likely to occur? What are the rates of harassment complaints, and do they parallel reported rates of harassment? In answer to these questions, a lot or a little knowledge is claimed, depending on the study. Data about the epidemiology of harassment often are difficult to interpret for a variety of reasons: the conduct is not clearly defined; reliance is placed on self-reports; the studies use very different target populations; and the studies are not of representative samples or when they are representative, response rates are low. Perceived rates of sexuality or sexism in employment or in the academy are quite high—in most studies, from one-half to two-thirds of women report harassment of some kind—and perceived rates of unwelcome pursuit, bribery or threats, and assault are lower but not negligible. Reports of the actual frequency with which harassment charges are made and the frequency of litigation, however, are extremely low—a small fraction of the reported rates, even the rates of sexual bribery, coercion, or assault.

The first comprehensive study of the frequency of sexual harassment was a survey of 10,648 women federal workers by the Merit Systems Protection Board (MSPB) in 1980.[26] In the survey, which defined harassment very broadly ("unwanted sexual attention"), about 40 percent of women reported having been harassed within the preceding two years; an update in 1988 reported a rate of 42 percent.[27] Men in the original MSPB study reported harassment rates of about 15 percent.

No similarly extensive studies exist for the academy. One recent study of women faculty did use a representative national sample and concluded that one of seven female faculty, in comparison with one of thirty-three male faculty, reported being harassed. Married women, women who teach at women's colleges, and women who teach in settings with higher concentrations of female faculty reported significantly lower harassment rates.[28] A recent study by the Centers for Disease Control and Prevention of the health behaviors of university undergraduates indicated that 84 percent of male undergraduates and 87 percent of female undergraduates reported having had sexual intercourse. About 4 percent of males and about 20 percent of females reported that they were "forced to have sexual intercourse."[29] This means that nearly one-fourth of female undergraduates who were sexually active and one-fifth of all female undergraduates believed they had experienced coerced sex. Several smaller studies, typically with local data sets and not easily comparable, indicated relatively high rates of perceived harassment. Efforts to generalize in the literature, based on reviews of these studies, put harassment rates at 20 to 30 percent, acknowledging that this is an estimated figure between higher and lower rates reported in different studies.[30] The figure probably should be regarded as an educated guess rather than a scientifically reliable result.

Some trends also seem to be apparent in the data. Graduate student women report higher rates of harassment than do undergraduate students, especially of seductive behavior. Among all students, rates of assaults, threats, or bribes are generally the lowest (one recent estimate is about 2 percent); rates of seduction are higher (one recent estimate is 8.9 percent); and rates of gender harassment are the highest (accounting for the bulk of the 20-to-30-percent reported rates).[31]

In comparison with rates of harassment reported in the survey data just described, rates of filed complaints are very low. The average reported rates of complaint frequency on college campuses in the early 1980s was 4.3 complaints per year at any given campus.[32] In the wake of Anita Hill's testimony in the confirmation hearings for Justice Clarence Thomas, rates of perceived harassment have increased somewhat.[33] A 1999 study likewise reports low reporting rates in comparison with estimated frequency.[34] Many explanations of moral importance have been offered for the low rates of reported harassment. Paramount among them are the costs to the victim of complaining and the cumbersome and frequently frustrating nature of the process. These issues also will be discussed in chapter 7, which addresses recommended procedures for dealing with harassment complaints.

PLAN OF THE BOOK

Liberal theory views the academy as serving two principal goals: the development and transmission of knowledge and the advancement of opportunity within society. Depending on how these goals are understood, they may not be fully compatible, and sexual harassment is an issue area that brings out tensions between the two goals. For example, if the development of knowledge requires uncensored debate but that debate makes some groups feel unwelcome and less able to participate in the academic community, then the goals of advancing knowledge and of advancing opportunity conflict. This is exactly the kind of conflict that may be present when sexually charged speech gives offense. It lies at the heart of debates over the understanding of sexual harassment within the university context. Radical and conservative theories see different roles for the academy in society: for radical critics, as transmitting power-entrenching ideology; for conservatives, as custodian of important social values and traditions. Chapter 2 lays out various accounts of the goals of the university as they affect the discussion of sexual harassment.

Sexual harassment developed as a legal theory in the domain of employment law. Beginning in the late 1970s, sexual harassment was recognized as a form of employment discrimination under Title VII of the Civil Rights Act of 1964. Title VII standards were initially incorporated into the law of Title IX, the equal opportunity in education title of the Civil Rights Act, although recent decisions of the U.S. Supreme Court have uncoupled the two. Because this background has done so much to shape treatment of harassment in higher education, it is central to the moral issues as well. Chapter 3 lays out central aspects of the law of sexual harassment in higher education, with particular attention to whether there are important differences between employment relationships—even within the academy—and educational relationships.

Chapters 4 and 5 turn to the central issues of the volume: developing an ethical account of sexual harassment in higher education. The account is based, first, on the wrongs resulting from harassment: interference with dignity and autonomy of the victim, emotional pain, and the denial of opportunity to participate fully in an education. Sometimes in conflict with these are values of academic freedom, individual liberty, and the development and transmission of knowledge. Balancing these factors must be accomplished within the context of the goals of higher education. The task of chapter 4 is to set out the ways in which sexual assaults, threats, and offers wrong their victims in a campus context. Chapter 5 focuses on seductive behavior, gender harassment, and the free speech issues these raise. Chapter 6 turns to a particularly contentious problem: consensual amorous relationships on campus.

The final chapter takes up the thorny issue of developing policies and procedures to deal with harassment complaints on campus. Serious problems of epistemology and fairness lie behind the development of such policies. On the one hand, there is the need to protect the subject of the complaint from unwarranted allegations; on the other hand, there is the concern to support the victim and protect her from being unfairly stigmatized in the complaining process. Both complainant and alleged perpetrator also have interests in confidentiality that ought to be protected.

The institution has interests as well: in the integrity of its processes, its reputation, and its institutional goals. The institution likewise has responsibilities, and a particularly difficult set of questions concerns the extent to which the institution bears responsibility for the behavior of those who work and act within it: employees and their supervisors, faculty and academic deans, and students and visitors to the campus. Appropriate remedies, who should bear their costs, and who should receive their benefits are a final set of issues that must be addressed in a theory of sexual harassment. Just to give a sense of the difficulties here: It certainly is possible that a remedy that would repair the loss of opportunity for a victimized student might impose costs—increased tuition, fewer spaces in a class, or loss of an opportunity to study with a favored professor—on other students or on the academy. The impact of sexual harassment is not confined to individual perpetrators and victims; it is an issue for the entire campus community, with resulting difficult moral choices.

2

The Roles of Education, Expression, and Freedom

The law school where I teach has a reading room crammed with study carrels for first-year students. Because the reading room is the remnant of a former library, it is overlooked by a glass-walled corridor serving faculty offices. Several years ago, one of our first-year students posted a *Playboy* centerfold on his carrel, right in the middle of the room. Several of my faculty colleagues—both male and female—requested removal of the poster, and in due course it disappeared. The requests and the removal seemed entirely reasonable to me at the time. The centerfold just was out of place in a study room intended for all students.

More recently, one of my law school colleagues presented a faculty colloquium on First Amendment protection for public library materials. For the colloquium, my colleague brought several art books from the local public library that had been the subject of complaints from patrons. Before passing the books around, she warned us that they were graphic and that we might find them offensive. An odd warning, I thought, to give to a group of faculty.[1] Then I wondered what made the warning seem so odd. Now I wonder as well about why I found the centerfold protest so normal but the colloquium apology so out of place.

Perhaps the difference lay in my knowledge that my colleagues had relatively high thresholds for offense. Certainly, none of them complained about the books as they had earlier about the poster, and popular commentators bewail our supposedly waning moral standards all the while. Perhaps the difference was that girlie posters seem tacky for the academy, whereas art books are—well—*art*. (One of the books, however, was an illustrated account of Roman pornography; perhaps its ancient origins made the difference.) As I reflected further, the real explanation seemed to be a set of assumptions about academic freedom. On the one hand, I expected an academic colloquium to lie outside of the need to apologize for materials or ideas, to be a setting of robust academic freedom. On the other hand, I assumed that there were limits to that freedom, limits set in this example by the poster's potential to demean and exclude—to *marginalize*—some of those who saw it.

At the time, these assumptions were unexamined. Examining them requires developing a theory of academic freedom and, beyond that, of the role(s) of the academy. These are the tasks of this chapter. I begin at the most fundamental level, with a discussion of the role(s) of higher education in contemporary American society.

THE ROLES OF THE ACADEMY

Contemporary discussions of higher education, whether complimentary or critical, single out four roles of the academy: the development and transmission of knowledge, the furtherance of equality of opportunity, the nurturance and transmission of culture, and the perpetuation of ideology. The first two of these are associated with liberal writers about the academy, the third with conservatives, and the last with radical critics. As with any discussion of higher education, it is important to bear in mind the wide variety of different institutions, from two-year community colleges to mega-universities, that make up contemporary academia. Different roles might be more congenial to some kinds of institutions than to others; for example, the development of new knowledge might fit a large-scale research university far better than a two-year teaching college. On the other hand, some of these values might be important for all of higher education; it has been argued that equality of opportunity should matter as much for a research university as for a teaching institution.

Most of the recent debates about the role(s) of higher education have cast the liberal view in opposition to the conservative and radical traditions. But there are increasing strains between the two values associated with the liberal academy itself. Is the freedom required for the development and transmission of knowledge consistent in practice with the goal of equality of opportunity? What if maintaining the university as an open forum for speech results in hate speech, harassment, or discussions that marginalize groups for whom access is particularly central? What if insistence on access deflects attention from the development and transmission of knowledge? Complex theoretical and empirical disagreements underlie both the questions and the answers that might be given to them. This section begins with a discussion of the liberal account of the knowledge goals of the academy.

Liberalism: The Knowledge Values of the Academy

The creation and transmission of knowledge are the "knowledge values" of the academy. Both historically and today, these have been the preeminent reasons for the academy. From ancient Alexandria, through the Arab world and medieval Europe, the academy was the center of learning. These functions have grown to a vast new scale since the 1950s, though not in the judgment of everyone entirely felicitously.[2]

The knowledge values are reflected in the standard research and teaching functions of contemporary higher education. The panoply of scholarly journals and monographs, together with the nearly $22 billion spent on research and development in universities in 1995 ($13 billion from the federal government alone),[3] a figure that has been increasing almost every year until recently, testify to the immense commitment to the development of new knowledge in the contemporary academy. This huge research engine is certainly not without its critics. Some claim that much of what is written is worthless—not knowledge but only pretense. Others argue that "research" masks professorial self-indulgence that has left the teaching function in the lurch.[4] Despite these criticisms, however, the production of new knowledge remains a major goal of research universities in particular and of at least some other colleges as well.

Today in the United States, there are more than 14 million students enrolled in institutions of higher education. Overall, about 78 percent of these students attend publicly funded colleges and universities.[5] There is a renewed interest in the nurturing of undergraduates on contemporary American campuses. The optimistic view of this revival of undergraduate education is that universities have rediscovered a central part of their academic mission. The more cynical explanation is that, as research funding dries up, there is more competition for the private philanthropic dollar and universities compete with prisons and the poor for a declining share of state budgets.

The knowledge goals of the academy have been defended on several grounds, and the differences matter when considering how these goals relate to other views about the aims of education. One picture is that knowledge is intrinsically valuable, part of the good life. Another is consequentialist, looking to the benefits of learning. In *On Liberty*, the classic defense of full freedom of inquiry, John Stuart Mill argued that the free exchange of ideas would further "the permanent interests of man as a progressive being."[6] Mill's defense of liberal education thus was linked specifically to the development and transmission of knowledge and ultimately to human progress.

A related consequentialist view, associated notably with John Dewey, links education to democracy, not just by creating literate people but by creating the conditions for social cooperation. For Dewey, education is the means of the "social continuity of life."[7] Formal education transmits the resources and achievements of a complex society to the young. Through interplay among different groups, a context of shared interests, values, and understandings is created.[8] Isolation of a particular group, for example in a private school devoted to fostering the culture of that group, "makes for rigidity and formal institutionalizing of life, for static and selfish ideals within the group."[9] On Dewey's vision, groups should be educated together, challenging and coming to know about one other. Dewey is thus not a communitarian of the contemporary kind who supports a program of school vouchers in preference to public schools, to allow the development of separate communities. Dewey's view is that democracy works when the groups within it find common ground.

In the spirit of Dewey, Amy Gutmann has defended two principles as basic to a democratic theory of education. The principles explicitly link the knowledge and the opportunity goals of education. First is the principle of nonrepression, which provides that the state (or any group within it) should not "us[e] education to restrict rational deliberation of competing conceptions of the good life and the good society."[10] The second is the principle of nondiscrimination, that "no educable child may be excluded from an education adequate to participating in the political processes that structure choice among good lives."[11] The principle of nonrepression requires open discussion in educational forms of different kinds of lives, from the traditional to the experimental; the principle of nondiscrimination requires the inclusion of all (at least, all who are educable) in such discussions. According to Gutmann, compulsory primary and secondary education should enable students to acquire the basic intellectual skills needed for participation in democratic life, and the character traits of tolerance, respect for the truth, and a predisposition to nonviolence. Voluntary higher education has two more particular roles to play. The first is helping students to learn "how to think carefully and critically about political problems."[12] The second is protecting democratic society against the dangers of majority tyranny by fostering the discussion of novel or threatened ideas. This latter role leads Gutmann to a defense of academic freedom for individual scholars, conceived as an aspect of the role morality of scholars and of the freedom of the academy from political control. Because this freedom of the academy serves the activities of scholars within a democracy,

Gutmann argues, it is limited properly by restrictions on sexual and racial discrimination. Gutmann's defense of academic freedom and the freedom of the academy, and its consequences for a theory of sexual harassment, will be developed more fully in the final section of this chapter.

Both Dewey and Gutmann thus envision education as demanding interaction and inclusiveness. In these twin goals lies the link between liberty and equality in the liberal picture of education. The marginalization of some groups would be deeply problematic on this view, because it would significantly impoverish the process of the creation of shared values, both for those who exclude and for those who are excluded. If sexual or racial harassment, for example, effectively limited the participation of some groups in the educational dialogue, it would seriously undermine education itself.

Liberalism: The Academy and Equality of Opportunity

From the Second World War until quite recently, particularly in the United States, higher education has been a basic source of opportunities—a secure means of entry to the middle class. The university has opened doors, first for the lower-middle class, then for women and minorities.[13] The GI Bill brought millions of returning soldiers to school. Affirmative action policies brought the numbers of women to majorities in some law schools and to near-majorities even in some medical schools. Blacks have enjoyed this inclusiveness too, particularly for women but to a significantly lesser extent for black men. Entrance into the professoriate also should be viewed as a form of equality of opportunity, and there have been significant increases here as well.[14]

The meaning of equality in education itself is an ongoing subject of debate. Typically, in liberal theory, equality in education is taken to mean equality of opportunity. But the argument also is made for the relevance of equality of results, in terms of the role of education in making changes in the relative or absolute status of particular social groups. Affirmative action is sometimes chastised (for requiring a "quota"), yet sometimes praised (for bringing groups into mainstream American life) when it aims at equality of results. The link between affirmative action and social equality has been largely severed in recent American law, but the argument still is made with some force that the role of the academy, particularly public higher education, is to train leaders for a variety of communities to function effectively in society. This concern to foster the advance of diverse communities, for example, was invoked as a principal defense of continuing affirmative action in the University of California system.

Writers such as Dewey and Gutmann present the knowledge and opportunity goals of the academy as complementing each other. This liberal paradigm may be falling apart, however, as rifts grow between the knowledge goals and the opportunity goals of the academy.[15] One obvious rift is admis-

sions policy—as opportunities expand, some contend, excellence dimin-
ishes, with deleterious consequences for the knowledge goals.[16] This may be
the source of a rift between the research and teaching goals of the academy,
if opportunity is regarded as the dominant goal for community colleges and
four-year institutions whereas the production of new knowledge is taken to
be the dominant goal for research institutions. A parallel rift may form in appointments policy, if such factors as the importance of diverse role models
are paramount for teaching institutions but preeminence in the field takes
the lead for research institutions.

These rifts raise significant questions for sexual harassment policy. To the
extent that free speech is necessary for the knowledge goals of the academy
yet cuts into the opportunity goals, decisions must be made about which
should take precedence. These balances need not be struck in the same way
in all contexts and at all institutions. Quite possibly, academic freedom
should take different forms in largely teaching institutions from the forms it
takes in research institutions. Conceivably, a wider range of materials and
more robust debate can be made available, without compromising equality
of opportunity, in academic communities that have developed cultures of
tolerance and the ability to separate the academic from the personal. To take
another example, perhaps consensual relationships between faculty and students should be permitted in research settings where students are more like
peers, but banned in predominantly undergraduate colleges, where they are
more likely to be perceived as coercive and as impeding equality of access.

This diagnosis of conflicts between opportunity and equality is itself contested. Sexist conduct such as belittling the contributions of women to team
results in a laboratory almost certainly undercuts both opportunities for the
women and the effectiveness of the laboratory team. More generally, the
judgment that there are conflicts between the advancement of opportunity
and the advancement of knowledge depends on assumptions about what
opportunity and knowledge require as well as about the causes of impedi-
ments to their advancement.

Central to the controversy here is dispute about what equality of opportunity means: If it is simply neutrality on the part of officials, much less is demanded than if it implies transformation of social attitudes.[17] Correspondingly, the broader conception of equality would support intervention to alter
the social attitudes that lead to harassment.

Conservatism: The Academy and the Transmission of Culture

On the "conservative" view, the role of the academy is to nurture, develop,
and perpetuate what is of most value in a culture. Scholarship should advance the understanding and enjoyment of materials that are canonical to the
culture and convey that understanding to the young. This commitment to

cultural transmission rests on beliefs about the substantive value of the culture or cultures at issue.[18] In contrast, Dewey's view that people need to learn about a variety of cultures to foster respect and inclusivity would be regarded as mere instrumentalism at best and as an invitation to cultural leveling at worst. For conservatives, it is important that the identified canon be given pride of place in the curriculum; calls for multiculturalist education must be resisted. A variation of this conservative view is that the role of education actually is to participate in creating the cultural canon.[19]

As outlined so far, the conservative view values the preservation of what might be called high culture. A significant variation of this view, associated with communitarian political philosophies, is that a goal of education is the preservation of traditional cultures. On this view, schools and universities play important roles in fostering cultural survival. An example is the role of francophone education in maintaining Quebecois culture.[20] In what follows, I refer to this view as *communitarian conservatism,* in contrast to the *canonical conservatism* just described.

Communitarian conservatives might see a more diverse range of roles for higher education than canonical conservatives. Public and private institutions, for example, might be conceived of quite differently. A principal function of private schools, both secular and religious, could be to allow different cultural forms to flourish. This is no less true in higher education than it is in primary and secondary schools, although their respective contributions differ. Higher education can provide the opportunity for advanced study within the commitments of a culture, can train future leaders of the culture, and can research and develop the cultural canon. Religious institutions of higher education—Catholic Notre Dame University, Jewish Yeshiva University, Baptist Baylor University, and Latter-day Saints (Mormon) Brigham Young University—are predominant examples of this type in the United States. Perhaps some former all-black colleges—Howard University, Morehouse College, Spelman College, and Tuskegee University, for example—play something of this role in nurturing African-American culture. Women's colleges such as Wellesley College and Barnard College, although not separate culturally, do make distinctive contributions to understanding women's roles, the status of women, and more recently feminist analysis, although it is arguable whether these activities involve the production and maintenance of a distinct culture.

If the project of cultural conservatism does support different roles for culture-promoting institutions, there will be issues about the applicability of general regulatory schemes in these circumstances. For example, although it might be inappropriate for religious criteria to play a role in the award of government-funded benefits in public institutions, private religious colleges participating in these programs might wish to take faith into account in making awards. Regulatory regimes such as Title VII (prohibiting employment discrimination) and Title IX (prohibiting discrimination in education) some-times have explicit exceptions for religion and may need to do so to comply with the establishment clause and the free-exercise clause of the Constitu-tion. There are many open questions about whether private institutions should be able to impose constraints (or recognize liberties) on faculty, stu-dents, staff, or curriculum that are not imposed in the public sector. To take one example, professional organizations such as the Association of Ameri-can Law Schools or the American Philosophical Association have struggled over how to apply the principle of nondiscrimination to religious schools when homosexuality is against the tenets of the relevant faith. Should such schools be permitted to deny employment to gay faculty—or even admission to gay students—while continuing to enjoy federal scholarship support or continuing to use the placement services of a professional organization? Di-rectly relevant here is the issue of whether different standards regarding sex-ual harassment should be permitted at private and public institutions.

If private institutions are to provide the functions of cultural transmission attributed to them by some commentators, it would seem to follow that they should be able to insist on at least the levels of distinctiveness required by this cultural project. But there may be direct conflicts between the goals of higher education as they are conceived in the liberal tradition and such cul-tural transmission. These conflicts have indeed been apparent at private re-ligious institutions in the United States. Brigham Young University, for ex-ample, has been criticized for allegedly constraining the academic freedom of feminists or historians critical of the Church of Jesus Christ of Latter-day Saints. Grove City College, a Presbyterian institution, was denied federal funding in a guaranteed student loan program for refusing to comply with Title IX.[21] Conservative and liberal commentators take understandably dif-ferent positions about how such conflicts should be resolved. To take an ex-ample of cultural conservatism, William Galston, defending diversity within the structure of a liberal society, concludes that private institutions should be able to shape their own values, at least when opportunities can be had else-where.[22] Canonical conservatives' preservationist concerns also may be thought to require more stringent rules about academic debate and conduct.

It also is worth noting in this discussion—and perhaps the connection to culture is the most relevant place—that the university serves important social functions for some students, particularly of the so-called traditional variety. Serious writers about the academy do not say much about this function, but football games, fraternities and sororities, proms, demonstrations, and spring break speak eloquently. For some students, however their numbers are dwindling, going to college is still what to do after high school that is socially legitimate, when there doesn't seem to be anything else to do. It's where stu-dents live away from home for the first time, discovering a more mature sense of self or at least the ability to do laundry. It's the center of social life—

of dating or hopefully mating. Indeed, the university is a vast gathering place of people between the ages of eighteen and twenty-five—perhaps the largest set of such gathering places outside of episodic rock festivals. This social function of the university certainly is relevant to questions about sexual harassment—for example, to such questions as whether a policy that would prohibit dating on campus can be reasonably defended.

Radical Critiques: The Academy and the Perpetuation of Ideology

Like conservatives, radical critics of contemporary higher education see its function as the reproduction of culture. Where radicals part company with the conservatives is in viewing cultural reproduction as repression rather than as the preservation of value. For radical critics, the selection of a cultural canon is a political choice through which hierarchies retain power. Liberal visions of free inquiry and open opportunity are ideologies of neutrality that mask the function of the university in serving the interests of the powerful. Of course, this is to some extent a caricature of radical criticism; radical critics disagree in analytical frameworks and critical diagnoses. But they agree that the claims that the university preserves inquiry, or opportunity, or culture, cannot be taken at face value without an understanding of the social function of the university in the preservation of power.

Although the materialist view that high culture is a manifestation of economic forces has been defended at least since the publication of Marx's *The German Ideology*,[23] the radical critique of the contemporary American academy assumed its contemporary shape during the war in Vietnam. Critics of the war, such as Noam Chomsky, alleged that universities, dependent on funding from industry and government, had become central cogs in the "military-industrial complex."[24] In his *The Ideal of the University*, written in 1969, Robert Paul Wolff argued that the academy had become much less a sanctuary of scholarship and much more a training camp for the professions; a social service station feeding market-generated preferences and dependent on federal or industry dollars; and an "assembly line for establishment man," in the simplistic mocking language of student radicals. Wolff yearned for the ideal of the academy as the center for scholarly critique and equality of opportunity and put forth such proposals as randomized admissions procedures in pursuit of those goals.[25]

More recently, critics of the academy have focused on the debate over "the canon." William Spanos' historical critique traces the origins of the "Great Books" movement at Columbia to the service of Americanism in the post–World War I period.[26] Spanos further argues that the movement toward general education, spawned at Harvard after the Second World War, similarly was enlisted in the service of American hegemony; he notes, scathingly, the omission of Marx from the account then-provided of the Western canon. Perhaps the best-known contemporary voice raised in critique of the hegemonic nature of the contemporary canon is that of Stanley Fish. In Fish's view, the adoption of a common curriculum is a recognition of "the normative and therefore coercive force of education."[27] Moreover, because of its apparently neutral content, education may be a particularly insidious form of domination.[28]

Arguments that the traditional curriculum marginalizes African-Americans, women, and a wide range of minority groups have played major roles in the debates over multiculturalism and affirmative action. The contention that the process of canon selection is utterly political has been advanced in support of considering factors such as race in admissions and in curricular design. In reply, liberals such as Amy Gutmann argue that politicization of the canon is self-defeating for those who lack political power. If, on the one hand, curricular design really is all political, then marginalized groups lose because they lack political power. If, on the other hand, curricular design is not all political and there are standards by which new materials are to be included in the canon, then the marginalized no longer have the grounding on which to argue for the inclusion of a wider range of important cultural materials.[29]

Indeed, some contemporary critical race theorists have defended viewing the role of the university as producing cultural change. Mari Matsuda, for example, argues that universities play an emancipatory role for students.[30] Charles Lawrence likewise argues that the university especially has a transformative role to play regarding attitudes toward race.[31] These scholars go beyond the idea that the university's role is to promote equality of opportunity; they see the university as changing American attitudes toward race.

These four views of the roles of the university—knowledge, opportunity, cultural transmission, and cultural imposition—have predominated in contemporary discussions of a wide range of issues of academic policy. Academic freedom is no exception. The background to understanding academic freedom, however, is freedom of expression itself, and it is to this issue that I now turn.

FREEDOM OF EXPRESSION

Harassment typically has expressive components: Indeed, conveying a point of view about the target may be precisely the point of threats, importunings, or sexist comments, to take a few examples. The contemporary debates about sexual—as well as racial—harassment thus bring issues of freedom of expression to center stage. This is not to say that harassment is simply a special case of freedom of expression; the activity involved in harassment may go far beyond speech.[32] It is to say that an understanding of the basic issues in the debates over freedom of expression is critical to an understanding of the treatment of sexual harassment, on and off campus.

Freedom of expression is, of course, a salient and a contentious issue in a democracy. From the absolutism of Justice Black—the First Amendment literally means that there shall be no law restricting freedom of expression[33]—to the instrumentalism of Justice Harlan—freedom of expression should be balanced against compelling state interests such as protection against insurrection[34]—the role of free expression has been contested in political philosophy and in jurisprudence. Two sets of interrelated issues have been central. The first concerns whether principled lines can be drawn between speech—or, construed more broadly, expression—and action. The second concerns whether restrictions on speech or expression require a special sort of justification not required for restrictions on other kinds of conduct, and if so, what kind of justification that might be. For example, does protecting people against expressions of violence or pornography or sexism ever override the case for freedom? As Kent Greenawalt notes, "No one doubts that freedom of speech and of the press is a cornerstone of liberal democracy."[35] Yet how this cornerstone is to be architecturally fitted with equality, opportunity, and other liberal values in particular situations remains deeply controversial. What follows is a brief survey of positions about freedom of expression that are most relevant to understanding the sexual harassment debates.

Distinguishing Speech from Action

If restrictions on expression demand special justification, expressive conduct must be distinguishable from other behaviors. Drawing a conceptual rather than a normative line around expressive behavior would avoid entangled problems of legal and moral justification, such as whether it is ever permissible to restrict speech for the message it conveys. The apparently easiest conceptual line to draw is whether words are used, but that line has not been thought to coincide comfortably with the purpose of giving special protection to the exchange of ideas. On the one side, some verbal behavior seems to be all action and no content: the epithet, the oath, or the curse. On the other side, some behavior is intended primarily to convey a message: adopting traditional styles of dress; burning symbolic objects such as the flag, a draft card, or a cross; or acting in performance art. Redrawing the expression/action line to take examples like these into account may better fit the goal of protecting genuine expression.

The identification of some speech with pure action was introduced in a holding of the United States Supreme Court in 1942 that "fighting words" are not speech. Words that "by their very utterance inflict injury or tend to incite an immediate breach of the peace," the Court said, can make no claim to special protection.[36] The case involved Chaplinsky, a Jehovah's Witness, who was warned by a public official for proselytizing and responded by calling the official a "goddamned racketeer" and a "damned Fascist." The Court's characterization of Chaplinsky's name-calling actually relies on two points. As tending to incite violence, the speech is condemned for the harm it is highly likely to cause. Viewed in this way, Chaplinsky's utterance is speech; the issue (discussed in the next section) is whether the harm it may cause is sufficient justification for regulation or prohibition. As the injury itself, the speech is characterized as conduct, akin to a blow. Viewed in this way, it is not speech at all and thus commands no special protection.

The recent debates about hate speech on campus have revitalized the "fighting words" idea. If hate speech is just action, after all, the case for prohibiting it is vastly easier. Yet the situations in which a word is literally a blow are infrequent; indeed, if public officials are expected to be a bit thick-skinned, it hardly seems that Chaplinsky's own utterances bore the force of punches. Moreover, what makes a word a blow is the context, particularly the understanding and reaction of the victim. But as Greenawalt points out, this approach makes the identification of "fighting words" dependent on the stoicism of the victim. Greenawalt defends instead what he calls a principle of the "equalization of victims," that the classification of speech should depend on the reactions of many listeners, not on the predicted response of the actual victim.[37]

Along with other commentators, therefore, Greenawalt has developed a theoretical account of the expression/action line that goes beyond the concept of "fighting words." Greenawalt's proposal is to classify "situation-altering utterances" as conduct rather than speech. Such utterances "change the normative environment," creating new obligations or claims. They include promises, threats, and offers. Greenawalt would thus classify "I'll give you a good grade if you come to bed with me," and other quid pro quo utterances, as pure conduct. In between situation-altering utterances and ordinary assertions, Greenawalt identifies what he calls "weak imperatives": requests and the like that do not alter the normative environment but that are aimed at action. Weak imperatives would include "please go out with me," in a context of rejection that becomes harassing. Such speech, on Greenawalt's view, warrants intermediate levels of protection—not as much protection as pure speech receives but at least some protection for its expressive aspects. Although it is true certainly that threats and harassment, like defamation, have not enjoyed legal protection as speech, it is hard to see how they fit Greenawalt's characterization. Threats change the environment but not normatively in any ordinary sense; they make their victims worse off but certainly not by obligating them.

Andrew Altman employs J. L. Austin's theory of speech acts to argue that acts of subordination should not be categorized as expression. Austin termed what speech does in virtue of being said—the speech act—its "illocutionary force," in contrast to its "perlocutionary force"—what is done through it. The illocutionary force of "come to bed with me or you'll fail the course" is to threaten; the perlocutionary force may cause many reactions in the hearer: fear, insult, or self-loathing. Altman concludes that speech with subordination as its illocutionary force is a harmful act that may be prohibited.[38] Speech that causes harm also may warrant regulation, but that is part of the problem, discussed below, of when to regulate speech for its consequences.

Altman's focus is campus hate speech; as a radical feminist, Catharine MacKinnon's targets are pornography and sexual harassment. MacKinnon argues that speech that depicts sex or violence against women is discrimination or even rape.[39] MacKinnon describes how the words of pornography are experienced as the action of abuse in the real lives of women. "Only words," they are not; to defend them as such is to "de-realize" the lives of women. As a matter of law, the words used in discrimination or harassment—"help wanted, male" or "sleep with me and I'll recommend you for a fellowship"— have standardly been treated as discriminatory acts with no effort to separate what they say from the damage they cause. By contrast, the words used in pornography have been protected as artistic speech, with regulation limited to supposedly separate harmful behavior. These analytic paradigms clash over hate speech on campus, with the speech paradigm used to defend academic freedom and the action paradigm to condemn harassment. Both pornography and hate speech, however, MacKinnon argues, are performatives, in J. L. Austin's sense of speech that acts, and both are properly understood as harmful acts. By analyzing speech and equality in separate tracks, we have failed to see how harassing speech is inequality, and by the same token how inequality—crucially in education—suppresses speech. One reading of MacKinnon's argument is that, like Altman, she is using the theory of performatives to understand harassing speech as action; another reading, discussed shortly, is that she is denying any distinction between speech and action.

On the other side are actions that are expressive in purpose and effect. If all actions can be viewed as expressive, however, as Frederick Schauer points out, the idea of speech as special will be lost. Nonetheless, some actions clearly are at least closely analogous to speech, if not purely expressive. To single these out, Schauer suggests looking at the communicative aspects of action, because it is the communicative aspects of speech that give it the claim to special protection.[40] Moving outward from language, which is the clearest case of communicative action, Schauer includes within expression the use of signs or symbols that have linguistic equivalents—codes, for example. Commonly understood symbols, such as a peace symbol or a gay pride banner or a black armband, also are expressive in function.[41] And Schauer argues that conduct with communicative intent should be analogized to expression, partly as a way to encourage the invention of new forms of communication. The hardest case for Schauer to classify is conduct with communicative intent that also clearly should be viewed as action: burning a cross[42] or picketing an abortion clinic, for example. Here the message is opposition to integration or to abortion, but the action is intimidation or violence. Schauer concludes that in these cases there is both speech and action and the positive good of protecting the speech should be weighed against the negative consequences of permitting the action.[43]

In another example of viewing action as communicative, Charles Lawrence reads *Brown v. Board of Education,* the school desegregation case, as condemnation of the racist message conveyed by segregated schools.[44] By analogy, sex discrimination may convey the message of inferiority, as it does when athletic scholarships are set aside for men but not for women. Lawrence concludes that "[r]acism is both 100 percent speech and 100 percent conduct," and so the prohibition of segregation under the equal protection clause exemplifies the regulation of speech.[45]

The use of words thus is neither sufficient nor necessary for the definition of a category of expression. Words wound and acts talk. But is the line-redrawing described above really a neutral conceptual enterprise? Some critics contend that there are no lines between speech and action; all speech is action and all action is expressive. This claim has been made by critical theorists such as Charles Lawrence or Catharine MacKinnon at least for contexts of inequality: "Discrimination does not divide into acts on one side and speech on the other. Speech acts. It makes no sense from the action side either. Acts speak. In the context of social inequality, so-called speech can be an exercise of power which constructs the social reality in which people live, from objectification to genocide."[46]

Others have argued that what is speech and what is action is highly contextualized. Although his goal is to find a way to single out some speech as acts, Greenawalt indicates that the determination depends on the hearer and the setting: An epithet that insults in a way that challenges to a fight would be a performative—a dare—but depending on the hearer might be heard as an insult or a criticism.[47] Stanley Fish argues that speech/action categorization is a political judgment: "'Free speech' is just the name we give to verbal behavior that serves the substantive agendas we wish to advance; and we give our preferred verbal behaviors *that* name when we can, when we have the power to do so, because in the rhetoric of American life the label 'free speech' is the one you want your favorites to wear."[48] If these critics are right, what is needed is a normative theory about when expression should be protected, to what degree, and why, constructed as part of a more general theory of the moral limits of the law.

Justifications for Protecting Expression

The traditional liberal view favoring special protection for expression, espoused by Mill, is that it is never justified to restrict liberty of expression because of the message it conveys, no matter how wrongful or hurtful. Mill maintained that expression should be protected to promote the development and transmission of knowledge within society—what I have identified within the university as its knowledge goals. In developing knowledge, Mill maintained, we can never be certain that what we accept is the whole truth: It might be part of the truth, or frank error. So we should assume uncertainty and never suppress an idea on the ground that we have every reason to believe it is false. This assumption is an heuristic device for Mill, a reminder of the historic links between progress and the refusal to stand pat with the received wisdom of the day. Unfortunately, Mill's view often has been mistaken by his critics for skepticism about either truth or the possibility of knowing it.[49] But this is a confusion. Mill is not maintaining the metaphysical position that there are no truths to be found, or even the epistemological position that we are not in a position to be able to recognize truths when we find them. His is the practical position that we will do better at knowing more if we act on the assumption of uncertainty.[50]

With respect to the transmission of knowledge, Mill likewise believed that with open criticism ideas will be better understood, held not as "dead dogma" but as living truth. Critics sometimes draw from Mill the recommendation that all major competing paradigms be given equal educational time, so that creationism must be taught alongside evolutionary theory in biology, traditional sex roles alongside feminist critique, and the doctrine of original sin alongside Freudian psychology. Both this defense of diversity and the criticism that it abandons intellectual rigor have been revived forcefully in the contemporary conflicts about multiculturalism in education. But educational leveling or equal time was not Mill's proposal (nor is it the view of many defenders of multiculturalism); Mill believed quite firmly that we progress in our knowledge of the truth by setting errors aside.[51] Mill's objection was instead to the attitude toward accepted doctrines that would revere them as received wisdom.[52]

The Millean view that diversity is helpful to the development of understanding assumes that students can learn about different views without adopting them. This gap between what might be called exposure and indoctrination is assumed in the contemporary defense of tolerating speech most when it expresses views we hate—even sexual or racial harassment.[53] Critics of the liberal ideal of tolerance are on their strongest ground at this point. For it would be disingenuous for liberals to contend that ideas are inert: Their very goal is "living" truth. To be sure, on the liberal view, reading Marx, or Locke, or Hayek is mediated by rational critique. Reading isn't believing, but when ideas stand up to challenge, minds should and will be changed. That minds will be changed is precisely the concern of communitarians, who fear the erosion by education of groups from the Amish to the Zuni Pueblo.[54] Changed attitudes also are the concern of traditionalists who worry that women will abandon the home as well as of feminists who argue that sexual harassment leads women to believe they do not belong in higher education or in the workplace.

Indeed, even Millean liberals agree that there are times when the harm caused by speech may warrant regulation. The principle advanced by Mill to govern the regulation of action has become known as the "harm principle": Coercion by the state is only justified to prevent harm to others. Two examples of kinds of speech linked to harm are commonly given. First is speech that is itself a harmful act: the racist or sexist epithet or the act of libel; the appeal of the "fighting words" doctrine was that it made some speech into direct action. Second is speech that is so highly likely to cause immediate danger that the only way to prevent the danger is by restricting the speech itself. Mill's own example was inciting a riot in front of the corn dealer's; Justice Holmes's was shouting "fire!" in a crowded theater. An example in the sexual context would be urging on comrades in a gang rape. Liberals following Mill have generally agreed that where the harm can be separated from the speech, the only justified strategy of intervention is to regulate the harm without affecting the speech. An interpretation of the liberal view that is even more protective of speech is that when the speech causes the harm through persuasion, it should be protected as the expression of an idea, but not when it causes the harm in some other way, such as by threatening.[55] In opposition to this approach to the regulation of pornography, Catharine MacKinnon argues that the speech itself is the harm.

Millean liberalism thus requires an especially strong case to bring speech within the scope of the harm principle. In a recent paper critical of this liberal attachment of extra value to speech, Frederick Schauer considers whether the harms caused by speech, or the ways in which speech causes harm, do make speech a special case for the application of the harm principle.[56] Schauer critically evaluates several purported reasons for thinking speech is different from conduct. The first concerns how speech effects harm: Speech, it is suggested, typically harms through an intermediating agent, who should be held responsible for the resulting harm. Schauer points out, however, that agents mediate the impact of conduct too—the gun seller or the bartender, for example—and that in either case complex judgments about third-party responsibility are at issue. A second possible difference is that the direct harm from speech is different from the direct harm from conduct. But Schauer argues that there are no characteristic differences in permanence, intensity, or duration between the pain of a punch and the pain of an epithet. Indeed, the psychological pain from an epithet may prove far more damaging than the transient bruise from a punch. Another possible difference lies in how mental and physical pains are experienced; mental distress is likely to be "belief-mediated"—although not always, as Feinberg's example of scratching on a blackboard, explained below, suggests. To the extent that beliefs or their effects on feelings are controllable, Judith Jarvis Thomson suggests, people can "steel" themselves against the pain of an epithet.[57] Schauer replies that people can learn to steel themselves against physical pain too. Moreover, the psychological damage from the effort to repress the effects of hateful speech can be severe. So can the loss of opportunity, if the distress is dealt with by avoiding the harassment (not taking that class) or changing beliefs (coming to believe it really would be better to be a physician's assistant rather than a physician). Schauer concludes that the sense of "harm" used in the argument that the victim should be strong rather than that the harasser should be suppressed is "ascriptive," representing a normative conclusion that some harms ought to be controlled or remediated but others must be left alone.[58]

A persistent difficulty in the interpretation and application of the harm principle has been the development of a theory of harm. Mill's own account looked to physical harm and the violation of rights. (The idea of rights may be problematic for a utilitarian to accept, an issue that has been much debated among Mill scholars.) There is general agreement among liberal theorists that damage to persons or property, or threats thereof, are harms the law rightly may prevent. If harm is a significant invasion of a legitimate interest, however, other kinds of damage seem equally problematic. Of particular importance to the discussion of harassment are psychological harms. Lowered self-esteem, depression, anxiety, and other psychological conditions can be just as debilitating as long-term physical disabilities—and certainly worse than transient physical damage—in their impact on a person's life. The case for adding psychological damage to the list of harms that the law rightfully may prevent would therefore seem to be strong. Alternatively, some commentators worry that including psychological damage under the harm principle unacceptably broadens the range of permissible legal prohibition.[59] Can psychological damage be distinguished from hypersensitivity? Should we expect targets of verbal abuse to armor themselves against it, as in the children's refrain, "Sticks and stones may break my bones but words will never hurt me"? Are there overriding reasons that support protecting ideas that cause psychological harm that do not apply to ideas when they cause physical damage?

Joel Feinberg's careful study of the moral limits of the criminal law argues that some cases of psychological harm justify legal restriction. "Harm," for Feinberg, is the wrongful invasion of an interest.[60] Significant psychological damage such as clinical depression, lowered self-esteem, or chronic anxiety are harms in Feinberg's sense, if they are wrongfully produced. The "harm principle," as Feinberg formulates it, provides that a good reason for using the criminal law is that it effectively would prevent harm to others and that this prevention cannot be achieved by equally effective means with lesser costs to other values. "Offense" is the wrongful causing of a disliked mental state;

Feinberg's list includes disgust, shame, hurt, anxiety, and the like.[61] Feinberg defends an offense principle that would permit legal restriction of serious offenses to others. Under Feinberg's principle, mere offenses or wounded feelings—nuisances—such as those caused by a transitory rude remark, do not warrant legal intervention because their effects on interests are minimal.[62] The production of extremely unpleasant sensations, however, like the experience of hearing nails scratched on a blackboard, may be discomfiting enough to warrant regulation. Offenses to sensibilities that literally sicken—such as watching someone deliberately eat his own vomit—legitimate intervention. Feinberg identifies as a significant problem for any view along these lines the case of visceral reactions that are cognitively mediated by a personal sense of disapproval; some people report such reactions from seeing interracial or same-sex couples, for example. Feinberg handles this kind of case by arguing that the behavior at issue is both reasonable and deeply important to the couple involved, and these factors mediate against letting the felt offense justify legal intervention. On the other side, the offense felt by victims of racial or sexual epithets warrants prohibition of the speech unless the conduct on the other side has value in its own right (as, for example, political speech would have but the mere expression of epithets would not). Also legitimating intervention are "profound offenses," offenses that are deep, abstract, impersonal, and morally motivated. As an example of profound offense in this sense, Feinberg describes the women mineworkers who discovered that their male colleagues had carved a peephole into their dressing room. The women in this example may have been psychologically damaged by the discovery—in which case prohibition of the harassment would be warranted by the harm principle—but they may have suffered the profound offense of mortification, thus bringing the offense principle into play. There is certainly much to question about Feinberg's account—for example, whether he gives an adequate account of the differences between the offense felt by an observer of an interracial couple and the offense felt by the victim of a racial epithet—but the efforts to distinguish offense from harm and to separate out different kinds of offense are helpful in the analysis of instances of harassment.

In the debates over hate speech, feminists and critical race theorists have described powerfully the hurtfulness of words. Here is just one story from Mari Matsuda:

> An African-American worker found himself repeatedly subjected to racist speech when he came to work. A noose was hanging one day in his work area, a dead animal and other threatening objects were placed in his locker. "KKK" references were directed at him, as well as other racist slurs and death threats. His employer discouraged him from calling the police, attributing the incidents to "horseplay."[63]

Here is a story from Catharine MacKinnon:

> In a case involving pornography as sexual harassment, the employer argued
> that pornography at work was protected expression, something the workers at
> Jacksonville Shipyards wanted to *say* to first-class welder Lois Robinson, their
> opinions about women and sex. Their "views" included naked women suppos-
> edly having sex with each other; a woman masturbating herself with a towel; a
> nude woman on a heater control box with fluid coming from her vaginal area;
> a woman with long blonde hair (like Lois) wearing only high heels and holding
> a whip (one welding tool is called a "whip"); and countless women in full labial
> display. When Lois Robinson protested, the men engaged in more of what the
> ACLU brief against her termed "speech" by posting a sign stating "Men Only."
> Suddenly, because Lois Robinson's sexual harassment complaint centered on
> pornography, her sexual harassment claim invoked the First Amendment, at
> least so far as relief was concerned.[64]

These stories have in common speech that is graphic, demeaning, excluding,[65] and threatening. They also have in common responses that tend to
trivialize the impact on the victim: The speech is "horseplay," or expression of a valuable point of view. Critical theorists have urged that such
speech be prohibited employment discrimination, subjected to suits for
damages[66] or even criminalized. In reply, defenders of free speech worry
that we will lose our commitment to the pursuit of knowledge—Mill's
great concern for the long-term interests of mankind as a progressive
being—in the effort to protect people against hurt feelings.[67] But the critical theorists are not arguing for a generalized ban on cruel speech; they
are arguing that when there are structural or historical conditions of inequality, there is a special case for prohibiting words that wound.
Kimberlé Crenshaw adds intersectionality to the discussion: Black feminists should not be forced to choose between race and sex but should
"construct and empower a political sensibility that opposes racism and misogyny simultaneously."[68] Several proposals for limited restrictions on hate
speech have been put forward. Matsuda, for example, proposes that hate
speech that is clearly harmful should be prohibited when the message is
racial inferiority; is directed against an historically oppressed group; and is
persecutory, hateful, and degrading.[69]

In sum, the issues of sexual and racial harassment have posed significant
challenges to traditional liberal defenses of freedom of expression. The line
between speech and action may be normative rather than conceptual, if indeed it can be drawn at all. Expression may warrant special protection for
the role it plays in the development of knowledge and the exchange of
ideas, but this role may be difficult to disentangle from individual or social
harm. There may be nothing special about the way speech harms. Indeed,

the psychological harm of words of harassment may be just as severe as the pain of physical injury, particularly when the words are targeted to victims of historical or structural discrimination. Nonetheless, freedom of expression remains a central tenet of democratic liberalism, just as liberals struggle to balance it with values of humanity and justice.

ACADEMIC FREEDOM AND THE ROLES OF THE UNIVERSITY

Liberty of expression within the academy—academic freedom—must be viewed within the context of these general debates. But academic freedom is not simply a special case of expressive liberty within, as it were, the very cradle of the development and transmission of knowledge. It also is part of what might be called the self-definition of the academy and the role morality of academic life. Professionals—academics included—have role moralities constructed in light of the goals and circumstances of a given profession. These role moralities may license behavior that would otherwise be prohibited—as physicians are permitted, in emergency situations, to examine and treat others without consent. Or these role moralities may prohibit behavior that would otherwise be permissible or even obligatory—as lawyers are prohibited from revealing clients' confidences even when disclosure might be enormously beneficial to others, an obligation of confidentiality that also might apply to teachers. The argument I advance here is that academic freedom should be viewed as part of the role morality of professionals in the academy, understood in turn in light of the goals of higher education. This argument opens up the possibilities that more—or less or different—freedom of expression should be permitted within the academy than outside. For example, because of their duties to foster learning, teachers might have duties to be particularly circumspect in expressing their views about the quality of student work (not, "What a fool!" which might be said more readily of a nonstudent). On the other hand, universities often play central roles in defending intellectual freedom against assault from outside.

Liberal theories of the academy have been exemplified in the regulations of the American Association of University Professors (AAUP) protecting academic freedom and its more recent struggles to integrate these regulations with the protection of equality of opportunity. The university's role in protecting traditional values can be seen in the effort to exempt religious institutions from AAUP regulations. On some campuses, critics of the AAUP have succeeded in introducing tough regulations restricting hate speech, although at state universities these regulations have not survived legal challenges.

The Knowledge and Opportunity Goals
of the Academy and the AAUP

The AAUP has been a major force in shaping the protection given academic freedom in contemporary higher education.[70] The establishment of the AAUP in 1915 was part of a wider movement toward organization of the professions in the United States. Responding to a call from professors at Johns Hopkins University, 650 select faculty at prestigious institutions—among them John Dewey—became charter members of the AAUP. The initial articulated goals of the organization were to protect the academy—then undergoing rapid growth—from supposed debasement of standards and to insulate the professoriate from administrative interference. In pursuit of these goals—which were at once both high-minded and protectionist—the AAUP insisted on faculty governance and the protection of academic values. Committee A, on academic freedom and tenure, was established in the AAUP's first year and has remained remarkably active ever since in setting and enforcing standards through investigation, exposure, and sanctions.

The 1940 Statement of Principles on Academic Freedom and Tenure contains the AAUP's core understanding of academic freedom in terms of the knowledge goals of the academy: "Institutions of higher education are conducted for the common good and not to further the interest of either the individual teacher or the institution as a whole. The common good depends upon the free search for truth and its free exposition." Academic freedom is "essential to these purposes and applies to both teaching and research." Freedom in research is needed to advance truth; freedom in teaching is critical to both the rights of the teacher and the interests of the student in learning.[71] The principle of academic freedom is to be enforced by means of recommended institutional regulations, which provide extensive safeguards for faculty faced with retention, promotion, or dismissal decisions.

The foreword to these recommended regulations paints a distinctively liberal position, albeit one that analogizes free inquiry to free trade: "A college or university is a marketplace of ideas, and it cannot fulfill its purposes of transmitting, evaluating, and extending knowledge if it requires conformity with any orthodoxy of content and method."[72]

The endorsement of academic freedom in the 1940 Statement of Principles is tempered by the AAUP's understanding of academic responsibilities, however. Some of these responsibilities can be grounded in the academy's knowledge goals. Research should be conducted with an open mind. Teachers are entitled to full freedom in research, subject to their obligation to perform other academic duties—presumably in the classroom. At the same time, the principles provide that teachers "should be careful not to introduce into their teaching controversial matter which has no relation to their subject."[73]

The Interpretive Comments added to the Principles in 1970 assert that this statement is not intended to discourage controversy, which is the heart of academic inquiry, but to prohibit the genuinely irrelevant. There appears to be no recognition in the Principles that judgments of relevance are themselves contested; indeed, arguments about relevance have been central to some highly publicized harassment complaints. For example, the writing instructor in New Hampshire who compared sexual intercourse with focus in writing claimed that the imagery met the standards for academic relevance and prevailed in court on this claim.[74] However, it is clear that the AAUP regulations contemplate disciplining faculty for cause in cases of unfitness as a teacher or researcher.[75]

Other responsibilities of teachers and researchers specified in the Principles apparently are protective of the interests of the institution. Academics have the responsibility to research with an open mind, but research "for pecuniary return" should be based on "an understanding with the authorities of the institution."[76] Perhaps the most controversial responsibility imposed on faculty in the Principles is the responsibility not to put their institution in a bad light. Faculty are not simply citizens; their "special position in the community imposes special obligations. As scholars and educational officers, they should remember that the public may judge their profession and their institution by their utterances. Hence they should at all times be accurate, should exercise appropriate restraint, should show respect for the opinions of others, and should make every effort to indicate that they are not speaking for the institution."[77] Extramural statements by faculty, such as allegedly racist or sexist remarks, remain a thorn in the side for the AAUP. A Statement dealing with extramural utterances, issued in 1964, reaffirms that teachers have the freedom of citizens and that extramural remarks cannot be grounds for dismissal unless they "clearly demonstrate the faculty member's unfitness to serve." The Statement also sets out stringent procedural safeguards, including a faculty committee, to govern disciplinary proceedings against faculty for extramural remarks.[78] Still contested, however, are standards for what really does demonstrate unfitness, such as the controversy over his remarks about Jews that led to the dismissal of Leonard Jeffries, the head of African-American studies at the City University of New York.

The AAUP also has issued a ringing endorsement of academic freedom in the arts. The statement was motivated by concerns that public standards of offensiveness were being used to restrict artistic expression on campus. It asserts that although freedom is important to the scientific enterprise, it is even more important to the imagination. The endorsement explicitly protects artistic freedom in classrooms, studios, performances, and exhibits. Moreover, it regards ideologically based limits on government funding for the arts as impermissible censorship. Like the 1940 Principles and the Statement on extramural remarks, however, the AAUP's endorsement of artistic freedom is joined with limits of questionable import. "Reasonable content-neutral" regulation of the time, place, and manner of artistic expression are permitted, so long as they "do not impair freedom of expression or discourage creativity by subjecting artistic work to tests of propriety or ideology." Although the academy is obligated to foster creativity, it does not thereby endorse all that is produced; "institutional neutrality" does not "relieve institutions of general responsibility for maintaining professional and educational standards."[79]

Within the past twenty-five years, the AAUP also has turned its attention to gender equality on campus. The first step was a statement opposing general bans on hiring members of the same family, adopted in 1971 with the specific goal "to define and safeguard the rights of women in academic life."[80] In 1976, the AAUP issued a short statement condemning discrimination, including discrimination on the bases of sex, marital status, or sexual preference.[81] Model policies for dealing with complaints of sex discrimination soon followed, noteworthy for a discussion of difficulties in proving motive.[82] Also during the 1970s, the AAUP produced an extensive Report on affirmative action, supporting inclusive recruitment and reexamination of appointments criteria but disavowing quotas or strategies that would diminish quality. The Report was optimistic that "the further improvement of quality in higher education and the elimination of discrimination due to race or sex are not at odds with each other."[83] This optimism was based on the redefinition of quality to include diversity and balance and the hope that reexamination of criteria will reject traditional self-replicating criteria that have been barriers to women and minorities. But the Report did not address the inevitable disputes over the understanding and measurement of quality that have proved endemic in affirmative action efforts. Indeed, the idea of academic freedom, which has been the basis for objections to some affirmative action plans, was absent from the Report. This is not to say that academic freedom is either in conflict with affirmative action or should outweigh it. It is to say that the Report seriously underestimated how perceived conflicts between the academy's knowledge and opportunity goals would play out in actual situations.

By the time the AAUP issued its suggested Policies and Procedures concerning sexual harassment in 1990, the potential for conflict with academic freedom had become clear. The Policies are prefaced by a reaffirmation of the commitment to academic freedom.[84] The preface then indicates that it is unprofessional conduct to use academic freedom to exploit students for private advantage, sexually or otherwise. The preface also notes that conduct that intimidates or harasses on the basis of sex violates the academic freedom of those it affects. The Policies themselves provide that sexual advances, requests for favors, and other sexual conduct are harassment when (1) they are made in circumstances suggesting any kind of a quid pro quo; (2) they are so repeated or offensive as to contribute to an unprofessional academic environment or interfere with educational opportunity; or (3) they are abusive of others or create or imply discriminatory hostility toward personal or professional interests based on sex. These Policies track what the EEOC has called quid pro quo (#1) and hostile environment (#2 and #3) harassment. The accompanying procedures recommend due process for all members of the academic community and provide for faculty to sit in judgment when complaints are directed against faculty. The Policies do not, however, discuss any more specifically the possibility that there might be conflicts between allegations of harassment and academic freedom.

The AAUP's endorsement of academic freedom in pursuit of the knowledge goals of the academy has thus been long standing and unwavering. Less clear, however, have been AAUP efforts to deal with hard cases of potential conflicts between liberty of expression and instructional duties, long-term institutional stability or independence, or the opportunity goals of the academy. Working out these conflicts in the development of policy or the adjudication of cases has posed difficult ethical dilemmas for American institutions of higher education.

Conservative Accounts and Liberty of Expression

As the AAUP developed its documents about academic freedom, an ongoing issue was their application to religious institutions. In a compromise between respect for the role of religious institutions and freedom of the individual instructor, the 1940 Statement adopted a disclosure requirement for religious institutions: "limitations of academic freedom because of religious or other aims of the institution should be clearly stated in writing at the time of the [faculty member's] appointment."[85] Examples might have included teaching about sex roles, sexual orientation, contraception, or abortion. The 1970 interpretive comments to the Statement disavowed this exception, opining that most church-related institutions neither "need nor desire the departure from academic freedom."[86]

The AAUP's disavowal of the distinctive needs of religious institutions, however, is not shared by all defenders of religious tradition. Congressman Henry Hyde's legislative proposal to protect campus free speech (the Collegiate Speech Protection Act), motivated by opposition to codes prohibiting hate speech, exempted religious institutions.[87] Michael McConnell, a prominent defender of the role of religion in American life, argues that even the values underlying the commitment to academic freedom tell against extension of the standard model to religious institutions, at least in the contemporary American context of secular dominance. McConnell's argument is that the secularist himself should admit that religious institutions present healthy challenges to secular assumptions. But if the standard model of academic freedom is applied to religious institutions, these institutions may be hard pressed to maintain their methodologies of "reference to authority, community, and faith, and not just to individualized and rationalistic processes of thought."[88] Religious institutions should, in McConnell's view, be free to settle questions of doctrinal orthodoxy, to insist on behavioral standards for faculty and students that are consistent with the tenets of the faith, and to select faculty and students based on faith-related criteria. With respect to sexual harassment policy, McConnell's view would conclude that religious institutions should be permitted to impose limits on what is said in the classroom or elsewhere—restricting, for example, the teaching of sexualized material. Religious institutions also should be free to set standards governing relationships, such as restricting extramarital affairs, same-sex relationships, or premarital sex. Even dress codes insisting on standards of modesty for religious reasons would be appropriate.

Religious institutions thus might argue for distinctive standards for sexual behavior to protect religious community. How far this argument goes, however, is a difficult question. Although defenders of religion such as McConnell argue that what is faith-related is itself a religious rather than a secular question, it is arguable that there are some judgments that should not be left solely up to the faith community. An example might be the judgment that membership in the religious community is limited to people of a given race. McConnell's argument is that secular regulatory bodies, such as the AAUP in its censure decisions, should not second-guess faith-based judgments, even about what is a faith-related reason. McConnell makes no exceptions, nor would it be theoretically easy for him to do so; what is a matter of faith is itself a matter of faith. McConnell's position is most defensible if diverse opportunities are available and faith-based institutions are difficult to sustain. Even so, this argument may not justify public support of the kind offered secular institutions, such as research grants or scholarships. Recognizing that public dollars may bring with them applicability of at least some general regulatory regimes, such as antidiscrimination, some religious institutions have opted to depend entirely on private, including religious, funding.

The defense of regulating speech and behavior on campus is not limited to religious conservatives, however. The communitarian Allan Bloom attributed the rise in observation of sexual harassment to cultural breakdown. Bloom believed that defenders of sexual liberation have in a sense gotten what they wanted—broken down barriers—and then complained about the results.[89] Bloom believed that differences between men and women should help to determine their roles; he thought that women and men should not just be "airplane pilots together" and cited Socrates for the understanding that if women were to be Socratic guardians of the state, modesty would be the first casualty.

Radical Critique

Stanley Fish writes provocatively:

> Take the case of universities and colleges. Could it be the purpose of such places to encourage free expression? If the answer were "yes," it would be hard to say why there would be any need for classes, or examinations, or departments, or disciplines, or libraries, since freedom of expression requires nothing but a soapbox or an open telephone line. The very fact of the university's machinery—of the events, rituals, and procedures that fill its calendar—argues for some other, more substantive purpose. In relation to that purpose (which will be realized differently in different kinds of institutions), the flourishing of free expression will in almost all circumstances be an obvious good; but in some circumstances, freedom of expression may pose a threat to that purpose, and at that point it may be necessary to discipline or regulate speech, lest, to paraphrase Milton, the institution sacrifice itself to one of its *accidental* features.[90]

Fish's point is that freedom of expression is only a means to selected goals of the university—and may not even be that. Neutrality among points of view is a sham; universities always further some social goal or another. The determination of academic orthodoxy is political; selection of the canon illustrates the "normative and therefore coercive" function of the academy.[91] Whether Fish's own view is utterly relativistic or amounts only to the judgment that there is no universal perspective from which all theories can be evaluated is not entirely clear; what is clear is that deconstructionist critique is committed to laying bare the repressive function of underlying values but not to a positive account of what the academy should be.

Other radical critics, critical race theorists particularly, see the university as socially transformative. Recent proposals for hate speech regulation on campus are a good illustration. In the late 1980s, in response to a significant number of ugly incidents of racism, sexism, and homophobia on campus, several institutions adopted hate speech codes. The events truly were shocking: They ranged from images of "niggers" and the jungle, and included escalation to mob violence and death threats. Some of the responsive regulations were drawn very narrowly, designed to protect access to educational opportunity for individual students who quite reasonably might have felt threatened by the hateful speech. Other regulations, however, were broader in scope and apparently aimed to prohibit the expression of racist, sexist, or homophobic points of view altogether.

Narrowly drawn hate speech regulations, targeted at derogatory language directed to specific people, further the opportunity goals of the academy. An example was the regulations at Stanford, which provided that students could be disciplined for "insults addressed directly to a person and involving 'fighting words.'"[92] Similarly narrow regulations at the University of California authorized discipline for fighting words, words that "were 'personally abusive,' were 'directly addressed to any ordinary person,' and were 'in the context used and as a matter of common knowledge, inherently likely to provoke a violent reaction whether or not they actually do so.'"[93]

Other campuses adopted much more sweeping prohibitions. The University of Michigan, for example, prohibited people from "stigmatizing or victimizing" people on the basis of race, ethnicity, religion, sex, sexual orientation, creed, national origin, ancestry, age, marital status, handicap, or Vietnam-era veteran status.[94] The regulation applied to conduct by students or faculty, anywhere on campus, including the classroom. It was interpreted broadly by the university in bringing charges against a graduate student in social work who had stated in class his view that homosexuality was a disease and that he planned to counsel gay clients to become straight. Another student was disciplined for reading a homophobic limerick during a public speaking class. Still another example of discipline involved a predentistry student who said he had heard that minorities had a difficult time in a particular class and were not treated fairly. In concluding that the Michigan regulations were impermissibly vague, the district court cited these examples for the failure to articulate a principled distinction between protected speech and sanctionable speech.

Siding with its vision of the knowledge rather than the opportunity goals of the academy, the AAUP adopted a resolution against all campus speech codes in 1992. The Michigan regulation and more narrowly drawn Wisconsin regulations were both rejected in court. The Supreme Court's *R.A.V.* decision effectively prohibited content-based regulation of speech. So speech codes effectively are dead as a way to restrict campus sexism or racism or homophobia. Nonetheless, the project of higher education as a means of transforming attitudes and values remains viable.

CONCLUSION

Depending on the point of view, contemporary American universities thus are considered to serve at least four goals: providing knowledge, opportunity, community, and radical transformation. Commitments to freedom of expression and knowledge goals have predominated in shaping campus regulations and the role morality of members of the academy. By contrast, the legal prohibition of sexual harassment has become a commonplace of employment discrimination law, almost without concerns about the liberty of expression affected. The next chapter presents the development of the legal theory of sexual harassment as a form of employment discrimination and the application of this theory to educational discrimination. The law of employment discrimination stands in such sharp contrast to the understanding of academic freedom that employment discrimination paradigms do not translate comfortably to the academic setting.

3

+

Sexual Harassment
in the Law

In the spring of 1992, Anita Murillo was a student at San Bernardino Valley College, enrolled in English 015, a remedial class. San Bernardino Valley College is a community college that serves a high percentage of older students returning to school, sometimes after long absences. Many of the students are Hispanic and many come from relatively low socioeconomic levels. San Bernardino is an important first step into higher education for many of these students, an institution in which the opportunity goals of the academy are central.

Dean Cohen, the faculty member assigned to teach Ms. Murillo's class, was a tenured faculty member in English and film studies who had taught at San Bernardino Valley College since 1968. He had deliberately adopted what he described as a confrontational pedagogical style. Assignments typically included reading such controversial essays as Jonathan Swift's political satire, "A Modest Proposal," a bitterly ironic condemnation of Britain's policies toward Ireland. (The "modest proposal" was to solve the problems of famine and overpopulation with one master strategy, an infant in every soup pot.) Assignments also involved examining pornography. Professor

Cohen used profanity in class, stated that he wrote for *Hustler* and *Playboy*, and read to the class some of his own film reviews for these magazines that described personal reactions to pornographic movies in graphic physical detail. Cohen then assigned his class to write an essay with the topic "Define Pornography."

Ms. Murillo was offended by the profanity and the emphasis on the subject of pornography. She asked for an alternative assignment but Professor Cohen refused her request. She stopped going to the class and was given a failing grade. Ms. Murillo then complained to the English department and filed a formal student grievance alleging sexual harassment. In addition to objections to the profanity and obscenity, her complaint alleged that Professor Cohen "would look down her shirt, as well as the shirts of other female students, and that he told her she was overreacting because she was a woman." She also alleged that Professor Cohen told her that if she met him in a bar, he would help her get a better grade.[1]

The college grievance procedure resulted in a ruling in favor of Ms. Murillo. It concluded that Professor Cohen had created a hostile learning environment that unreasonably interfered with Ms. Murillo's academic performance. The administrative decision was based on the testimony about Professor Cohen's conduct of the class and apparently did not rest on Ms. Murillo's claims about the remarks directed to her individually. Discipline imposed on Professor Cohen included the requirements that he provide a syllabus describing his teaching methods and materials, attend a sexual harassment seminar, undergo a formal evaluation procedure in accord with the collective bargaining agreement, and modify his teaching strategy to become sensitive to the needs of his students.

Far from responding meekly to the discipline, Professor Cohen went to court, arguing that the college's sexual harassment policy violated the First Amendment to the United States Constitution. He lost at the district court level, with the court opining that "Lacking definition or guiding principle, the doctrine [of academic freedom] floats in the law, picking up decisions as a hull does barnacles."[2] The district court concluded that the college had a substantial interest in the education of all students and that the discipline was narrowly tailored and reasonable. The court suggested that a case of termination or direct censorship would pose a different question, however.

Not satisfied with the district court's ruling, Professor Cohen appealed, and the Ninth Circuit Court of Appeals agreed with him that the college's policy was unconstitutionally vague as applied to his conduct. The problem, as the court saw it, was that Professor Cohen was not on notice that a teaching style he had used for many years violated the newly adopted sexual harassment policy. Discipline thus amounted to a "legalistic ambush." The court did not, however, attempt to work out the boundaries of a legitimate harassment policy and confined itself to noting that the policy at issue was not itself clear or precise or construed precisely enough by authoritative interpretive guidelines.[3]

This case is typical in many ways. The charges involved offensive conduct in a classroom setting. The allegations were principally that the classroom was sexualized and thus offensive. In the end, the law was used by the faculty member as a shield, not as a sword by the student originally bringing the complaint. The student lost and the faculty member won, but only after a long, wrenching process.

The development of sexual harassment policy in higher education largely has been driven by the law. Legal requirements—or perhaps even more importantly, perceptions of what the law requires—continue to pose ethical dilemmas for higher education. At the same time, the law on sexual harassment in higher education is not entirely settled. Although in 1998 the United States Supreme Court decided a quartet of critical sexual harassment cases, there continue to be opportunities for ethical analysis to influence the direction in which the law evolves. This chapter provides an understanding of how the treatment of sexual harassment within the university has been framed by the law and discusses the problems this raises for the ethical treatment of sexual harassment in higher education.

TITLE VII: SEXUAL HARASSMENT IN EMPLOYMENT LAW

Sexual harassment as a legal theory originated as an aspect of employment discrimination law. Its development was initially structured by Title VII of the Civil Rights Act of 1964,[4] which governs employment discrimination based on sex, and by the Fourteenth Amendment's guarantees of liberty and of equal protection as they apply to state agencies, including institutions of higher education.[5] As litigation developed under Title IX, which governs discrimination in federally funded educational programs, it increasingly followed already-explored Title VII precedents. In 1998 and 1999, however, the Supreme Court handed down several important decisions that divided Title IX from Title VII for purposes of liability. These cases involved a suit brought by a student against a school district, seeking damages for sexual advances by a teacher,[6] and a suit brought by a student against a school district, seeking damages for the district's failure to stop harassment by another student.[7] In each case, the Court applied a stricter standard under Title IX than it would have applied under Title VII to find harassment by a supervisor or by a coworker. It now appears that the Supreme Court is interpreting the statutory schemes of Title VII and Title IX to give more protection to employees than to students, a result that might appear perverse if students are thought to be more vulnerable than employees and if education is thought to be a particularly central factor in equality of opportunity.[8] It is also a result that may prove difficult to apply when students are also employees, such as teaching or laboratory assistants. These developments pose significant questions about the extent to which Title VII paradigms will continue to dominate Title IX law more generally. Nonetheless, Title IX law must be understood against the backdrop of employment law from which it emerged.

Title VII prohibits discrimination on the basis of sex in the terms or conditions of employment. With the 1976 case of *Williams v. Saxbe*,[9] courts began to view sexual favors, sexual threats, and sexual banter in the workplace as terms or conditions of employment that had the potential to violate Title VII. In 1980, in amending its guidelines on discrimination because of sex, the Equal Employment Opportunity Commission (EEOC) distinguished two forms of sexual harassment.[10] When sexual advances or favors are traded for employee evaluations, promotions, or other job benefits, the harassment is "quid pro quo." When sexual conduct creates difficult working conditions, the harassment takes the form of a "hostile environment." Distinguishing a hostile environment from "mere incivility" has been a particularly contentious issue as the law has developed, notably when women challenge long-standing workplace norms of sexually explicit behavior. The EEOC guidelines on harassment were followed by many of the lower federal courts, but their authority was questioned without word from the United States Supreme Court. In 1986, in *Meritor Savings Bank v. Vinson*,[11] the Supreme Court recognized sexual harassment as a form of employment discrimination under Title VII and followed the EEOC regulations delineating quid pro quo and hostile environment harassment. Mechelle Vinson, the plaintiff, alleged that she had had a long-standing, coercive sexual relationship with her supervisor, which was consensual only in that she had agreed to some of the sex out of fear of losing her job. On her account, the relationship had ended when she got a steady boyfriend. The supervisor claimed that there never had been a sexual relationship and that Vinson had made the charges to retaliate for an adverse business decision. The bank contended that even if the sexual relationship had existed, it was unknown to them, so they should not be held responsible for the acts of the supervisor. The Supreme Court concluded that conduct that is severe or pervasive enough "to alter the conditions of [victim's] employment and create an abusive working environment"[12] is actionable as employment discrimination and remanded the case to the District Court with directions to consider whether the "unwelcome" sexual conduct had been serious and pervasive enough to alter the victim's conditions of employment. "Serious and pervasive" was not spelled out further, although the District Court was given additional important guidance on two points. It was not to limit its analysis to economic harms of the quid pro quo variety in assessing hostility. And it was to consider the "unwelcomeness" of the supervisor's behavior to the plaintiff, rather than the "voluntariness" of any particular sexual encounters between them. All of these terms—"quid pro quo," "hostile environment," "serious and pervasive," "voluntariness," and "unwelcomeness"—are terms of art in sexual harassment litigation in education.

In developing standards for determining when an environment is sufficiently hostile to alter working conditions, lower courts took different paths after *Meritor.*[13] Some courts required plaintiffs to show that they had suffered actual psychological harm,[14] at least one court assessed hostility from the perspective of a "reasonable woman,"[15] and other courts looked to whether an androgynous "reasonable person in the victim's position" would have suffered damage.[16] This tension between charges of oversensitivity (of complaining women) and undersensitivity (to real women's lives) has continued in the development of Title VII law and has carried over into the development of sexual harassment law in higher education.

In 1993, in *Harris v. Forklift Systems,*[17] the Supreme Court held that hostile environment harassment is not limited to cases in which the employee suffers actual psychological damage. Title VII prohibits discrimination in the conditions of employment, including an environment that is abusive enough to alter working conditions. Occasional utterances that offend or conduct that does not create an environment that a reasonable person would find hostile do not rise to the level of employment discrimination. In *Harris,* the Court also insisted that the plaintiff make a subjective showing that the complained-of conduct was offensive to her. This conclusion has been criticized for taking the victim's character into account by the back door; if the victim has become hardened to conduct that would horrify any reasonable person, she cannot recover for harassment.

In the 1998 quartet of sexual harassment decisions, the Supreme Court continued to emphasize the distinction between hostile environment harassment and workplace incivility. In holding that same-sex behavior could be sexual harassment if it was discrimination because of sex, the Court opined that the plaintiff

> must always prove that the conduct at issue was not merely tinged with offensive sexual connotations, but actually constituted "discrimination. . . ." And there is another requirement that prevents Title VII from expanding into a general civility code: . . . the statute does not reach genuine but innocuous differences in the ways men and women routinely interact with members of the same sex and of the opposite sex . . . it forbids only behavior so objectively offensive as to alter the "conditions" of the victim's employment.[18]

Likewise, in holding that an employee who refuses unwelcome, coercive advances but suffers no adverse job consequences can sue under Title VII, the Court opined that unfulfilled threats can constitute a hostile environment, if the plaintiff shows "severe or pervasive" conduct.[19] In the latter case, the plaintiff had sought to characterize her claim as quid pro quo harassment, despite the nonfulfillment of the threats, to take advantage of the apparently more favorable rules governing employer liability in such cases.

Indeed, the other highly controversial issue in the development of sexual harassment law that was resolved by the Court in 1998 was the employer's responsibility for harassing behavior by supervisors or fellow employees. Title VII defines "employer" to include "agents."[20] Relying on this language, the EEOC regulations provided that employers were responsible for harassing acts by supervisors, whether or not the employer knew or should have known of their behavior. In *Meritor*, the Court expressed general approval of the use of agency law—that is, law governing when one person should be held to have acted on behalf of another—to determine whether the employer should be vicariously liable, leaving it open to lower courts to fashion standards case by case. The prevailing view that emerged was that employers should be vicariously liable in cases of quid pro quo harassment by supervisors; courts were more divided, however, on whether in hostile environment cases the plaintiff could rely on agency principles or needed to show that the employer had known of the harassment and been negligent in failing to correct it.

In the 1998 quartet of cases, the Court used principles of agency law to set out uniform standards to govern employer liability in both types of cases. The basic premise of agency law is that the acts of the agent are attributed to the principal if the agent is acting "within the scope" of his or her authority. An agent's "frolic or detour"—a sexual dalliance is the textbook example— is not within the scope of the agent's authority.[21] If agency principles are applied to sexual harassment law, therefore, the plaintiff will either need to show that the agent was acting within the scope of responsibilities or will need to establish some other basis for attributing the agent's conduct to the principal. If a supervisor carries through on threats—that is, in a case of genuine quid pro quo harassment—the employer is liable because the supervisor is acting within the scope of responsibilities in changing the terms of employment. In hostile environment cases, including those in which the supervisor makes unfulfilled threats, the employer is liable if the supervisor is acting within the scope of his authority, if the employer knows of the harassment and negligently fails to correct it, or if the harassment is aided by the employer. In the last case, the employer may assert an affirmative defense by showing that the employer exercised reasonable care to prevent and correct harassment and that the employee unreasonably failed to take advantage of preventive or corrective opportunities.[22] In the wake of these decisions, commentators are recommending to employers that they scrupulously promulgate sexual harassment policies and complaint procedures to take advantage of the affirmative defense should a complaint arise.

The structure of this affirmative defense is entirely Court-created. It represents the Court's view that Title VII was designed not to punish employers but to encourage antidiscrimination policies in the workplace. The Court reasoned that grievance procedures are encouraged by allowing employers to defend themselves against sexual harassment suits on the basis that they have provided reasonable corrective opportunities. Moreover, limiting employer liability when employees unreasonably fail to take advantage of grievance opportunities will encourage victims to report harassment and employers to take corrective steps before it becomes pervasive or severe. Critics are sure to argue that the Court's approach favors employers in practice when grievance procedures are in place on paper but are underutilized by plaintiffs who are too embarrassed, too afraid of retaliation, or too intimidated by the process itself. In the 1998 decision analyzing the vicarious liability of educational institutions, however, the Court regarded Title VII and Title IX as having very different goals and refused to apply agency principles at all to Title IX. The result is to leave students in educational institutions even worse off than employees in those same settings when it comes to suing for harassment and to call into question the developing practice of regarding the two statutes as analogous.

TITLE IX: SEXUAL HARASSMENT IN EDUCATION LAW

Adopted in 1972, Title IX of the Civil Rights Act prohibits discrimination in educational programs receiving federal funds. Its exact language reads: "No person in the United States shall, on the basis of sex, be excluded from participation in, be denied the benefits of, or be subjected to discrimination under any education program or activity receiving Federal financial assistance."[23] Title IX thus is more limited in scope than Title VII: Its domain is the federal dollar and it keeps federal dollars from supporting discriminatory educational programs. That it is not a more general attack on educational discrimination quite possibly is because of this country's tradition of local control over education. Title IX's limited reach has discouraged some religious institutions in particular from nibbling the federal carrot.[24]

Threshold Issues

The fact that Title IX operates as an aspect of federal funding for educational programs generates complex threshold issues about the structure of sexual harassment litigation in higher education in terms of the following questions: Who can sue under Title IX, when can they sue, what can they sue for, and whom can they sue? To the extent that courts have given restrictive answers to these questions, potential plaintiffs in sexual harassment suits have resorted to legal theories that bypass Title IX. These include the Fourteenth and First Amendments to the United States Constitution; Section 1983 (the Reconstruction Era federal statute that authorizes damage suits against people for violating constitutional or statutory rights under color of state law);[25] Title VII; and various state law statutory and common law claims such as breach of contract or defamation. Just as in the area of employment discrimination, this complexity brings with it the possibility of significantly different treatment of state institutions—subject to constitutional limits—and private institutions.

The question of who may bring suit under Title IX was the first to be answered, in 1979; the United States Supreme Court held that individuals such as students could sue to enforce the rights given them under Title IX.[26] It was not until 1992, though, that the Court ruled on another of the questions, what they can sue for, holding that money damages could be the remedy in a Title IX suit brought by students.[27] Even now, it is not legally settled whether other actors in an educational setting—such as Dean Cohen, the disciplined instructor with which this chapter began—can recover damages under Title IX. (The alternative remedy would be injunctive relief, a court order mandating or prohibiting action such as the discipline imposed on Cohen by his college.) As for the answer to when plaintiffs can sue, they may be required to use university processes before they can resort to the courts, and they face a significant risk that if they are not careful, their claims will be barred because they were not brought quickly enough.[28] Moreover, because Title IX prohibits discrimination in educational *programs*, it does not authorize suits against private individuals such as a teacher or a counselor. Potential plaintiffs must either find a way to hold an institution responsible for the acts of individual harassers, such as a classroom teacher or even fellow students—an approach made less likely to succeed under 1998 and 1999 decisions of the U.S. Supreme Court—or call on another theory of liability.

The legal alternatives to Title IX are significantly richer when suit is brought against a public rather than a private institution. Against private institutions, the only real alternatives to Title IX are Title VII if the plaintiff is an employee (in which case the defense to a Title IX suit may be that Title VII is the exclusive remedy); state tort law (suits for damages for negligence, infliction of emotional distress, or libel, primarily); breach of contract; or one of a variety of state antidiscrimination statutes. Against public institutions, both federal and state constitutional theories are available as well as Section 1983 suits for damages against individuals for deprivation of civil rights under color of state law. The Fourteenth Amendment prohibits state action depriving citizens of the equal protection of the laws; public institutions are state actors, subject to suit under the Fourteenth Amendment. Section 1983 allows suits for damages against individuals acting under color of state law to violate the constitutional or statutory rights of another; typically, individuals acting in private colleges do not act under color of state law but individuals acting in public institutions do. Dean Cohen, for example, sued officials of San Bernardino Valley College for damages under Section 1983, alleging that they had violated his First Amendment rights to free speech.

When they are sued, however, public actors can avail themselves of defenses not available to private actors. Chief among these are the varieties of immunity provided states and their employees. ("Immunity" means that an individual or an entity is insulated from a given lawsuit.) States can claim immunity under the Eleventh Amendment from suits for damages (although not from suits for injunctive relief); the federal Constitution protects state treasuries, unless the states themselves waive their sovereign immunity or are otherwise subject to federal legislation. Thus Dean Cohen's effort to sue San Bernardino College itself for damages under Section 1983 for violation of his constitutional rights failed, whereas his suit for an injunction against the imposition of discipline succeeded. As for suits against employees of state institutions, state officers enjoy what is called "qualified immunity" (immunity under limited circumstances) from suits for damages under Section 1983 when they are exercising discretionary functions. This means they cannot be sued for damages unless they violate clearly established constitutional rights. Particularly contentious issues in this situation have been whether students have clearly established constitutional rights to be protected by school administrators from harassment and whether teachers have clearly established First Amendment rights to academic freedom. Again the *Cohen* case is an example: The court held that individual officers of the college did have qualified immunity from his suit for damages because the right to academic freedom was not clearly defined. Cohen's victory thus was limited to an injunction against the discipline the college sought to impose on him. The perhaps ironic result of the qualified-immunity doctrine is that the first lawsuit will be met by a successful immunity defense but will establish the constitutional right, and subsequent lawsuits will recover damages.

This tangle of legal possibilities, in many cases not yet fully defined, creates a variety of different worries and incentives for campus actors. All quite naturally want to avoid the trouble of litigation, much less the costs of damage awards. With the tendency of institutional lawyers to give conservative, institutionally protective legal advice, universities have reacted by trying to create policies and procedures that avoid their being held liable for the behavior of their employees. Individual administrators at public institutions may worry about their liability for damages under Section 1983, although their institutions typically will pay any judgments for actions taken in good faith. Defensiveness has been the norm shaping administrative practice, although data indicate that it may well be an overreaction.

A survey of legal databases indicates that between January 1, 1994, and July 1, 1997, the federal courts issued rulings in fifty-six reported cases litigating sexual harassment claims against institutions of higher education. Twenty-nine of these involved the use of federal law as a shield—that is, the plaintiffs who were accused of sexual harassment or disciplined in a situation involving a sexual harassment charge claimed that they had not been afforded appropriate legal process or had otherwise been denied their legal rights. The plaintiff was successful in six of these "shield" cases, including five brought by disciplined faculty members and one brought by a disciplined student. Dean Cohen's case once again is an excellent example of the successful use of federal law as a shield against discipline. Nineteen of the twenty-seven "sword" cases (in which the plaintiff used the law to allege victimization by harassment) were brought by students charging that they had been victimized by harassment. In four of these nineteen cases, the students also were college employees, and the harassment took place in the employment setting. Students won in four of the twenty cases over all (the one shield case and three of the nineteen sword cases). To be sure, cases that end up in federal court represent only a small fraction of the reported incidence of sexual harassment. Many other cases are settled for damages without resulting in a publicized court decision. Nonetheless, this database survey suggests that very few students sue their universities, and few of them are successful when they do so. Perhaps because of the economic stakes involved, sexual harassment law has been used more frequently by faculty members who have been denied tenure, dismissed, or disciplined.[29]

The Supreme Court Decisions in 1998 and 1999

In 1998 and 1999, the Supreme Court decided two critical cases for the understanding of Title IX. These cases involved the highly contentious issues of whether an educational institution can be held vicariously liable for harassing actions of teachers (or other employees) or students. (Because suits under Title IX must be directed against educational programs rather than individuals, they frequently raise significant problems of "vicarious liability"— liability in which the acts of individual "agents" are attributed to the institution.) In both cases, the Court held that Title IX and Title VII are not analogous for purposes of liability. Title VII prohibits employment discrimination and its principal goal is employment opportunity; Title IX was enacted under Congress's power to direct how federal money is spent. The authorization of suits for damages may thus be required to meet stricter standards under Title IX than under Title VII.

In the first of these cases, *Gebser v. Lago Vista Independent School District*,[30] the Court took up vicarious liability of educational programs for the acts of teachers. As discussed above, under Title VII, employees are treated as "agents" of their employers, who can then be held vicariously liable for harassing actions performed within the scope of employment. Flatly rejecting the analogy to employment law, the Court held that under Title IX, educational institutions could be held vicariously liable for damages only when an official with authority to correct the alleged discrimination has "actual knowledge" of it and "fails adequately to respond," with the failure amounting to "deliberate indifference."[31]

The facts of the *Gebser* case are important to understanding the reach of the decision, so they are recounted briefly here. Alida Gebser was in the eighth grade when she was asked by a teacher to join a high school reading group. At this time, her sexual relationship with the teacher began. Other parents had complained to the principal about the teacher's sexually suggestive behavior, although Gebser had not; the principal advised the teacher to be careful in class but did not report the complaints to the district's sexual harassment officer. Gebser herself was afraid to complain because she wanted to be able to enroll in the teacher's advanced placement English class. Much of the sexual relationship took place during class time, when Gebser was the only student present, although not—this must have been a relief to the school district—actually on school property. Lago Vista School District had no sexual harassment policy at the time and no established grievance procedure.

In rejecting the analogy to Title VII, the Court relied first on the differences in language between the statutes: Title VII defines "employer" to include "agent" and Title IX applies to educational programs. More deeply, the Court saw Title IX and Title VII as having quite different goals. Title VII provides expressly for damage remedies and is designed both to root out employment discrimination and to compensate victims.[32] The right of individuals to sue for damages under Title IX is judicially implied and must be construed to further the purposes of Title IX. Title IX's goal is to prevent discrimination in programs receiving educational funds from the federal government; programs receiving federal funding in effect contract with the federal government to meet its terms. It would "frustrate" the purposes of Title IX, the Court said, to allow individuals to sue school districts for damages when the district had no actual knowledge of the harassment or opportunity to correct it.[33] The supposedly "frustrated" purposes are to avoid the use of federal funds to support discrimination and to provide individual citizens effective protection against discrimination.[34] As Justice Stevens pointed out in dissent, however, it is hard to see how these purposes would not be *furthered* by allowing individuals to recover damages.[35] The Court's position was that Title IX was structured by Congress to allow the federal government to withdraw funding when a recipient had actual notice of a deficiency and failed to correct it. To allow damage recoveries in other cases, the Court feared, would risk undoing the very purpose of federal support for education by putting school districts at financial risk for liability judgments far beyond what they had expected under the "contract" with the federal government. A reply to this concern is that once principles of vicarious liability were firmly established, school districts would know exactly what they were getting into in accepting federal funding for education.

In 1999, the Court followed *Gebser* in a case involving harassment by a fellow student. In *Davis v. Monroe County Board of Education*, the Court held that educational institutions could be held liable for student-to-student harassment only if they knew of the behavior and acted with "deliberate indifference" to it.[36] Once again, the facts alleged in the case depicted a pattern of behavior remarkably threatening to the student's education. LaShonda Davis—a fifth grader—complained that she was repeatedly subjected to harassing behavior from a classmate from December through May. The harassment ended only when the classmate was charged with sexual battery and pleaded guilty to the charges. The alleged behavior included vulgar language, seductive language ("I want to go to bed with you"), attempted touching, quite graphic mimicry of sexual actions, and actual physical contact (rubbing his body up against hers). LaShonda complained repeatedly about the behavior to three teachers and to the principal, but no disciplinary action was taken; more than three months passed before she was even allowed to change her classroom seat so that she was no longer next to her harasser. As in *Gebser*, Justice O'Connor, writing for the Court in *Davis*, left the door open for the plaintiff to make a showing that would allow her to recover damages. But the opening was limited: Davis would need to show that the school district had in effect "made an official decision" not to remedy the violation, thus demonstrating its "deliberate indifference" to it.[37] It would not be enough to show that the district had negligently failed to take action in her situation. The *Davis* decision was marked by considerable acrimony on the Court. Justice Kennedy's dissent characterized the door as left open very wide and as federalizing educational standards: "The Nation's schoolchildren will learn their first lessons about federalism in classrooms where the federal government is the ever-present regulator. The federal government will have insinuated itself not only into one of the most traditional areas of state concern but also into one of the most sensitive areas of human affairs."[38] Justice Kennedy's dissent would have distinguished *Gebser*—involving harassment by someone under the authority of the educational institution—from *Davis* as involving harassment by a student over whom the education institution had no authority. In announcing the decision of the Court, Justice O'Connor replied to the dissent that far from "teach[ing] little Johnny a perverse lesson in Federalism," the decision would assure "that little Mary may attend class."[39] Commentators on the *Davis* decision remain divided about the extent to which it allows plaintiffs a realistic chance of succeeding in a lawsuit alleging peer harassment.

The result of these two decisions is that educational institutions are not held to the same standards employers are to remedy harassment. Plaintiffs seeking damages for teacher or peer harassment from educational institutions under Title IX are thus worse off than employees would be seeking damages for the same harassment under Title VII. Moreover, it is unclear whether the Court will disanalogize Title IX from Title VII in other areas in which the two statutes have been regarded as parallel.

The Department of Education Sexual Harassment Guidance Document

Another major step toward clarifying unresolved questions under Title IX was the issuance in March 1997 of a document titled "Sexual Harassment Guidance" by the Office of Civil Rights of the Department of Education. The document takes positions on many of the most contentious issues in the cases litigating sexual harassment in education, such as defining harassment, integrating harassment prohibitions with protection of academic freedom, characterizing female-male and same-sex behaviors as forms of sexual harassment, and structuring grievance procedures to protect confidentiality and due process for all concerned. Although the document's position on teacher harassment was rejected by the Court in *Gebser*, many of its other positions may still be legally viable, and it provides a useful framework for discussion of these issues.

Vicarious Liability: Harassment by Teachers and Fellow Students

Let me turn first to the Guidance positions on vicarious liability. On teacher harassment, as just indicated, the Guidance would have applied agency principles, the approach rejected by the Court.[40] On harassment by fellow students or other peers, the Guidance position was closer to that of the Court's in *Davis*. Recognizing that students are not agents of the educational institution, the Guidance rejected the application of agency principles to institutional liability for their actions. The behavior of students, or for that matter of visitors to educational institutions, may, however, create a hostile environment for others. If the behavior does so, and the educational institution knows about it, it will be liable if it fails to take "immediate and appropriate corrective action. However, the type of appropriate steps the school should take will differ depending on the level of control the school has over the third party harasser."[41] The Guidance continued by specifying that if an educational institution did not have a grievance procedure in place, and thus lacked a mechanism for detecting and remedying harassment, it could be held liable for harassment that was severe enough to create a hostile environment even if it did not know of the harassment. This treatment of peer harassment parallels *Davis* in rejecting agency principles and in requiring that the educational institution have actual knowledge of the harassment before it could be held liable. It applies what may be a weaker standard to the action required to avoid liability, however: "immediate and appropriate corrective action" in contrast to failure to act with "deliberate indifference." Moreover, the Court concluded in *Gebser* that the lack of a grievance procedure would not in itself give rise to liability, although federal agencies might impose such a requirement administratively.[42]

Defining Harassment

Like the EEOC guidelines for Title VII, the Guidance provides that both quid pro quo and hostile environment are prohibited forms of sexual harassment under Title IX. Quid pro quo harassment occurs whenever an agent of an institution conditions a student's participation in an activity on submission to unwanted sexual behavior. Good examples are an assistant coach's refusal to let a recent graduate work out with the cross country ski team after she refused his sexual advances,[43] or a professor's conditioning an exam retake on a student's willingness to be spanked if she failed to obtain a specified grade.[44]

To create a "hostile environment," conduct must be "sufficiently severe, persistent, or pervasive to limit a student's ability to participate in or benefit from an educational program or to create a hostile or abusive educational environment."[45] In thus setting standards for severity and persistency that affect the ability to benefit from one's setting, the Title IX Guidance tracks Title VII standards. Also like the Title VII understanding of a hostile environment, the Guidance incorporates both subjective and objective aspects. Ability to participate in education actually must be impaired and must be so in a way that is rooted in problematic features of the situation rather than in the oversensitivity of the plaintiff.

In the suggestions it makes about applying this account to educational situations, however, the Guidance singles out factors that would not be relevant to employment settings, suggesting that both the age of the students and the size of the educational institution are relevant to determining whether a hostile environment was created. Sexual relations by professors, other staff, or older students with younger students may be judged to be harassment even when they were apparently consensual. In smaller colleges, harassing actions may loom larger than in universities where they can be avoided more easily. These examples indicate possible differences between what equal opportunity requires in education and in employment, although they are tougher on educational institutions and thus might be regarded as legally problematic after *Gebser*.

Courts interpreting Title IX, however, have not been as attentive as the Guidance document to these differences between education and employment settings. For example, court decisions applying severity and pervasiveness in Title IX cases have in general drawn on Title VII characterizations of environments as repeatedly offensive in a way that affects working conditions, but what affects working and learning conditions may differ.

The tendency is for courts to insist on a series of actions to create a hostile environment rather than a single event, although there are examples of cases concluding that one event will suffice.[46] Perhaps the most extreme example of a case holding that one event will not suffice was the determination by a federal district court in Virginia that a rape by a fellow student was not sufficiently pervasive. Nor was it enough that the rape was followed by allegedly half-hearted use of the college disciplinary process to allow the offending student to continue to play football.[47]

Even with a series of events, courts are likely to discount the seriousness of "horseplay" or "teasing" and to accept the quoted views of school administrators that "boys will be boys," particularly as the administrations' explanations for failure to respond to incidents of alleged harassment.[48] Critics of this leniency, however, have argued that because the goal of Title IX is to create equal opportunity in education, these decisions apply standards that are inappropriate, especially where secondary school students or undergraduates are involved. If courts rule in their favor, the tougher approach advocated by these critics would further the opportunity goals of education.

Unwelcomeness

Under the Guidance document, welcomed conduct is not sexual harassment. The idea behind this doctrine is consent and autonomy: How can conduct be harassment if it is invited, enjoyed, a source of pleasure, or if it is reasonable for the actor to believe it is so considered? The doctrine is clearly endorsed for employment law,[49] but there are major difficulties in applying it to education. The Guidance follows *Harris* in distinguishing welcomed behavior from participation and acquiescence; "going along" does not always signify welcomeness. But critics of this distinction point out that it is hard to sustain in relationships marked by significant power imbalances, such as between younger students and much older or admired faculty. The reactions of immature students to advances may be ambivalent, and some overtly welcomed conduct still may be inappropriate. Following the *Harris* approach in the Title VII cases, the Guidance specifies that a student's active involvement—say, participating in the give and take of banter, or even the choice of provocative styles of dress—without a hint of distress quite likely will defeat a harassment claim.[50] The Guidance also observes, however, that students may choose not to resist or object to sexual advances out of fear or concern that the situation will get worse. The Guidance cautions too that with younger children "it may be necessary to determine the degree to which they are able to recognize that certain sexual conduct is conduct to which they can or should reasonably object and the degree to which they can articulate an objection."[51] Presumably this caution is not meant by the Guidance to apply to college students, and the typical advice given to them is to speak up when conduct makes them uncomfortable, the same caution given employees under Title VII.[52] But immaturity and power imbalances exist on campus, too, and the application of the Title VII paradigm about welcomeness to Title IX cases in higher education cases well might be questioned.

The Guidance advice governing actual sexual relationships between employees and students does depart from the Title VII model. Relationships between elementary-school-age children and adult school employees can never be consensual, according to the Guidance. Relationships between secondary school students and adults are presumed to be nonconsensual. The presumption may be overridden in unusual cases for older secondary students, again according to the Guidance. The factors considered in overriding the presumption are the same factors the Guidance identifies for determining whether relations with postsecondary students are welcome: the nature of the conduct and the relationship of the employee to the student, the degree of authority the employee has over the student, the student's legal ability to consent, and practical barriers to consent such as disabilities or impairment. There is at least one case in which a court held that whether a sexual relationship between a secondary school teacher and a student was "welcome" was a fact question for the jury,[53] and there is at least one holding that a consensual sexual relationship "gone sour" between an undergraduate and a faculty member was not a Title IX violation.[54] "Consensual relationship" policies are a contentious issue on many campuses, and it seems likely that as the law of Title IX develops, there will be more litigation about the appropriateness and the understanding of the unwelcomeness requirement in higher education.[55]

Perspective

What is the standpoint from which to assess severity and pervasiveness, unwelcomeness, or other aspects of a hostile environment? The Guidance, like the Supreme Court in *Harris*, requires both objective and subjective elements. The objective element is alteration of the educational environment; the subjective element is the student's finding it more difficult to function in that environment. Insisting on both objective standards of reasonableness and subjective harm does not settle, however, what the objective standard might be and whether it is or is not itself gendered.[56] The Guidance takes up the issue in a puzzling footnote, first observing that *Harris* used the reasonable person standard and then opining that the standard has been interpreted to take into account the sex of the victim. As authority for this last claim, the footnote cites *Ellison v. Brady*,[57] the case that adopted a "reasonable woman" standard specifically instead of a "reasonable person" standard.[58] Perhaps the footnote's apparently contradictory nature can be explained by recognizing that in formulating a standard of objective reasonableness to apply to students there is room for taking differences into account: differences in age, ability, and arguably gender. Although the idea of a gendered standard apparently has faded in employment discrimination litigation, this argument from difference suggests reconsidering it in education.

Same-Sex Harassment

Neither Title VII nor Title IX prohibits discrimination based on sexual orientation. The Guidance states explicitly that heckling or advances based on sexual orientation are not prohibited by Title IX. At the same time, the Guidance provides that same-sex harassment or harassment against gay or lesbian students is sexual harassment if it is discrimination based on sex. As examples, the Guidance describes sexual graffiti by girls directed against the sexuality of other girls or sexual advances by males against lesbian students.

In March 1998, the United States Supreme Court held that same sex behavior can be discrimination "because of sex," provided it was severe enough to create discriminatory conditions of employment.[59] At least one Title IX case also has reached the conclusion that same sex harassment can be sexual discrimination.[60] One consequence of concluding that same sex harassment could not violate Title IX would be to preclude relief for students who are propositioned by administrators or faculty of the same sex, a result at odds with Title IX's goal of equal educational opportunity and the opportunity function of the university.[61]

Fair Procedures and Confidentiality

The Guidance requires institutions to provide "prompt and equitable" grievance procedures that are publicly known, timely, impartial, and reliable. They should allow the opportunity to present witnesses and other evidence, have adequate mechanisms to prevent recurrence and retaliation, and provide the parties with notice of the outcome of the complaint. All of these requirements seem fair, but not surprisingly, there have been significant legal disputes about many aspects of Title IX procedures. Commentators, moreover, noting extremely low reporting rates, are critical of whether Title IX procedures really work as they are supposed to.[62]

Under *Gebser*, as noted above, lack of grievance procedures will not itself give rise to legal liability for damages. This decision has drawn criticism as compounding already-questionable processes for dealing with sexual harassment complaints.

One major procedural concern is the extent to which the confidentiality of the complainant should be protected. The Guidance document indicates that complainants should be told that requests for confidentiality may limit the institution's ability to investigate or respond to complaints. It may be difficult to investigate without implicitly revealing the source of a complaint, and eventually the alleged harasser will need to be offered the opportunity to respond to the complaint. It should be stressed to complainants, though, that Title IX prohibits retaliation. However, the Guidance recommends that despite requests for confidentiality, institutions should investigate complaints when necessary to provide a nondiscriminatory educational environment. As cases have been litigated, defendants have sought access to the complainant's past history or psychological state, raising issues of appropriateness comparable to those in rape cases.[63] These situations create inevitable conflicts, when complainants believe their confidentiality was inappropriately breached either by revealing their identities or by digging into their past histories, but the subjects of the complaint believe they have interests in the availability of the information.

From the view of the alleged harasser, several disciplined faculty or school employees have contended that the procedures applied to them have been unfair. Cases have alleged that inappropriate publicity about harassment complaints has caused damage to reputations or led to trumped up charges.[64] They have alleged that the person accused of harassment was not given a fair hearing or the opportunity to respond.[65] These issues will be discussed in more detail in chapter 7, which describes the development of morally defensible procedures for handling sexual harassment complaints in higher education.

The Constitution and the First Amendment

How to interpret the U.S. Constitution, especially the First Amendment, is a recurring legal issue in the litigation of sexual harassment complaints in higher education. Enforcement of Title VII against harassing speech in the workplace has encountered little successful First Amendment challenge.[66] Nonetheless, there is significant criticism in law reviews of Title VII's impact on workplace speech.[67] Because a plaintiff may allege that a hostile environment was created by the statements of many people, the employer has the incentive to urge everyone to be overcautious in what they say; the result may be a significant chilling effect on workplace speech.[68] Such a chilling effect, some argue, is of even more concern in education, given the knowledge values of the academy.

Indeed, fueled by the protection of academic freedom, enforcing prohibitions on sexual harassment in higher education has met with robust constitutional challenges. As with the *Cohen* case that began this chapter, many harassment cases involve either a First Amendment defense or the allegation that disciplinary processes violated due process rights. Rather delicately, the Guidance document refuses to announce hard and fast rules to govern the

First Amendment implications of sexual harassment litigation. Commentators and cases have not been as shy, however.

As chapter 2 discussed, protecting academic freedom plays a major role in the American Association of University Professors' suggested regulations for institutions of higher education; they are generally written into university regulations and incorporated by implication into job contracts of university faculty. Faculty who are disciplined for sexual harassment typically raise contractual objections either to the processes used or to the imposition of restrictions on what they can say or do. The success of these objections depends on the terms of the contract and, of course, presupposes a contract; contractual theories are not available to "at will" employees, who are hired for an indefinite term and may be terminated at any time or for any reason. Although university faculty generally are hired on a contractual basis, other employees, such as maintenance workers or clerical staff, often have at-will status and thus are not able to use contractual theories against charges of harassment.

In addition, employees of public institutions have constitutional protections that far outstrip their contracts. Public institutions are state actors, subject to the Fourteenth Amendment. They may not deprive their employees of property or liberty without due process of law, and they may not deprive them of the equal protection of the law. Tenured faculty have property interests in their jobs, protected by due process; tenure-track faculty have property interests in being considered as the contract provides in the tenure review process.[69] Other expectations of job renewal also may rise to the level of protected property interests, although yearly appointments of instructors do not. Everyone on a university campus—faculty, students, employees, or visitors—has First Amendment rights to freedom of expression. If these rights are violated, public institutions may be sued for damages for violation of constitutional rights under section 1983.

Free speech rights are not absolute, however. They may be restricted by narrowly tailored regulations furthering a compelling state interest. Not surprisingly, state agencies have argued that they had compelling interests in regulating the speech of their employees. The so-called *Pickering* test, named after the initial case holding that public employees have free speech rights on the job, is the standard formulation courts use for delineating these rights.[70] If the employee's speech comments on a matter of public concern and the employee's interest in the speech is not outweighed by the government's interest in efficient management, the speech is protected.

What is a matter of public concern has been a highly contested issue. Employee dissatisfaction is not a public matter. A college basketball coach who attempted to motivate his players in the locker room by urging them to play "like niggers," found to his chagrin that such talk was not of public concern: "A coach's distress about the degree of aggressiveness shown by his players on the basketball court is a reasonable matter of concern, certainly, to the coach, but not the kind of question that is fairly cast as a 'public' issue." The coach was attempting to pick up on slang used by the players in a positive way to urge them to be tough, and at least some of the players sided with the coach. The United States Court of Appeals for the Sixth Circuit, on the other hand, was openly critical of the mixed messages and covert racism in the coach's urging players to be "niggers" on the basketball floor but not in the classroom. The critique was framed broadly: "What the First Amendment does not do, however, is require the government as employer or the university as educator to accept this view as a valid means of motivating players. An instructor's choice of teaching methods does not rise to the level of protected expression."[71]

In its analysis, the Sixth Circuit court considered carefully and distinguished between two cases involving City University of New York (CUNY) professors who were disciplined for racist statements made in public. In the first, Professor Levin published letters in the *New York Times* and two journals that denigrated the intelligence of African-Americans.[72] In the second, Professor Jeffries made an anti-Semitic speech about racial bias in New York public schools; he was relieved of his chairmanship of the Black Studies department as a result.[73] In both cases, the court concluded that the speech, however disagreeable or controversial, contributed to the public debate. In Professor Jeffries' case, however, the discipline was upheld on the balancing part of the *Pickering* test, as of less value than the disruption it was likely to cause CUNY.

Other cases brought by faculty also have construed "public concern" broadly. A court ruled that criticism of the academic standards and accreditation problems of a university were public, even if they also involved personal animosity: "while personal disputes may have generated many of the events in the chemistry department, the record reveals that at least some of the controversy concerned questions of educational standards and academic policy of a scope broader than their application within the department."[74] In another case, a controversial photo display identifying faculty with their areas of interest in military history was held to be public.[75] In this case, the controversy was over whether the photo display in the department was informative or offensive.

Government agencies that suppress employee speech outside the *Pickering* test are subject to liability under Section 1983. Several damage suits of this kind have been filed. The first time they appear in a jurisdiction, they generally lose, because Section 1983 only allows damage awards for violation of clearly established constitutional rights.[76] This was the outcome of Dean Cohen's damage claim, although he succeeded in his efforts to enjoin the discipline imposed by San Bernandino Valley College. Once a jurisdiction has adopted a ruling such as the *Pickering* test, however, government employees may well expect to recover damages for wrongfully suppressed speech. University faculty at state institutions have not been slow to take up this possibility and have scored several recent highly publicized successes, including Cohen's.[77]

CONCLUSION

The law of sexual harassment under Title IX is evolving rapidly with respect to institutions of higher education. Whether the law in this area is evolving wisely is questionable. Models from employment law may be insensitive to the unique populations and goals of higher education. The Supreme Court's recent rejection of employment law analogies for suits seeking damages from institutions, however, leaves students with less protection than the employees of these very same institutions. At the same time, threats of litigation have encouraged defensiveness on the part of administrators, even though the data suggest that successful lawsuits by students are rare. This situation is an apt reminder that rules of law and ethics are different but good ethical analysis may be helpful in suggesting directions for the law to take. It is to that ethical analysis that I now turn.

4

Sexual Harassment as a Moral Wrong: Assaults, Threats, and Offers

This chapter begins with a day in the life of Jane, an undergraduate at a large state university. She wakes up early and goes for a run in the neighborhood of student apartments where she lives. Jane chooses her route carefully, avoiding fraternity row and a park where a friend of hers was jumped several months ago. It's a good morning for a run—clear and cool—and for the first time in weeks nobody whistles at her or makes fun of her speed.

Jane is a junior majoring in English and is thinking about going to law school. Her first class of the day is the twentieth-century British novel; the discussion is of *Lady Chatterley's Lover*. The book seems quaint to the students. On the way to her next class, Jane runs into an old friend. He greets her with a hug and a "Hiya, beautiful!" Her next class is philosophy of law; the topic is the legal enforcement of morality and they talk about censorship and 2 Live Crew, complete with some of the words from the album *Nasty as They Wanna Be*. Jane pays close attention to the discussion because she has an assignment due on the legal decision that invalidated the Indianapolis antipornography ordinance drafted by Catharine MacKinnon. Some of the students are clearly shocked by the Crew lyrics; one, who works at a media store, explains that the group has gone out of fashion. At the end of class, the student sitting next to Jane asks her if she wants to do something sometime. She doesn't and tells him so politely. Jane's third class of the day is her science requirement; she's avoided taking science until now and signed up for a reputedly easy course called "Common Medicines." This week the topic is contraceptives; the public policy questions raised by Norplant, the long-acting implantable contraceptive, are treated seriously by the instructor but meet with a few giggles from students. Most agree that it would be wrong to require women convicted of child abuse to have Norplant implanted.

As she heads to her car, Jane passes the AIDS Awareness Week booth and is handed a condom. She stops by her apartment to pick up her mail and get ready for work. Examining her mail, she notices idly that someone has left a catalog from Frederick's of Hollywood on top of the mailboxes. Jane is paying her way through school by waitressing at a local restaurant with the theme of a rustic country estate. Her uniform features a tight, low-cut bodice under which she wears a push-up bra, supposedly the garb of a country wench. Several men tip her heavily, commenting on her figure as they do so. On her way home, she picks up her boyfriend as he gets off work. He's also a student at the university. They spend the night together. Jane's apartment-mate sleeps on the couch; their understanding is that anyone with a guest gets the bedroom.

Sexuality and sexual relationships are part of the lives of college students and their campuses, from old-fashioned jokes about Mrs. degrees to the stock reports of marriages between classmates in college alumni magazines. A campus that insulated students from all references to sex would be distinctive but boring, impractical, and in social denial. But when is sexuality on campus to be celebrated, or at least tolerated, and when is it to be condemned as sexual harassment? To answer this question requires accounts of when sexuality itself is morally problematic as well as accounts of when a campus setting makes a difference. Some forms of sexual behavior—such as rape—are clearly wrong wherever they occur. But what of others, such as all the sexually charged events in Jane's day? Are any of them unlawful? Immoral? How bad are they? Does it matter whether they occurred on or off campus?

It is not easy to sort out which of the events are entirely innocent pleasantries and which fall into one of the categories of harassment. Jane experienced no sexual assaults or threats, assuming her relationship with her boyfriend was genuinely consensual, a topic for chapter 6. In this, she is quite typical; rates of sexual assaults and threats are lower than reported rates of other forms of harassment, although one-fifth of all female undergraduates report being forced to have sex.[1] If her overtipping customers really were seeking flirtation, she may have encountered a mild form of sexual bribery. The fellow student who asked her out exemplified a standard, nonaggressive form of seductive behavior. But depending on what actually went on in her classes, in her apartment complex, and in her encounters as she went along her way, Jane may have experienced a great deal of what some critics characterize as gender harassment.

Using the examples from Jane's day, this chapter examines the kinds of moral wrongs inflicted by sexual harassment, starting with the most serious case of a sexual wrong, sexual assault, and arguing that it violates the safety, privacy, and autonomy of the victim; that it harms the victim's intimates; and that, if prevalent, it undermines campus community. Whether sexual threats and offers involve similar types of wrongs is then considered, and the chapter concludes by asking whether the campus context makes a difference, using the example of date rape on campus: Should it be regarded differently from date rape off campus? Chapter 5 continues the discussion, dealing with seductive behavior and gender harassment—all the moments of sexuality and sexism in Jane's day—and strikes a balance between the knowledge and opportunity values of the academy. Chapter 6 considers the special case of consensual amorous relationships on campus.

THE WRONGS OF SEXUAL ASSAULT

Fortunately, Jane was not a victim of sexual assault. During her run, she wasn't jumped from behind, pushed into a bush, and penetrated. Nor was she overwhelmed in the parking lot as she went back to her apartment to change for work. Had this happened, she would have been the victim of what has been described as "real rape," violent sexual penetration by a stranger.[2] There is an extensive literature about whether acquaintance or date rape is similar to such "real" rape.[3]

Sexual assault is, first of all, assault. Like all assaults, it interferes with bodily security and integrity. If the assault is rape, the victim has been literally penetrated. The attack may have been violent or have threatened violence. It may have been painful, leaving the victim with serious injuries or permanent impairments. Invaded once, a victim has confronted her sense of vulnerability and the inability to assure personal safety.

Sexual assault is, second, sexual. To the wrong of the assault, it adds incursion on aspects of the body significant for the establishment of intimate relationships, for the experience of erotic pleasure, and for reproduction. Twisting ankles may cause severe pain, but twisting breasts or testicles both agonizes and degrades in a special way. Victims of sexual assaults frequently find themselves unable to recapture the pleasures of intimacy or eroticism. Some cultures may react by rejecting rape victims, treating them as damaged goods unfit for marriage.

Third, sexual assault violates autonomy. It forces intimacy on the victim. The liberty to choose whether to enter a sexual relationship, with whom, and to what end, is an especially important personal liberty, often conceptualized as liberty privacy. Decisions about sexuality and reproduction are central to a person's conception of who she is and the kind of life she wants to lead. The victim of sexual assault has not had these very central choices respected. She even may become pregnant and face all the dilemmas and stigma of an unwanted child.

Those close to the victim have interests that may be violated as well. A victim damaged by assault, physically or emotionally, may be unable to work or to care for children. A victim whose intimacy has been invaded may be fearful of being a sexual partner to anyone, even a spouse. Someone who has lost autonomy privacy may lose the sense of value or the ability to participate in chosen relationships. For injuries like these to a spouse, it is not uncommon for states to allow suits for damages for what is called "loss of consortium" in the old-fashioned language of the common law.[4]

The violations of bodily security, intimacy, and autonomy principally are wrongs to the victim and those close to her. Sexual assault also may create fundamental inequalities for the victim, and these inequalities wrong both the victim and other women. If cultural factors encourage the rape of women, women encounter risks that are disproportional to those encountered by men.[5] Even the sense that walking back to a dormitory room is like running a gauntlet places burdens on women students that male students may escape entirely. Public safety policies also may raise questions of equality. How much to spend on public safety and where to spend it are public policy issues that may be resolved in ways that disadvantage women. For example, a university may choose to devote scarce public safety dollars to crowd control at football games rather than to night patrols in parking garages. In addition, the communicative message of rape is a general one of violence against all women. Knowledge of the risk of rape may decrease the ability of any woman to function or to participate in valued activities. For example, it may be rational for women to avoid areas of campus that are educationally vital but unsafe, such as laboratories at night. If in response to the assault the victim modifies her life, she loses out on basic opportunities. A woman who is sexually assaulted on the job and quits because she cannot face her fears of a recurrence, or a student who leaves school after being raped in a dormitory or in the library stacks, are examples. This was the case with the female athlete at Virginia Polytechic Institute who left school after she was raped by a football player— while he returned to his scholarship after a brief suspension.[6]

There are ways in which sexual assaults wrong everyone. They express a lack of respect for personal safety, integrity, and autonomy. They may thus contribute to a more general social climate of disrespect. They may increase fears for safety and the sense of social disintegration. If sexual assaults are directed toward particular social groups, such as Muslims in Bosnia, they wrong that group in a manner akin to genocide. The location of sexual assaults also may matter to how they wrong the community. If rapes occur largely in private homes, people's sense of security may falter. Rapes in public places such as parks may drive people inward and degrade the quality of public spaces. Fears about safety, particularly at night, seriously may damage community at universities with large areas that are difficult for police to patrol. Anyone who has lived on a campus with an uncaught serial rapist will recognize the devastating effects on community. When the University of Michigan at Ann Arbor faced a series of rape-murders about twenty-five years ago, women students were warned against going out on blind dates, making male acquaintances at student events, and sharing rides posted on campus bulletin boards—all apparent ways in which the rapist had met his victims. Normal student pleasantries became infinitely threatening; indeed, the assailant eventually was identified as a student at a neighboring college who met his victims at campus events.

These, then, are the wrongs of sexual assault: wrongs to victims and their intimates, wrongs of inequality, and wrongs to communities. Each of these wrongs is a matter of degree. The other categories of sexual harassment outlined in chapter 1—sexual threats, sexual offers, seductive behavior, and gender harassment—can be viewed in terms of the degree to which they involve any or all of the wrongs of sexual assault.

SEXUAL THREATS

Sexual threats use the indication of an intent to inflict harm to induce sex. An example would be the threat to fail a student unless she enters a sexual relationship. Unless the victim resists and the person making the threat carries it out, threats do not actually inflict the harm. If the victim complies with the threat, there is at least some sense in which the sex obtained is consensual; the victim chose it as a lesser evil than the threatened harm. This has been regarded as the possible moral difference between threats and assaults, and it is central to understanding whether sexual threats are unlawful in the same ways as sexual assaults. There are at least four possible results for the victim of a sexual threat: (1) she resists the threat, rejects the sexual advance, and the threatener carries through with the harm; (2) she resists the threat, rejects the sexual advance, and the threatener backs off and does not carry through with the harm; (3) she gives in to the threat, has the sex, and avoids the harm; and (4) she gives in to the threat, has the sex, and the threatener inflicts the harm anyway.

One moral question is raised by (1) and (4), whether it is wrong to follow through on the threat. An example would be a professor's carrying out a threat to write a poor reference for a student unless she responds sexually. In academic life, threatened harms are likely to be judgments of desert: grades, awards, letters of reference, appointments, tenure decisions, job performance evaluations, raises, and promotions. If the poor judgment is unwarranted—in the example, if the poor reference is not warranted by the student's work— the recipient is wronged by not getting what she deserves. If the poor judgment is deserved, the recipient is not wronged by the judgment itself—it is what she deserved. But she still may have been wronged by the threat.

Ironically, even in case (4), when she gives in to the threat but the harm is inflicted anyway, the recipient is not wronged by a deserved judgment itself. She is, however, wronged by having been duped; threats have something of a promissory character that the threat will not be made good on if the victim responds. More importantly, the background of threats and sex cast doubt on whether any judgments of the recipient's merits made by the threatener could be fair. Evaluations of the quality of academic work—the originality of a doctoral dissertation, for example—are notoriously subjective. If the evaluation was preceded by sexual threats, it cannot be regarded as trustworthy, whether the subject gave in to or rebuffed the threats. It is probably not accidental that some of the most acrimonious harassment cases feature scenarios in which sexual relationships and high regard soured together. The story line is predictable: The professor-student relationship flourishes, the student is highly praised, the relationship becomes sexual, the sex ends, the student's work is criticized, and the student cannot continue to find support in the program. In these cases, it is often unclear whether the earlier favorable judgments were inflated by the sexual interest or the later critical judgments were deflated by the rejection (or by an eventual loss of interest in the relationship). Either way, the threat's recipient is wronged by the doubts cast on the process of evaluation.

So are others affected by the tainted evaluative processes. When an evaluative process is infected by sex, all evaluations are suspect, because those subject to the same process cannot trust that evaluations they receive are fair. If word gets out more generally, everyone subject to the process may be hurt; no one will trust evaluations from the tainted source. The effects on the careers of women students can be severe if their advisor has the reputation of praising women in response to their succumbing to sexual pressure— even if they themselves have never been sexually pressed.

Regardless of her response, sexual threats themselves also wrong the victim. Arguing for this claim requires a fuller look at the moral wrongfulness of threats. Threats wrong because they are coercive; sexual threats wrong because of the coercive means they employ. On standard analyses, coercion involves the threat of harm in the effort to influence choice. Michael Bayles, for example, gives the following account of coercion: X coerces Y to do A if (1) X intends that Y do A; (2) X intends to harm Y if Y does not do A; (3) X threatens Y with harm if Y does not do A; (4) Y does A; (5) Y could have done otherwise had Y so chosen; and (6) Y would have chosen otherwise had Y not been threatened by X.[7] Now, the fact that coercion interferes with choice certainly raises a moral red flag, but the interference does not show conclusively that coercion is wrong. As a matter of background morality, much but not all use of coercion is wrongful. For example, suppose a landlord threatens a tenant with eviction—a harm—in the effort to induce payment of overdue rent—a payment the tenant would prefer not to make or is unable to make. Or suppose a tenant threatens a landlord with legally available methods for withholding rent in the effort to compel the landlord to make repairs needed to bring the building up to code. Both of these threats are coercive in Bayles's sense of the announcement of a harm designed to influence choice. Yet neither is wrongful. The landlord has a right to evict a tenant who does not pay rent, and the tenant has the moral right (and the legal right in some jurisdictions) to sequester rental payments for an uninhabitable apartment. Other types of threats under the same circumstances would clearly be wrongful. Neither the tenant nor the landlord has the right to threaten to shoot the other for nonpayment of rent or for poor maintenance of the apartment; the landlord does not have the right to threaten the tenant with eviction if the tenant does not have sex with him; and the tenant does not have the right to threaten the landlord with nonpayment of rent for refusing to provide the tenant with expensive leather furniture (unless the lease so stipulates). To generalize from these examples, the morality of the coercion rests on whether the person making the threats has the right to inflict the harm at issue, whether the person threatened is properly subject to the harm, and whether the choice at issue is one the threatener may properly influence by imposing the given harm, among other factors.

There are examples of the permissible use of coercion in academe along the lines of the landlord-tenant example. A teacher might threaten a student with failure if work isn't turned in on time or doesn't improve. A student might be threatened with involuntary withdrawal from a class for nonattendance. A faculty member might be threatened with nonrenewal if his teaching or research does not improve. A department secretary might be threatened with dismissal for absenteeism. In each case, the threatener has the right to make the judgment at issue, the person threatened is the appropriate subject of the threat, and the threatened harm is relevant to the goal sought to be achieved by means of the threat.

But there are no permissible examples of the use of sexual coercion in academe. I say this with some trepidation, because negatives are notoriously hard to prove. Sexual threats simply are never relevant to the goals of academe, be they the advancement of knowledge, the development of opportunities, or the furtherance of community. Academic officers are not legitimately placed to make the threats, and their recipients are not appropriate subjects. Even Jane Gallop's celebration of the sexiness of education, reprinted in Part II, chapter 14, does not support linking sex to qualitative judgments; it argues at best that learning is sexy and is enhanced by sexiness.

The argument here relies on the inappropriateness of sexual threats in an educational context. A more sweeping argument could be made that it is never morally permissible to use the threat of harm to induce someone to choose to engage in a sexual relationship. There are hard cases in which the threat of harm could be relevant to the provision or withdrawal of sex. Perhaps the hardest might be a threat by a husband or wife to end a marriage if the partner does not take steps to improve their sexual relationship. If this threat is not permissible—and I argue that it is not—it is hard to imagine when sexual threats would be permissible. It is reasonable to assume the partners in a marriage are morally permitted to seek mutual sexual satisfaction and to expect each other to work together to that end. For a variety of reasons, including physical or psychological disabilities, there may be limits on what can be achieved, even with cooperation. On some views of the obligations of marriage, it is morally permissible for a partner to leave the marriage if the other does not cooperate in trying to improve the sexual relationship. On other views, although this is more controversial, it is morally permissible to end the marriage if the sexual relationship cannot be made fulfilling. (Think of tragic cases of a severely injured partner, one who remains in a persistent vegetative state; a partner who remains in the relationship is commonly described as a moral saint.) The question here is whether a partner legitimately may use the threat of leaving to affect choices about the sexual relationship. If the value of sexual choices, in their own right and to the people involved, depends on their being made in an unpressured manner, threats are arguably inappropriate. But even within marriage, compelling sex by the threat of harm is wrongful because of the intimacy and personal importance of the choice. That is why marital rape is now viewed as a crime: Marriage is no longer assumed to confer a rightful expectation of sex. One corollary may be that partners have a right to expect each other to try to work together to improve the quality of a sexual relationship and to end the relationship if such efforts are not forthcoming. This corollary depends on the mutuality of the obligation to try to improve the relationship, however, not on the legitimacy of sexual threats.

Thus sexual threats, to whatever end and in whatever context, even within marriage, are morally wrong. They announce that the recipient's bodily intimacy and her autonomy with respect to that intimacy are subject to the threat of harm. Sex is not properly up for bargaining; it should be the result of voluntary and joyful choice.

In addition to wronging the victim, sexual threats in academe wrong the victim's intimates. Whether the victim resists or gives in, she may be left fearful, dysfunctional, unable to enter into satisfying sexual relationships, or be forced to violate the trust or uniqueness of other ongoing relationships.

Threats also express a lack of respect for the relations of intimacy the victim now has by treating her intimacy itself as the subject of interference. The anger spouses or lovers of victims of sexual assaults or threats feel on their own behalf (in addition to on the victim's behalf) by may be explained in this way.

The effects of sexual threats on the victim's equality are similar to the effects of sexual assaults. Threats manifest disrespect for and objectify their victims. People who are threatened, particularly if the threats occur repeatedly, may rationally choose to avoid the locus of the threats. Over and over again, women's stories of sexual harassment report giving up jobs or abandoning educational plans in response to threats of harm if they do not engage in sex. Significant losses of opportunities are the result.

Because threats are most likely to be directed at selected people rather than at a generalized group, their impact on the use of public spaces may be more limited than the impact of sexual assault. At the same time, it is possible for threatening contexts to be created that undermine community. On certain jobs, women may avoid places where men congregate because they are threatened with physical harm or verbal abuse unless they respond sexually, such as the office coffee pot or water fountain, the lunchroom, or an exercise area. Women may thus be effectively excluded from places where useful information is shared, where camaraderie and networking occur, or simply where amenities are available.[8] At universities, dormitory hallways or living rooms may become spaces where women reasonably feel threatened. Weight rooms or the track may be off limits. Areas of the student union—as well as local bars—may be effectively inaccessible. Certain public walkways or gathering places may be better avoided. For women students, the results may range from no impact (who wanted to go to that bar anyway?), to mild inconvenience (why not take a different route to class?) to serious educational barriers (how can I finish that paper if I can't be safe in the library at night?)

Sexual threats thus wrong women when they inflict harms as they are carried out, when they devalue intimacy and autonomy, when they limit opportunities, and when they diminish the accessibility and livability of public spaces.

SEXUAL BRIBES AS COERCIVE OFFERS

Jane's day illustrates only one possible example of sexual bribery, the excessive tips, depending on what their offerors intended and expected. Some heavy tips are simply expressions of pleasure or concern for the waitress, others reflect crassness or drunken overenthusiasm, and still others intend to induce a response. Tips held out and then pulled back with an accompanying smirk of "give us a kiss," or tips put down the wenchly bodice with a moment's pause and a glance seeking assent, followed by a long, tight hug, are sexual bribes. At universities, reported forms of sexual bribes include sex for grades, sex for letters of recommendation or job placements, and sex for job promotions or good job evaluations.

At first glance, it may seem that the chief problem with bribes is their unfairness to others—the students who aren't offered the opportunity to improve their grades, for example. How is the potential recipient wronged by the offer of a benefit—which can be refused—in exchange for sex? Michael Bayles argued further that "sexual offers"—note the change in terminology from "bribes" to "offers"—are not coercive and indeed augment the range of choices available to the recipient:

> Assume there is a mediocre woman graduate student who would not receive an assistantship. Suppose the department chairman offers her one if she goes to bed with him and she does so. In what sense has the graduate student acted against her will? She apparently preferred having the assistantship and sleeping with the chairman to not sleeping with the chairman and not having the assistantship.[9]

Libertarians argue that unless such sexual offers involve force or fraud or otherwise violate rights, there is nothing at all morally wrong about them. If Jane is offered an extra $20 tip for a kiss, she is given more possible choices than she otherwise would have had. She can kiss and get the $20. Or she can refuse the kiss, tossing it off with a pleasant—or not so pleasant—laugh. Depending on what is said and what ensues, she can consider the incident to be of little consequence—just an off-color joke, all in a night's work. Of course, Jane most likely won't get the tip if she doesn't give the kiss, but the tip is not something she was entitled to anyway, assuming it's not a tip automatically included for good service. Nor is the offer to Jane of an extra tip a wrong to other waitresses, at least in the sense that it takes anything they were entitled to and gives it to Jane. What more might make the offer problematic?

A threshold issue about offers is whether they can be distinguished from threats; if they cannot be, the discussion of the wrongfulness of threats will apply directly to the discussion of the wrongfulness of offers. Offers propose a benefit to be foregone if sex is not forthcoming; threats propose a harm unless sex occurs. Many writers on harassment work within the intuitive framework that a difference exists between suffering significantly undesirable consequences and missing out on a benefit.[10] Yet there is real question about whether the underlying distinction can be sustained. For example, is there a difference in principle between threatening a student with the loss of a scholarship if she does not have sex and offering a student a scholarship in exchange for sex? In both cases, the foregone item is the scholarship. Characterizing the loss as a harm and the award as a benefit assumes a baseline situation from which the recipient is being made worse off or better off. Characterizing the harm as a wrong makes the further assumption that the recipient can legitimately expect continuation of the baseline situation. Leaving aside sexual offers for a moment, suppose, for example, that all scholarships are competitively awarded on an annual basis, without any expectation of renewal. This year's recipient who does not receive a scholarship for the next year because other candidates are judged more meritorious might more reasonably be described as having lost out on a benefit than as having been dealt a harm. Which characterization is correct—harm or benefit—depends on the expected baseline situation. The harm/lost benefit distinction is thus arguably itself a moral judgment that the libertarian would need to defend to separate threats from offers.

Nonetheless, much of the discussion of the morality of sexual offers does assume that offers can be distinguished from threats, and it is important to address this literature directly. First of all, it is arguable, even on libertarian terms, that sexual offers or threats violate rights or duties, most likely, obligations assumed voluntarily by promise or contract. For example, a university might commit itself by public announcement to the terms of a scholarship award. Applicants for the scholarship would then be entitled to be considered for the award on the announced terms, an entitlement that would be violated by an awards committee member's supporting a particular candidate in return for a sexual relationship. This would wrong the favored candidate as well as all of the disappointed candidates, for all are entitled to be considered on the announced terms. Or a university might incorporate grading policies and policies restricting relationships with students in contracts with faculty; faculty signing the contracts would thereby agree to be bound by these policies and would be in breach of contract if they violated these policies.

Such contractual terms, however, do not cover all aspects of the moral status of sexual offers. Contracts may not anticipate some kinds of offers—perhaps a faculty member implicitly offering a student generous conversation and expertise in the field rather than a better grade, in exchange for sex. And they do not provide a moral reason for including terms about sexual offers and whether such terms should or should not be incorporated in university contractual arrangements. What more might wrong the beneficiaries of handsome offers in exchange for sex?

Critics answering this question have developed responses to Michael Bayles's example of the woman graduate student, quoted above. Bayles contends that when the department chairman offers the student an assistantship in exchange for sex, she is not coerced; she chooses what she most wants from an enlarged set of options. That there is an undesirable aspect of the desired package—sex with the chair—does not show that the choice overall was coerced. To be sure, there are cases that differ Bayles's scenario, in which the offer is combined with a threat, such as the department chair offering the assistantship in exchange for sex and at the same time making it clear to the student that if she does not take the package, she will be dismissed from the program. This "offer you can't refuse" really is a threat mixed with an offer and is wrong because of the threat it contains.

But what if there is, at the time it is made, no threat implicit in the offer? What if the department chair in Bayles's case genuinely does not intend to threaten the student with harm if she refuses? Several writers have argued that the student's situation has nevertheless been made worse by the offer and that she has thereby been coerced. Nancy Tuana, in the selection reprinted in Part II, chapter 10, shows that where the offeror is in a position of authority, it is reasonable for the recipient of the offer to believe that she will be harmed if she does not respond positively. Despite his current intentions, the department chair may react to a refusal of his offer with the desire to retaliate or with changed attitudes toward the student, to her ultimate detriment. His ego, after all, is on the line. And she is in a very vulnerable position: a student, already labeled "mediocre." Such offers, Tuana contends, are just as coercive as threats: The student would not have chosen sex with the chair absent the offer, and the student accepts the offer because she reasonably fears the refusal will make her worse off in the long run.[11]

It also is arguable that sexual offers are wrongful even if there is no broader threat of harm to be discerned in the context. Suppose, for example, that a rich man in the community offers to pay the student the equivalent of an assistantship in exchange for sex. He has no connection with her department and no power over her. What he does is not coercive: It is a pure offer, no strings attached. Yet there are still reasons why it might be judged wrongful. It offers the effective equivalent of a scholarship on the basis of unrelated criteria. By comparison, an alternative use for the money is a contribution to the university's scholarship fund. The man has no obligation to make such a contribution, but it does not follow that it is morally desirable for him to open his own private scholarship fund in exchange for sex with the students he supports. Consider the impact on attitudes toward scholarships if this practice of private funding became widespread. Such a practice of awarding scholarships treats sex as a commodity up for sale for an education.

Sexual offers also wrong others who do not have access to the offers on the terms indicated. These may be wrongs to students of both sexes who do not get what they deserve when the fellowship goes to the student who responds favorably to the offer rather than to the student with the better record.

John Hughes and Larry May point out that sexual offers are wrongs that are done to all women.[12] In the earlier example, the department chair has demonstrated, by making the offer, that he is willing to use his academic power arbitrarily. This may in turn affect attitudes toward all women in an academic program who find their positive recommendations discounted because the program has a reputation for corrupted recommendations and women are thought to get ahead by sleeping their way to the top. As Hughes and May point out, if sexual offers become widespread, sexual discrimination is the result.

The coercive interference with autonomy and the exacerbation of sex discrimination are the chief wrongs of sexual offers. It is fair to say, however, that they are in other ways of lesser significance than sexual threats. They may insult the partners of the person receiving the offer, but unless they are unusually persistent or threatening, it is less likely that the offers would impair the resisting person's ability to enter into intimate relationships. It also is unlikely that sexual offers contribute to an atmosphere of danger or undermine community in the way that threats do. The conclusion to be drawn is that sexual offers are serious moral wrongs but wrongs of a lesser order than sexual threats or assaults.

THE SIGNIFICANCE OF A CAMPUS SETTING

The discussion so far has already suggested several ways in which a campus setting is significant to the ethics of assaults, threats, and offers. If sexual assaults or threats particularly are widely apparent on campus, community may be seriously undermined. For individual victims, the ability to learn and to benefit from an education may be impaired. If threats or offers infect the evaluation process, attitudes toward women's success may be altered and their ability to compete on fair terms may be compromised. Sexual assaults, threats, and offers thus are incompatible with the knowledge, opportunity, and community goals of the academy, and as discussed above, the case for their prohibition is clear cut. At the same time, some critics have offered arguments that a campus setting should alter the understanding of what is to be prohibited. Is it possible that a "no" on campus means something different from a "no" off campus?

Date Rape: Is the Campus Different?

The current controversy about whether date rape is "real" rape has been particularly heated on American college campuses. The varying positions in the date rape controversy are summarized as follows: At one pole is the strict view that date rape is exactly like real rape except that the parties know each other and it is less likely to be violent. Therefore, the two people contemplating sexual intimacy should discuss and agree upon it, step by step; this view is represented in the Antioch College policy, reprinted in Part II, chapter 17.[13] At the other pole is the more liberal view that a dating situation is at best ambiguous about consent, and women are responsible for making their objections known, loudly and clearly, if they do not wish to have sex.[14] In between are proposals to view date rape as a lesser wrong, as a wrong for which diminished responsibility should be attributed, or as a wrong that poses particularly difficult problems of proof. This discussion does not focus on the general issues raised by date rape, although my view is that given the ambiguities of some dating situations and the problems of proof, the law should move toward developing the lesser offense of nonconsensual sexual intercourse. The focus here is whether a campus setting changes the terms of the date rape debate. The hard questions about the understanding of sexual assault may be harder in a campus context: Is there any reason for believing sexual assaults should be defined differently, punished differently, or subjected to a different evidentiary standard on campus?

One reason for thinking that a campus setting changes the terms of the debate is that the rules of the dating game are unique on campus. According to this view, the presumption is that people are seeking mates or at least a little bit of fun. Therefore, consent to a sexual relationship is presumed rather than the reverse. This view might be offered to cover campus relationships in general or for specific campus situations noted for their sexuality. Suppose a secluded spot in the campus arboretum is well known as a place to establish sexual intimacy; going there happily with a boyfriend might be understood as consent unless consent is clearly withdrawn. Consent also might be presumed, absent a clear contrary expression, from attendance at notorious parties. These presumptions about consent would be rejected by the strict stance on the date rape debate, that consent must be explicit at every step of the way, regardless of the circumstances.

Now, suppose it is true that facts about campus life are relevant to the date rape debate, as just outlined. It does not follow, however, that this changes the concept of date rape. Date rape is nonconsensual sex imposed by one acquaintance upon another. What these examples show is that on the more liberal view, accepted campus norms and practices may make a difference as to what *beliefs* about consent are reasonable. If it is reasonable for one of the parties to believe that the other is consenting, even though the other is, in fact, not consenting, then the sex is not date rape. But the examples do not show that date rape should be *defined* differently on campus.

Another possibility is that a campus setting limits culpability for date rape. In *Real Rape*,[15] her well-known defense of the status of acquaintance rape as a serious invasion of the person, really rape, Susan Estrich supports reforms that introduce sexual offenses of lessened culpability, such as negligent sexual assault. A campus setting, it might be argued, is a perfect place to experiment with the delineation of such a category of offenses. Much of the acquaintance rape on campus is not sex that intentionally overrides the consent of the victim. It is sex that is careless about consent by people who are young, egged on by their peers, inexperienced, and quite possibly drunk. This is not to say that campuses should encourage a "boys will be boys" attitude or should let students off without recognition of the seriousness of the harm that has been caused. It is to recognize that there are sexual assaults in which the mens rea—the mental element of the offense—may be recklessness or negligence but is not intent. Such recognition of an offense of lesser culpability, however, should not be unique to college campuses; rape law everywhere has difficulty accommodating cases of nonconsensual sex that are not intentional rape. Colleges should recognize this possibility and formulate their educational and disciplinary processes to take it into account.

Relationships of Trust on Campus

These examples of date rape involve sex between peers, but there are special relationships of trust on campus within which acquaintance rape might be judged more culpable. Faculty-student relationships are the most important of these. Because these relationships are based on trust and because the participants in them are not equal, the parties with more power have a special duty to ensure consent. Trust may exist even in the case of a nominally peer relationship, such as one between a senior faculty member and an academic trainee listed with faculty status but under the senior's supervision. Indeed, many of these relationships are morally problematic even with apparent consent. These problems about consent and responsibility will be taken up more fully in chapter 6.

Special Responsibilities of the University

Another issue raised by the campus setting is the university's responsibility for the acts of those within it. As chapter 3 indicated, the Supreme Court has held that educational institutions may be liable for sexual harassment by their agents when they knew of it and remained deliberately indifferent;[16] they may also be liable for student-student harassment when they acted with deliberate indifference to known actions of harassment.[17] Vicarious liability is clear if the university ordered or knew about and condoned the harassment, but this is unlikely to be true at least initially for assaults, threats, and offers. Courts are divided about whether to treat faculty and staff as agents of the institution, as they would be regarded in employment law for purposes of Title IX, and so are divided about whether to attribute liability to the institution for anything that faculty and staff do. Some courts will hold the institution liable only if it failed to provide adequate grievance and supportive services for students. Courts are even more divided about peer harassment, with holdings ranging from the refusal to make schools liable unless they respond better to peer harassment against one sex than against the other, to holdings that schools are liable if they had constructive notice of the harassment and failed to act.

Whether universities should be held legally liable is, of course, a different question from whether they should be held morally responsible for the harassment of those who work and act within the ivory tower. The case for legal liability might turn on which entity is available and able to pay for damages. The case for moral responsibility should hinge on what it is reasonable to expect the university to do to prevent and investigate harassment.

Universities cannot and should not monitor faculty in every step of what they do. The knowledge goals of the academy require liberty of thought and action. Classrooms, laboratories, public spaces, and faculty offices are managed in a decentralized way; that is part of their charm and their effectiveness as a setting for the give and take of learning. At the same time, without interfering with freedom of inquiry, universities can use their powers of selection, education, and discipline to minimize the risks that faculty will engage in harassing behavior, important steps toward helping ensure that women students do not lose out on the opportunities of higher education. John Hughes and Larry May argue that active enforcement of prohibitions on sexual harassment is the flip side of the university's grant of discretionary power to faculty in evaluating students.[18] Universities have the power to discipline faculty and other employees, and they should use that power in service of the opportunity goals of the academy.

Universities also can provide supportive services for students who believe they might have been harassed, including readily accessible education, mediation, counseling, and grievance structures. Such supportive services are particularly important on campuses with young and inexperienced undergraduate populations who may experience increased levels of difficulty in recognizing and coming forth with concerns, but they are important everywhere.

When the source of the harassment is not a university employee but a student or a campus visitor, the university's ability to organize educational and disciplinary processes may be more limited. If the university has less ability to prevent the harassment, its levels of responsibility should be correspondingly lessened. Schools can, however, set examples, educate, and discipline students where there are clear incidents of harassment. Just as in cases of harassment by faculty, universities can have well-advertised and well-run services for students who believe they have been victimized by other members of the campus community. Universities cannot and should not police the private lives of their students, but they can create a campus climate that discourages harassment and that helps those students who have been its unfortunate recipients.

In further support of the university's moral obligation to undertake significant efforts to prevent and remedy harassment, it is worth comparing the situation of a university student with that of a university employee. Because of the accidentally different structures of employment and education law, university employees can receive damages for any quid pro quo harassment on the part of other employees and as well as damages for a setting in which harassment is pervasive enough to create an environment that is significantly uncomfortable or that interferes with job performance. Students are not nearly so fortunate. Depending on their legal jurisdiction, they may be able to get preventive relief only after the fact; if they can recover damages, it may be only when they can prove the university engaged in discrimination of its own. Yet access to the educational benefits of a university is surely as important to opportunity as access to employment, and students need as much protection as employees.

Unfortunately, the evidence does not suggest that universities are particularly good at discharging these vicarious obligations. Educational efforts about sexual harassment are typically directed at entering students, and complaint rates remain very low. Yet as discussed above, about one-fifth of women undergraduates report coerced intercourse. Recently universities have been criticized for being unlikely to share information about harassment histories with successor employers of professors found guilty of harassment.[19] The explanation for this failure may be fear of litigation or negative publicity for the university, or it may be concern about the fairness of the university's own processes. These are surely legitimate concerns for the faculty member, but if the university is concerned about the fairness of its policies, it should rethink those same procedures. Issues of process design are explored further in chapter 7.

The Campus Setting: Moral Responsibilities of Bystanders

Another issue of vicarious responsibility on campus is the responsibility faculty or staff bear for one another's actions. Suppose one faculty member has reliable information that a colleague has been sexually coercing students. Silence, perhaps bolstered by concerns about academic witch hunts or by questions about whether the evidence really is trustworthy, is the typical response. But it is arguable that the response is morally wrong and that faculty in particular bear responsibility for failure to take even the most minimal action in response to a colleague's harassment, at least when they can do so without significant costs to their own careers.

Other professions, such as law, impose some level of responsibility on colleagues for their peers' behavior. Supervisory lawyers are responsible for making reasonable efforts to ensure that their subordinates do not violate the rules of professional conduct.[20] Any lawyer having reason to believe that a colleague has committed an ethical violation that casts serious doubt on honesty or fitness to practice law has a duty to report it to the bar.[21] Unlike lawyers or physicians, university faculty lack the tradition of a professional

role morality that would encourage them to take responsibility for one another's behavior. There are good reasons for this absence, academic freedom
paramount among them.

Nevertheless, to dismiss outright any kind of coprofessional responsibility among academics in the name of academic freedom can be considered
a regrettable and serious violation of faculty obligations to students. Faculty
are at times in supervisory relationships with each other: department chairs,
area committee chairs, or formally assigned mentors. In these roles, they
have formal responsibilities to help their colleagues meet their professional
obligations.

Even without such formal responsibilities, faculty have fiduciary responsibilities to their own students and perhaps to other students as well. Their
most direct fiduciary obligations are to students in their own classes; these
obligations would certainly include not harassing their students; working to
create a successful classroom-learning environment, including discouraging
student-to-student harassment; and counseling students about legitimate academic concerns. But the fiduciary obligations of faculty extend beyond the
students in their immediate classes, at least to students who are majors and
graduate students in their departments. Providing educationally successful
undergraduate and graduate programs is a departmental responsibility,
shared at least by all regular faculty in a department. Sexual coercion on the
part of a colleague may leave graduate students unable to complete programs, majors unable to take crucial courses required for their degrees, and
other students unable to benefit from central courses offered by the department. These are very serious consequences for students' opportunities to
learn; to leave such a situation entirely untouched violates the fiduciary obligations of every faculty member to students in the department. Most generally, all faculty have an obligation to all students to work to create an educational climate that achieves the goals of the academy. The more direct the
connection of the faculty member to the student, the stronger the fiduciary
obligation; thus the strongest obligations would lie to a faculty member's
own students, advisees, and departmental majors and graduate students.

There are real problems of how these fiduciary obligations might be discharged. Faculty may hear reports of harassment that are unreliable; passing
on such gossip, particularly in the form of an official complaint, could be seriously damaging to careers. Harassment complaints can be used to political
ends and the threats to academic freedom are serious; yet academic freedom
does not provide a legitimate protective umbrella for sexual coercion. Faculty who challenge their peers' behavior may find their own careers threatened, a threat that is particularly serious for untenured faculty. Perhaps the
way to accommodate these risks is to conclude that coprofessional obligations should be discharged principally by supporting and educating students
(for example, helping them become aware of the resources available to them

on campus) and by encouraging recalcitrant colleagues to understand better when behavior is problematic. When a faculty member has clear, first-hand evidence of sexual coercion—for example, if she overhears a conversation through thin office walls—then the case for reporting is strongest. The student has a great deal at stake, and the offending colleague's conduct does not fall within the protective scope of academic freedom. With first-hand knowledge of the incident, the faculty member is less likely to be the unwitting agent of unwarranted gossip or political agendas. Reprisals against the faculty member and concerns about unfair practices remain concerns that universities can best allay by working to be sure their processes are fair and protective. These are controversial conclusions; I offer them with the goal of raising questions about whether faculty should take more seriously the possibility that they have obligations to respond to the misbehavior of their colleagues.

CONCLUSION

Sexual assaults, threats, and offers are serious moral wrongs to their victims and to others whose opportunities they may impair. Universities need to take their remedial and preventative responsibilities more seriously than they do. Faculty especially need to reconsider the extent to which they bear responsibility for responding to the acts of their peers.

5

The Wrongs of Sexual Harassment: Seductive Behavior and Gender Harassment

I continue now with the sexual aspects of Jane's day. As would be typical of a contemporary undergraduate, Jane experienced some seductive behavior and many reminders of sex. Whether any of these should be judged to be harassment, and thus morally problematic, is the topic of this chapter. I begin with seductive behavior, arguing that it is problematic in a university context when it interferes with learning or opportunity. I then apply the same analysis to determine which, if any, of the reminders of sex that Jane experienced are properly viewed as gender harassment. More than any other segment of the volume, this chapter illustrates the point made in chapter 1 that a judgment of sexual harassment is a normative conclusion rather than a mere description. A particular problem here is that both seduction and gender harassment involve speech and thus potentially implicate academic freedom. To restrict one also would restrict the other. The proper balance to strike is that with the exception of special academic communities, freedom of expression should be protected unless the speech serves minimal or no academic purpose and is clearly targeted to make particular students uncomfortable.

SEDUCTIVE BEHAVIOR

Jane's day contained two minor incidents of seductive behavior—her being asked out on a date by a classmate and the hug and "Hiya" from her friend—and another quite extensive one, her relationship with her boyfriend. Assuming the relationship with the boyfriend was consensual, it is the topic for the next chapter, on consensual relationships. The focus here will be the wide variety of sexual overtures—invitations, flirtatious behavior, admiring glances—that are common campus social occurrences. What distinguishes these from sexual offers is that no exchange of benefits is suggested.

Was there anything wrongful about Jane's being asked out on a date at the end of class by a very casual acquaintance? If there was, it would rule out of university life what are regarded today as normal social pleasantries. (In a world of different social conventions—say, the eighteenth-century world of Jane Austen—what are regarded as normal social pleasantries would not have been the same.) The background assumption should be that it is reasonable to think ordinary pleasantries are welcomed, absent an express disavowal. Unusual gestures—such as "looking down my shirt" or "ogling"—would not be included in this assumption.

In circumstances in which seductive behavior is clearly inappropriate and does not function as a normal social pleasantry, the background assumption would shift because the seductive behavior is out of place. Such seductive behavior, if it impaired the knowledge, opportunity, or community goals of the academy, would be harassment that is morally problematic in a campus community. One such circumstance is seductive behavior that persists in the face of a definite refusal; the refusal shifts the background assumption of reasonableness. Persistence in the face of refusal is not a normal pleasantry. It fails to view the recipient as an autonomous person whose expressed choices are to be respected. It also harms her: Having refused, possibly repeatedly, the recipient may be embarrassed by the ongoing attention. She may feel demeaned by the suitor's failure to respect her refusal: Her "no" doesn't mean no. Quite reasonably made uncomfortable by the importunings, she may avoid possible encounters with her pursuer. Attending class, going to work, or going to the library may become chores if the advances are persistent and intrusive enough, impairing her ability to learn and to benefit from the opportunities of the university. Pursuit that is clearly unwelcome meets the moral foundations of the unwelcomeness requirement in discrimination law:[1] It fails to respect the recipient, harms her, violates her private space if it is intrusive enough, and affects her opportunities as a result of her attempts to avoid it, and all this to no social end.

No doubt, this discussion will be met with anecdotal counterexamples such as the love relationship of a lifetime that began only after the woman had rebuffed her pursuer over and over again. Such anecdotes acquire their force by making the persistent behavior seem unusual, risky, or glamorous; perhaps gauche; or even over the edge of being rude. The stories are worth recounting precisely because the suitor's likelihood of success was slim. Far from justifying the behavior in the ordinary case, they suggest that the happy endings are surprising; the normal rules of behavior are overridden; the dogged suitor persists at his peril.

Seductions are often complicated, however, by the recipient's failure to express her displeasure forcefully. Differences in communicative styles and in perspectives can be critical. In such situations, if it was not reasonable for the seducer to realize that his advances were unwanted or otherwise morally suspect, perhaps because he was not told they were unwelcome, he does not act wrongfully. At the same time, if it was reasonable for the seduced to feel uncomfortable, say because of the persistence of the seducer's behavior, she may reasonably view herself as having been harmed in the same way as a victim who openly expresses her dislike of the advances. Her discomfort may well affect her educational opportunities. The bad results for her are the same as they would be had she expressed her dislike, although his level of responsibility for them may be much less.

These observations are not meant to relieve the seducer from the responsibility of making reasonable judgments about the timing, style, or persistence of social approaches. They are meant to cover situations in which the seduced knows things the seducer cannot reasonably be expected to know—such as her feelings about men of his type or facts about her romantic history that might affect her willingness to enter into relationships. Perhaps she says "no" with a friendly excuse because she cannot bear to hurt his feelings, and he asks again, not knowing that this invitation was unwelcome. To be sure, there comes a point at which it is no longer reasonable for him to think his invitations are welcomed, no matter how friendly her response, but that point may be long past the time at which she has been made seriously uncomfortable by his interest without his knowing.

The solution to such all-too-common misperceptions is not to blame or punish the seducer; that would be unfair, since he doesn't know and it was not reasonable for him to know his actions are hurtful.[2] But it is not to ignore the seduced, either; she has been genuinely harmed. Instead, universities should work to support and to educate both sides: women to have resources to deal with situations that are uncomfortable for them and to be better able to make their feelings known, and men to be better able to see the situation from the perspective of the person being approached. If complaints are filed in such situations, informal dispute resolution processes should be employed with the goals of educating, reducing conflict, and restoring lost opportunities. Chapter 7 discusses these issues more fully.

This kind of miscommunication can be examined in the example of Jane receiving the hug and "Hiya, beautiful!" from her friend. Effusive greetings often are understood to be a license permitted old friends, expressions of warmth that appropriately go far beyond the ordinary. But suppose such greetings are Jane's friend's style, his way of saying hello to any woman he knows reasonably well. Some women might be fully comfortable with the greeting, but others might not be, especially if the hug is accompanied by a squeeze or a pat on the behind. Or suppose the greeting is a fairly typical approach for men of Jane's friend's culture or generation but Jane's background is different. The greeting may seem entirely natural to Jane's friend, but years of engaging in such conduct are not necessarily legitimating. At the same time, it may be quite difficult for Jane to express discomfort about the greeting; Jane may think her friend would be hurt or humiliated if he knew her true feelings. (Indeed, if Jane's friend is a decent guy, the longer he has been greeting her with a hug, the more uncomfortable he will feel if he learns that his well-meant embrace has been a source of discomfort to her. Jane may know all this, feel even worse about not having said something earlier, and continue to tolerate the conduct that makes her uncomfortable.) The fairest answer to this apparent impasse is that Jane's friend should recheck the acceptability of such personalized behavior every so often—a hesitant "may I?"—if it is out of line with ordinary greetings or the cultural norms seem to be changing. Jane, in turn, might reply with a gentle, "I wish you would be a little less conspicuous." Reminders of the possibilities of such misperceptions about attitudes, particularly when norms of behavior are changing, are an important function of sexual harassment education programs. So are reminders of the need to recheck acquiescence in behavior that is overly familiar.

Context also can put people on notice that it is not reasonable to think their advances are welcome. Sexual advances are wrongful if they occur at a clearly inappropriate time. Suppose Jane is in the middle of an oral report that is important to her grade and a student in the class looks at her in a way that is clearly intended to evoke a sexual response. Perhaps she might have eagerly responded to the look had it only occurred at another time. Jane now finds it hard to concentrate on the report and her grade suffers; her educational opportunity is impaired by the ill-timed flirtatiousness. Or suppose Jane makes what she intends to be a serious contribution to class discussion and her professor responds, "You sure look cute when you argue like that." Or suppose Jane is a resident in the department of surgery and in the middle of a procedure, the attending physician asks her if she'd like to go out with him. These are examples of behavior that would fail to respect Jane as a person engaged in the educational process; such humiliation is harassment.

Additionally, sexual advances are wrongful if they are calculated to demean. Ogling, fondling, and patting may be done in a manner that suggests the intended is simply an object—that she has no choice about whether to enter into the proffered relationship. Or the advances may be imperious, assuming that she naturally will want to play along. Or they may be mocking, never intended for the object to take them up or greeted with a laugh if they are. Such belittling seduction fails to respect the autonomy and dignity of the victim and may, in a university context, impair her ability to learn and her educational opportunities.

Seduction also is wrong if the proffered relationship would be wrong. If it would be wrong for a teacher to enter into a relationship with a high school student, it is wrong for the teacher to invite the relationship flirtatiously. The goal of an established relationship cannot be met morally. The student may be enticed by the flirtation to believe that the relationship is a realistic possibility, to fantasize about its reality, and to be sadly disappointed to discover that it cannot be. Or the student may be led into the wrongful relationship itself. In either case, the results may be psychologically devastating.

A special case of such inappropriate seductions are relationships that are prohibited in unique university communities, such as a military academy where sexual relations are prohibited among officers or a religious institution with a particularly strict code of conduct. Another case might be behavior enticing a relationship that is forbidden by a university's rules about consensual relationships; the issue of such relationships is taken up in chapter 6.

Seductive behavior on campus that is known to be unwelcome or that is not reasonable under the circumstances wrongs the victim and may impair the knowledge and opportunity goals of the academy and conflict with certain special community goals, but it especially interferes with educational goals. In cases of especially intrusive seductive behavior, it may be as bad as sexual assault. Where seduction is unreasonable because it is clearly unwelcome or because of the circumstances, it should be disciplined by the university. Universities also should, through education and supportive services, work to reduce the incidence and impact of seductive behavior that may not be recognized as unreasonable but that reduces the recipient's educational effectiveness and opportunity.

GENDER HARASSMENT

Gender harassment, as the term is used in the literature of sexual harassment, is a catch-all category referring to both sexism and sexuality. Jane experienced many typical examples of sexuality during her day. She observed sexually explicit material (the Frederick's of Hollywood catalog), she was handed an object of sex (the condom), she spent the night with her boyfriend, and discussions in each of her classes touched on sexual themes. Whether she experienced sexism as well depends on whether any of these events was handled in a sexually discriminatory way. She was affected by sexism when she chose to avoid certain areas on her run because she knew she would be subject to demeaning comments. Gender harassment, as it is used loosely in the literature of sexual harassment, includes both these categories—inappropriate sexuality and sexism. Were any of the sexual moments in Jane's day harassment of these types? As with seductive behavior, the initial concern is whether there is any reason to believe the incidents were morally problematic: whether they evidenced sexism or sexuality (or both); whether they were targeted to a particular student or group of students; where they occurred (classroom, dormitory, public space, private residence, and so on); and whether they implicated other important moral values (such as the right to privacy or academic freedom). The university should be especially concerned about whether the morally problematic examples of sexism or sexuality affected Jane's educational opportunities.

Sexism as Gender Harassment

As indicated in chapter 1, "gender harassment" is a broad and controversially defined category of sexual harassment. Some advocate classifying any acts of sexism as sexual harassment of the gender harassment type. To classify sexist behavior in this way, however, regardless of whether it has any links to sexuality, in effect brings all unequal treatment based on sex within the umbrella of sexual harassment. For example, suppose a professor makes remarks demeaning a woman's intelligence; those sexist remarks would count as gender harassment, as would remarks about the size of her breasts. The result would be that the category of "gender harassment" becomes huge, as broad as the category of sex discrimination itself.

An alternative classification is to limit "gender harassment" to harassment relating to a person's body or sexuality, what could be called sexuality-based harassment. The advantage of this narrower view of gender harassment is that it allows different forms of harassment to be identified. It is possible to zero in on how derogatory references to a person as a sexual being affect them in particularly damaging ways. On the other hand, if the connections between sexism and sexuality-based harassment are lost, the ability to identify links and patterns is also lost. Derogatory references to a woman's intelligence may be combined with derogatory references to her breasts in a manner that makes her feel doubly rejected as a student worthy of respect.[3] Indeed, many of the highly publicized cases of sexual harassment include elements of both sexism and sexuality; the case of Professor Cohen, described in chapter 3, is an example.

From the perspective of how it affects educational opportunity, gender harassment is most serious if it occurs in academic programs. If one of Jane's professors regularly called on male students but not on female students, or only called on female students the day rape was the subject, it would be sexism that significantly limits Jane's opportunities at the university and would be a serious moral wrong as a result. Gender harassment also limits opportunities significantly if it occurs in core university facilities that students cannot easily avoid, such as the library or a dormitory room. If women are regularly subjected to wolf whistles on their way to the library, for example, they might feel unwilling to go there. Other examples of gender harassment as sexism are milder because their impact is less central and less severe, such as the catcalls directed at female (but not male) students out for a run. This is milder gender harassment because it is assumed that the catcalls can be avoided by a relatively simple route change; the impact on Jane's opportunity would be far more severe if she was subjected to ridicule on all routes. This illustrates how not all sexism is sexual harassment: persistent "ragging" really is harassment, in the ordinary language sense of the term, and it is sexual harassment if there is a gendered or sexual dimension to the ragging.[4] Sexism affects educational opportunity whenever it occurs, but its effects may be more significant when it is harassing in the further sense that it is sexual, an observation that is lost if all sexism is included under sexual harassment.

It also is important to note that some examples of gender harassment as sexism raise questions of conflicts with countervailing academic values. Suppose, for example, that Jane's English professor had peppered the discussion of *Lady Chatterley's Lover* with remarks reminiscent of the infamous assertion in the 1960s, that the only place for women in the civil rights movement was prone. The recent firestorm over the comments by University of Texas law professor Lou Graglia that African American and Mexican American law students are "not academically competitive," when he announced the formation of an organization opposed to race-based admissions criteria, is another example.[5] Professor Graglia's remarks were regarded critically by faculty and administrators at Texas, who feared that these comments would contribute to the hopefully erroneous perception that Texas is unwelcoming of minority students.[6] (Controversy over his use of the word "pickaninny" in class had cost Professor Graglia consideration for a judicial nomination during the Reagan administration.) At the same time, the American Civil Liberties Union and other defenders of academic freedom came to Professor Graglia's side. The balance here, between providing educational opportunity to students and academic freedom to professors, should be appropriate to the specific setting. In a classroom setting, students could reasonably conclude that a faculty member who consistently espoused or demonstrated sexist or racist views without entertaining different points of view or critique and without giving an academic justification for them, would judge students' performance based on their sex or race and thus compromise their opportunities. This is discriminatory behavior by a professor that lacks academic justification and that directly affects students; it should either be prohibited or restricted to settings in which students can avoid it if they choose (e.g., in elective courses, the nature of which is announced clearly beforehand). In a public forum setting, by contrast, outside of class where no evaluation of particular students occurs, values of academic freedom should predominate over educational opportunity, which is not being compromised.

Sexuality as Gender Harassment

Sexuality is a narrower category of gender harassment. Apart from the political theory that combines sexuality with the expression of gender dominance, such as that held by Catharine MacKinnon, sexuality and sexism are regarded as separable phenomena; not all examples of sexuality are discriminatory. Some references to sexuality are, however, used in a discriminatory manner, and it is these that constitute sexuality that is properly regarded as gender harassment. The difficulty with this form of gender harassment is distinguishing innocent from problematic references to sexuality. The goals of the academy can be used to distinguish innocent from discriminatory sexuality, illustrated by the examples of sexuality in Jane's day.

The first example is the Frederick's of Hollywood catalog left by the mailbox. It could be viewed as part of the general sexuality of American culture, what Jane might have seen had she turned on late-night television or browsed through the local shopping mall. Nothing about the catalog was aimed particularly at Jane, nor was it left in university facilities. Consider how different the impact might have been if a cutout of a body from the catalog had been taped to the door of Jane's dormitory room below a photograph of Jane's face. Under such circumstances, Jane might reasonably have felt humiliated, hit quite literally where she lived. Similar incidents in college dormitories have rightly been viewed as seriously unlawful forms of harassment because they stigmatize and wound individual students in a campus context central to those students' lives, the entry to their living quarters. Such an incident makes it much harder for these students to function in an educational setting on a par with other students.

The second example is Jane's decision to have her boyfriend spend the night. She and her roommate lived off campus, in a private apartment. They had an arrangement that couples got the bedroom—a not uncommon arrangement among college students. What they did was entirely their own business. But suppose they had lived in a college dormitory and the arrangement had become a nightly affair. Although many colleges have rules limiting the number of consecutive nights guests can stay in dormitories, these rules are difficult to enforce. Yet students, regardless of their levels of prudishness, who are forced to find other sleeping and studying arrangements because their roommates monopolize the dorm room or suite to have sex, are very much inconvenienced, and consequently their educational opportunities are impaired. Coercive strategies enacted by the university are less likely to be successful in such circumstances than consultative strategies; universities should have available such policies that aim to settle disputes between roommates or to help students exposed to this type of unwanted sexuality in their living situation.[7]

The third example is Jane's passing the AIDS Awareness Week booth. Here, the activities were clearly directed to making a political point. Although a person handed a condom to Jane, it was not targeted especially for her; the activist would have handed the condom to any passerby as a symbol of the importance of safe sex. Neither its aim nor its effect was to discriminate. Moreover, the person gave the condom to Jane as part of an effort to convey information about AIDS. Despite a sexuality she might have regarded as offensive, the condom was educational and not in any way discriminatory; this reference to sexuality should be judged as protected speech. (Compare this with a Klan symbol handed to all those going by; that is a much closer case, because at a minimum the effect would be to evoke images of discrimination. It is still taking place in an outside educational forum, however, and is not discrimination in a class, so it would come under the claim that the value of academic freedom predominates.)

The next examples come from the references to sex in all three of Jane's courses. In no case were the references aimed particularly at Jane or any other students; had they been, questions would have been raised about whether the references were academically appropriate. Moreover, these were academic courses, in at least one case a course that fulfilled a basic educational requirement. Jane certainly might have found some of the material offensive, however, and her reaction might have affected the extent to which she participated in and learned from the course. As in the case featured in chapter 3, Anita Murillo was deeply offended by the sexuality in the English course taught by Dean Cohen, and she eventually received a failing grade.

When are classroom references to sexuality academically appropriate? In cases in which gender harassment is alleged, because of targeted references to particular students or because of the level of sexuality, what standards should be used to distinguish hypersensitivity on the part of students from academic misconduct on the part of faculty? Some basic requirements that some universities have implemented can prevent misunderstandings from occurring or avoid sexually harassing behavior.

One requirement is that students should have fair notice beforehand of course content and course assignments. This requirement was actually an issue in the Cohen case; part of the discipline imposed on Professor Cohen was that he publish a syllabus that indicated his teaching philosophy and the materials and assignments he planned to use. Such notice gives students the opportunity to plan their education in ways that suit their own interests and concerns and thus respects their autonomy. A critic of this practice might observe that by allowing students to avoid ideas they may find challenging, this advance notice may compromise the knowledge goals of the academy. However, a far better way to ensure that students encounter thought-provoking perspectives is by structuring overall programs to include them, rather than by unannounced and potentially random surprises in courses.

A core standard of academic ethics is that professors be able to give academic reasons for the requirements they impose on students. This is a weak requirement of academic relevance and reasonableness and does not imply commitment by the university to any set of preeminent disciplinary norms. The knowledge goals of the academy are supported by a robust understanding of academic freedom, one that gives full scope to contested points of view and experimentation. But the knowledge goals are not supported by a view of academic freedom that allows faculty to teach whatever they want, choosing capriciously without any effort to tie what they are doing to academic goals. Thus the faculty member teaching Jane's English course should be able to give reasons for his choice of *Lady Chatterley's Lover* in terms of the goals of a course on the twentieth-century English novel. Discussion of contraceptives should be relevant subject matter in a course on common medicines, given the frequency of contraceptive use in society. The enforcement of morality is a central issue in philosophy of law, and in assessing arguments for and against legal moralism, students need to understand what might be restricted by laws that enforce morality. Dean Cohen was able to give academic reasons for some of the contentious materials he taught, such as Swift's "A Modest Proposal," and for the requirement that students write an essay on a controversial topic. Writing an essay in defense of a contested point of view is an important skill for college students. Cohen gave no academic reasons, however, for reading movie reviews to the class that described his own physical sexual reactions in graphic detail. The course was a course in remedial English, not one that had anything to do with erotic writing or expression.

Standards of relevance apply in other professions as well, such as in law. The Model Rules of Professional Conduct specify that in dealing with persons other than clients, lawyers should not "use means that have no substantial purpose other than to embarrass, delay, or burden."[8] In 1995, the American Bar Association adopted a resolution against using bias and prejudice, including words of bias against a client.[9] In the field of medicine, patients do not expect their physicians to discuss their own sex lives in graphic detail during an examination, and such behavior is forbidden.

Another academic moral standard is that faculty members conduct their classes in a way that treats students with even-handed respect and concern.[10]

Discussion that is targeted to make a particular student or group of students uncomfortable because of their sexuality violates this standard, especially if it is persistent or intrusive. The targeted student or students might reasonably conclude that they are less welcome in the classroom than others are for reasons that lack academic relevance, and as a result, lose out on educational opportunities.

There is no indication that any of the discussion in Jane's classes had targeted particular people or groups of people, but consider some ways it might have done so. Suppose that a particular woman in Jane's common medicines course had been questioned closely about whether she used Norplant. Putting a student on the spot in this way subjects that student to a level of intrusiveness and discomfort that other students in the class will not experience, compounded by what is arguably a violation of the right to privacy about intimate information. Or suppose that Jane's English professor had questioned women students probingly about whether Lawrence's descriptions of women's emotional lives mirrored their own experiences without raising parallel questions for male students. Or suppose Jane's philosophy of law professor had required African-American women students to describe how they felt after listening to 2 Live Crew, putting them but not others on the spot.

These examples of targeting are very difficult ones because they all can be defended on points of academic relevance. Reactions on the part of Norplant users—and their partners—are clearly relevant to the public policy question of whether widespread campaigns to encourage Norplant use are likely to be successful—or indeed are ethically justified. D. H. Lawrence's work is criticized for its misogyny. And there is a growing tradition of narrative scholarship in philosophy of law that examines the lives of real women to discuss the critical perspective to be taken on works that brutalize women yet are defended as therapeutic or culturally valuable.[11]

Nonetheless, faculty can raise these kinds of issues while at the same time treating students with equal respect and concern. For example, an individual student's experience with Norplant is anecdotal at best and of dubious relevance to epidemiological data about reactions to the contraceptive. Discussions can give students space to respond by asking for volunteers rather than by putting particular students on the spot. Such flexibility is especially important when intimate reactions are involved or when the student is a member of a small minority, for example, the only African-American woman in Jane's philosophy of law class.

Although treating students with evenhanded respect and concern is an important academic value, balancing it with issues of genuine academic inquiry is difficult. Imposing persistent questions on particular students, with limited academic gain achieved, should probably be viewed as gender harassment. But there are ways to accommodate efforts both to treat students with respect and to ask them to incorporate relevant individual experiences into academic discussions. Academic freedom requires allowing faculty room for experimentation in classroom techniques and so should predominate except where the material does not meet even minimal academic standards of relevance and where the burden on individual students is significant.

In sum, sexism and sexuality are problematic when they impede educational opportunity. They are most likely to do so in core campus contexts—classes, dormitory rooms—and when they are targeted to individual students. Faculty have obligations of publicizing their class content, ensuring academic relevance, and having equal respect and concern for students. At the same time, academic freedom is a crucial value, and there are many instances of misunderstandings in which punitive models do not seem to be fair. The next section focuses more specifically on some of these conflicts and defends the importance of accommodationist and supportive strategies in such cases.

ACCOMMODATION AND SENSIBILITIES

Suppose, however, we add to the story of Jane's day that she reacts with unusually strong sensitivities to what others might regard as ordinary pleasantries. Suppose she anguishes over her decision to turn down the boy in her class, literally loses sleep over it; or suppose she finds all references to her appearance demeaning, including even the blandest inquiry admiring the hand-knit sweaters she wears. Janes of this kind face a difficult choice. If they make their feelings known, they risk pejorative labels and critique: "hypersensitive," "prickly," "overreacting." If they do not make their feelings known, they suffer in silence, to their own likely quite serious detriment.

One policy response is to formulate campus sexual harassment rules to protect those with more sensitive reactions by prohibiting all forms of seductive behavior, sexual references, or sexist behavior. Such an encompassing rule has the advantage of protecting people with greater sensibilities from the difficult choice of making their feelings known. It has several disadvantages, however. Restricting what many people believe are ordinary pleasantries introduces a degree of awkwardness into social interactions. The rules at issue will be difficult to enforce. They are likely to be found irritating, even by some people of goodwill and certainly by others who are bothered by sexual harassment policy to begin with. However, dismissing the issue of unusual sensitivity by simply labeling it "excessive" ignores the very real issues faced by some students. These students will confront a gap between the behavior of others that is reasonable to regulate and the behavior of others that only they find harmful. To conclude that these students are out of luck, that they should be sufficiently grown up to deal with the rough and tumble of university life, is to leave them to deal with difficult personal issues on their own. Yet most colleges and universities today are expected to provide a range of services to enhance the educational opportunities of their students, including supportive services for students with disabilities and training programs for faculty and staff in understanding students with different backgrounds and learning issues. Students with cultural differences and other sensitivities that make them susceptible to feeling sexually harassed should be afforded similar services.

Two examples illustrate appropriate services. The first, addressing social issues, would be programs for women students to explore settings that make them uncomfortable and to practice skills of self-expression in such contexts. The second, for faculty, would be education (perhaps from a teaching center on campus) about how students from different cultural backgrounds may view controversial sexual material and how that material can best be presented to them educationally. Neither of these is a suggestion for discipline or repression; both are ways to try to allow the educational experience to be more fruitful for students who may feel themselves under assault.

CONCLUSION

Seductive behavior and gender harassment are problems for the university when they affect students' educational opportunities. These behaviors should be prohibited when they are unreasonable and the parties should be able to recognize their unreasonableness. In other cases, when the balance of fairness or academic freedom is tilted to protect behavior that unusually sensitive students still find hurtful, supportive services should be provided for helping students and faculty deal with these issues.

6

Consensual Sex on Campus

Joan is a graduate student at a top-tier university in her field. She is about to take her comprehensives and begin work on a cutting-edge dissertation. She's highly regarded by the faculty in her department: their rising star. The department is recruiting a new faculty member in her field; the top candidate is a man who, the professional gossip goes, just has been unfairly denied tenure at unquestionably the best department in the country. Joan meets the candidate during the interviews and they hit it off, both intellectually and socially. Joan learns that he is in the process of a painful divorce; he is sad because the tenure denial and move prevent him from remaining as involved in the lives of his two young children. Joan looks forward eagerly to his arrival and to her ability to work with him. This story has many beginnings, but it also has many endings.

Ending One. The candidate arrives on campus and becomes Joan's dissertation chair. Although it's clear that under other circumstances they might have become romantically involved, it remains unspoken between them that this would not be a good idea because of their professional relationship. Her chair publishes a brilliant book and becomes the object of much professional attention. When Joan goes on the job market, however, she finds herself fighting the suspicion that she and her chair have been having an affair, which is the reason she is so highly regarded by her department. The suspicions are based on what has by now become professional gossip that her chair's departure from his first institution was clouded by an affair with a student. Joan gets a series of temporary jobs and eventually leaves the field. (Or Joan gets a job at a small school too far away to have heard the professional gossip. Or, Joan gets a job at another research university, at a department willing to ignore the gossip. . . .)

Ending Two. Joan and her professor fall in love and are married within six months after his arrival on campus. At first, they experience domestic bliss; Joan works excitedly on her dissertation, gives department dinner parties, and enjoys her status as almost-peer. Their mutual interest in the field and the particular topics on which they are working give the pair subjects for endless hours of conversation. The professor publishes a brilliant book that makes him famous; although no one else knows this, Joan is the author of at least half the book. One child later, Joan finishes her dissertation and reconsiders her professional future. Her institution does not hire its own graduates and her husband does not want to move. After three years of teaching on a temporary basis for the university's extension program, Joan goes to law school. (Or Joan takes a job at the community college down the road. Or Joan goes on the job market, receives the job of her dreams, and she and her husband commute between universities one thousand miles apart. Or another top research university in the field offers them both "real" jobs, Joan on tenure track and her husband with tenure, and they live happily ever after. . . .)

Ending Three. Joan and her professor begin a passionate affair. At first it is wonderful. Joan makes great progress on her dissertation. Then the affair goes sour. The professor becomes very critical of Joan's work. It's hard to tell which happened first, the end of the affair or the dissatisfaction with Joan's work. Joan herself begins to lose confidence in her abilities. Joan seeks a replacement as her dissertation chair, and finds someone who is interested in the area but not an expert. At first, things improve and Joan believes she is beginning to do good work again. Then the new chair becomes very critical of her work, and Joan suspects it is because of derogatory remarks by Joan's first chair. Joan eventually is told that it is unlikely she will be able to complete a dissertation that meets the standards of her department. (Or after the relationship sours, Joan files a complaint of sexual harassment with the university's office of equal opportunity. The complaint charges that the relationship had been unwelcome from the beginning, that Joan had felt pressured to enter into it and had been afraid that the professor would refuse to work with her unless she gave into his demands. The complaint is investigated but found to have no merit because the relationship was voluntary and the EEOC office defers to the judgment of departments about the academic qualifications of their students. Or the complaint is investigated and the story comes out that the reason the professor was not given tenure at his former institution is that he had been notorious for having sex with graduate students. Joan is vindicated, but with a reputation as a troublemaker has great difficulty finding a job in the field. . . .)

These stories are all true enough, based on composites of the lives of people I have known, the backgrounds of many academic marriages, and the sad stories of failed careers and acrimonious litigation. What do they show about sexual relationships between faculty and students from varying moral points of view? What do they show about other sexual relations on campus: faculty-staff relations, faculty-faculty relations, staff-student relations, or student-student relations? Viewpoints here range from the position that Joan and the professor are both adults with rights to enter into relationships of their own choosing, to the position that all faculty-student relationships and many other relationships should be prohibited because of the power imbalance and opportunity for exploitation they embody. In this chapter, I defend the moderate view that sexual relationships within universities should be prohibited when one of the parties has direct supervisory authority over the other and should be strongly discouraged when there are significant power imbalances between the two. Moreover, the overt expression of consensual sexual relationships on campus—fondling in the library or intercourse in the dorm, for example—should not be treated as special but should follow other campus policies, such as those involving gender harassment or social life in dormitories.

CONSENSUAL RELATIONS: THE CASE FOR A PERMISSIVE POLICY

Chapter 4 argued that sexual assaults, threats, and even offers are wrong because they interfere with choice about important, intimate relationships. A policy that seriously limited consensual sexual relationships on campus also would interfere significantly with the liberty to enter into relationships. How, then, could such a policy be defended in the context of a commitment to autonomy about intimate relationships? Joan and her professor, for example, have the moral and the legal right to their intimate associations.[1] As the policy from Wellesley College—interestingly enough, an undergraduate institution—puts it: "When there is no supervisory relation between students, or between faculty members, or between faculty and staff members, or between staff members—any recommendations by the College concerning sexual relations would constitute an intolerable invasion of privacy" (part II, chapter 17). Privacy and associational liberty are the core of the argument for a permissive policy about sexual relationships on campus, but several other moral considerations also lend support to such a policy.

A corollary of the value of autonomy is opposition to paternalism. The critique of consensual sexual relationships between professionals and those who receive their services typically invokes paternalism, as demonstrated in the following way. The professional has experience and skills not possessed by those seeking his services: patients or clients. He is in a position of trust; they are in a position of reliance and dependency, often exacerbated by the life events—an illness, a divorce—that led them to seek professional services in the first place. The best way to protect vulnerable clients from abusive professionals is a prophylactic ban on sexual relationships, even apparently consensual relationships. This critique is, quite frankly, paternalistic in its assumptions about the recipients of professional services. Mischler (part II, chapter 15) argues that it infantilizes them as lacking the capacity of reasonable adults to make sexual choices. My fictitious graduate student, Joan, for example, might argue that a ban on professor-student relationships is an insult to her independence; she is perfectly able to make decisions about her personal relationships without any help from authoritarian protectionism. She might add that to the extent that such bans are seen as protecting her from her professors, rather than her professors from her, they are particularly demeaning to her.

A further, related concern about any bans on consensual relationships on campus is that they affect women unequally. As Mischler observes for cases involving lawyers and clients, such bans are constructed on the basis of assumptions of inequality: The imagined client is always a woman; the imagined professional is always a man. They thus play into perceptions of inequality, particularly for women. And they may create further inequalities in academic situations. If faculty demographics are largely male and graduate-student populations increasingly female, bans may preclude women students from a particularly desirable source of satisfying relationships. Or they may force women already in relationships to choose schooling at a different institution or in a different field. At the very least, a ban on consensual relationships between faculty and the students they supervise would force Joan to a hard choice: either seeking a new, possibly less intellectually appropriate advisor or sacrificing the relationship.

These considerations make the case for a permissive policy a very powerful one. It is supported by respect for the autonomy and the equality of women in the academic community. Why, then, have the calls for bans on consensual relationships, in the academy and in other professional relationships, been so persistent and so increasingly accepted? Are any of the arguments powerful enough to override the case for permissiveness?

The insistence of these questions can be understood by viewing the problem of whether consensual relations are sexual harassment as a problem of ethics under less than ideal circumstances. In *A Theory of Justice,* published nearly thirty years ago, John Rawls distinguished between ideal theory and partial compliance theory.[2] Rawls's point was that the principles of justice that apply under nonideal circumstances might differ from those that apply under ideal circumstances. Rawls's own view of ideal justice was that basic liberties, when they can be exercised effectively, take priority over the principle of equal basic opportunity. The argument for a permissive policy then could be viewed as a reflection of the priority of a basic liberty, the liberty to enter into intimate, consensual relationships. Critics of such a permissive policy, by contrast, might argue that in a less than ideal world, basic liberties do not take priority over values such as equality of educational opportunity.

In answering the ethical questions about consensual relationships in a university setting, it also is important to bear in mind the wide variety of such possible relationships on campus: faculty-student, faculty-staff, faculty-faculty, student-student, staff-staff, and staff-student. Yet another set of permutations appears if visitors are considered part of the university community: alumni, donors, guest speakers, patients at university hospitals or clinics, sports fans, theatergoers, and casual visitors. These permutations can be doubled if they are classified by the initiator of the relationship: faculty-student or student-faculty, for example. An additional complication is that groups on campus may not fit neatly into one or another of these categories. Should all students be classified together, the most senior of graduate students with the entering freshman, the oldest of nontraditional students with the early-entry sixteen-year-old? Are professionals in training programs, such as post-docs or medical residents, more like students or like faculty? What about staff members who are also students, possibly part-time students? What about alumni who return to campus for continuing education courses? What about teaching or laboratory assistants who are graduate students? Are instructors and research and part-time faculty like regular faculty? These permutations alone suggest powerfully that a "one size fits all" policy cannot be defended for consensual relations on campus and as well that different policies may be appropriate for universities that serve very different populations. With all of these differences in mind, I turn now to the reasons offered in support of restricting at least some types of sexual relations on campus. Although questioning the adequacy of consent is the predominant reason offered for regulating relationships, it does smack of paternalism. I begin, therefore, with two other concerns: quality of education and equality of opportunity. In assessing each of these concerns, my goal will be to see whether they are of sufficient moral importance to override the general argument for a permissive policy just presented.

CONSENSUAL SEXUAL RELATIONSHIPS
AND EDUCATIONAL QUALITY

The University of Iowa's consensual relationship policy begins with the observation that "the University's educational mission is promoted by professionalism in faculty-student relationships. Professionalism is fostered by an atmosphere of mutual trust and respect" (part II, chapter 17). The Iowa policy continues by linking the lack of professionalism to the abuse of power and failure of genuine consent, but educational aspects of the lack of professionalism also are important.

The first problem of consensual sexual relationships is distraction from teaching, learning, and research. Such distraction may affect the parties to the relationship and those who observe it. Any student who has sat next to other students fondling each other in class may recognize the difficulties such behavior poses for the overall success of the class. Even faculty may be distracted by the side show. (I once tried to lecture to a class when two students, sitting in the center of the front row, were quite obviously fondling each others' genitals. I didn't know whether it would be more distracting to try to ignore the situation or to ask them to desist. I tried to conduct the class as though nothing were happening, but I am certain that it was one of my less successful efforts.) The atmosphere in a research laboratory can deteriorate quickly when a major source of interest is figuring out who matches up sexually with whom. These distractions are manifest even when the relationships in question are entirely consensual and harmonious—in fact, too amorous, at least if they spill over actively in more serious contexts such as the laboratory. And imagine the intrigue that might follow if there were competitors for relationships among members of the same small group such as members of the same lab group.

Such problems in mixing the personal and the professional are commonplace, both within and without the university. Their effects are manifest, whatever the power levels of the involved parties: An overt sexual relationship between two students in a class can affect significantly both what they and what others learn. The effects are exacerbated, moreover, as the context becomes more intimate. An overt sexual relationship between two students in a small seminar or in an intense laboratory setting could be more distracting than a relationship among two students in a large lecture class. Ironically, because smaller settings within research universities are likely to be the province of more advanced students, these distractions may be more intense when the apparent need for paternalism is less.

These educational effects of romantic relationships also are exacerbated when one of the parties is the centerpiece of the setting: the senior professor in a laboratory or the instructor in a class. Even apart from the conflicts of interest and power imbalances discussed below, romantic interest on the part of a professor might take his or her own mind away from instruction. The student who is the object of affection might find it more difficult to concentrate. Other students also might be distracted if the relationship is in any way obvious or even known. It is more likely that educational quality would suffer in a small discussion section, a seminar, or a smaller research setting than it would in a large lecture. Both small and large settings might be negatively affected when one of the participants occupies a privileged position vis-à-vis the instructor. Behavior that overtly indicates a sexual relationship in an instructional or research setting is problematic because it interferes with core functions of the academy, the development and transmission of knowledge. Overt expression of a sexual relationship in class is inappropriate and should be regulated by the university in the same way that the university should restrict sexualization as a form of gender harassment.

Another difficulty with consensual sexual relations on campus is that a romantic relationship can create a conflict of interest that impairs the quality of professional services. At universities the most likely conflict is with evaluative functions: grading, awarding fellowships or scholarships, or making decisions about tenure or promotion. In other professions, the case for prohibition rests centrally on the nexus between the delivery of the professional services and the sex. Psychiatrists cannot treat their lovers. Dermatologists can, maybe, if the professional relationship is short-lived and does not involve confidences that could be exploited. Divorce lawyers should not become romantically involved with their clients during the divorce proceedings: Romantic involvement gives the lawyer a personal stake in the outcome and may compromise the client's position as well.[3] In education, it seems that there is a nexus between evaluation and affection.The teacher who is also a lover will both want his beloved to do well and be obligated to judge work impartially. He may find it very difficult to demand excellence from his lover—or, bending over backward trying to be fair, he may judge his lover too harshly. In either case, other students may reasonably fear that evaluations of their work are compromised by the professorial confusion. Such conflicts will be worse when evaluative judgments are highly subjective—as many in academe are—and less severe when evaluation is relatively mechanical, such as when processing a machine-scored multiple-choice exam.

Jane Gallop (part II, chapter 14) argues that education is sexy. Her point, put in a pedestrian way, is that there is no conflict of interest between sex and learning—indeed, there is a felicitous marriage of the two, in the style of Plato's *Symposium*. Perhaps the reason her joking remark, "My sexual passion is graduate students," fell flat is the evaluative aspect of contemporary higher education. Other graduate students may not have seen the sexiness of the learning when it was not directed to them. And the graduate student who was the immediate target of the remark also may have felt compromised. As a graduate supervisor of one of the students, after all, Gallop was in the position to make extremely important, but subjective, judgments about the quality of her student's work. From the perspective of other students, what Gallop was defending could seem more like massive self-indulgence than like a serious supervisory relationship.

Ironically, the impact of such conflicts of interest is probably the worst at the highest academic levels, where relationships are likely to occur; arguably taking an introductory logic class with machine-graded exams is more like filing routine legal documents or taking off a wart than like psychiatry. Such tasks are more mechanical, and so the difficulties raised by a mixture of personal and professional involvement might be less severe. One of the features of academic life, particularly at the graduate-student level and beyond, however, is the mixture of the personal and the professional. Small departments or laboratories become the centers of social lives. Although, there certainly are advantages to this mixture, the conflicts of interest generated where there are direct supervisory relationships seem highly likely to impair the quality of the professional judgments rendered in important academic matters.

In sum, educational quality can be impaired in several ways by consensual relationships. First, if the relationships are overt enough to be distracting, quality may suffer. Such distractions are most likely in smaller settings or where one of the parties to the relationship is the focus of educational attention, such as a professor. Second, if the relationships create conflicts of interest because of the supervisory or evaluative responsibilities of one of the parties, the relationship has the potential to impair the quality of the resulting judgments that affect all students. In either case, the knowledge functions of the academy are impaired.

EQUALITY OF OPPORTUNITY

The second problem of consensual sexual relations is their potential impact on equality of educational opportunity. These concerns are more likely to be raised by others outside the relationship, but the parties to the relationship also may find their opportunities are affected.

First, overt expression of sexual relationships in educational settings may make others feel uncomfortable, compromising their opportunity to participate in the class, laboratory, or other educational activity. This discomfort may arise whether those romantically involved are faculty members or students. To be sure, some people may be oversensitive to such relationships just as they are when sexuality of any kind is introduced into an educational setting. As discussed in the section on gender harassment in chapter 5, the treatment of such behavoir should be judged by the relevance of the sexuality to the educational topic at hand. It is hard to see what the relevance of an individual sexual relationship would be to a classroom or research setting. Nor are sexual relationships burdened very much by requiring that their overt expression should be confined to more private settings. Thus, making out in class is inappropriate and could be banned.

A harder question is posed by the occurrence of consensual sex in areas on campus that are not primarily academic in function, because the conflicts between the relationship and opportunity may be more or less severe. Consider Jane from chapter 5; with her roommate, she had worked out a mutually acceptable accommodation between their sexual lives and their abilities to function as students: Whoever had a guest got the bedroom. In cramped dormitories, it may be difficult to make such arrangements. Moreover, roommates may be assigned relatively randomly and may not share common views about the appropriateness of sex. Suppose, for example, two freshmen share a double room; one falls madly in love and her boyfriend, in effect, moves in. The other roommate both disapproves of the relationship and finds it very difficult to study when the boyfriend is around. The relationship is very important to the one roommate, but the other roommate's learning and grades suffer. This conflict should be treated like many other social conflicts that occur between roommates, over music, television, or even art on the walls. There is nothing special about sex here, unless dormitories are still to be viewed as an area where the enforcement of morality is appropriate. Sex is just one of many behaviors that can affect roommates' comfort, happiness, and, ultimately, educational performance. If there are nonsexual reasons for the university to prohibit aspects of sexual relationships or to otherwise make accommodations between roommates, they should be followed. An example would be one roommate's boyfriend moving in. There are general reasons to limit the length of time guests can stay in dormitories, whether or not the reason for the stay is romantic. For a start, students who pay for a space in a dormitory are paying for their own living space, not for someone else's. One's roommate's young sister—or mother, for that matter—living in a dormitory room intended for two may cause as many problems as a boyfriend. And colleges should make every effort to reassign roommates when incompatible preferences—whether over music or sex—threaten to make life particularly difficult for one of them. Otherwise, the college is not ensuring that all of its students receive maximum educational opportunities. The college should make sure that one roommate does not impose his or her preferences on the other, be it over sex or music, if reassignment proves impossible. Just as roommates should accommodate other differences, so should they accommodate differences in romantic relationships; at the least cooperative, this might mean one roommate gets the room one night until a reasonable time for sleep, the other gets the room the next night, and so on.

The most serious concerns about how someone else's consensual relationship affects the educational opportunities of others occur with evaluation. If one of those being evaluated has a romantic relationship with the evaluator, others may believe that they are unlikely to receive fair evaluations. Even if these perceptions are inaccurate, because the evaluator bends over backward to be fair or because the evaluation is entirely mechanical (as with a machine-graded test), these students' beliefs may still affect their opportunity, because they may not think their hard work will be rewarded and their motivation may suffer as a result. These perceptions are not unreasonable, because there are many ways beyond the actual moment of evaluation in which someone may benefit by a romantic relationship with a superior. My fictional Joan, for example, will have many opportunities to share wisdom about the field with her mentor. To be sure, students vary immensely in their ability to interact with faculty, as employees vary greatly in their ability to seek out and receive mentoring. Such differences are inevitable and probably should be left unregulated because of the importance of mentoring relationships, unless they fall into patterns under which identified groups find it very difficult to receive mentoring (women, for example, finding that men hold all of the powerful positions and will only mentor other men). But the problem here is not inequality in mentoring generally. It is the inequality resulting from the fact that the mentor, in a position of authority, has chosen to enter a romantic relationship with someone he is charged to evaluate. The whole evaluative process may be tarnished as a result.

This effect on the evaluative process, as it is and as it is perceived, also explains why the parties to the relationship cannot decide on their own to take the risks of a compromised evaluation. The concern here is not merely a paternalistic one. Joan might object, "I'm willing to take the risks that my supervisor will bend over backward to be hard on me, because I value the relationship. I'm also willing to take the risk that others in the field will believe I got ahead because I slept with my mentor. That's my choice, to conclude that the relationship means more to me than untarnished professional success." But the choice is not Joan's alone to make. If it becomes known that evaluations in a department take place despite romantic connections between the evaluator and student, observers may raise red flags about other evaluations, affecting the overall confidence in the evaluative judgments and hence compromising the opportunites of all those being evaluated. Equality of opportunity is a second reason for the university to restrict consensual relationships when those involved have positions of direct supervision and evaluation.

IMPAIRED CONSENT

A third issue about consensual relationships on campus is the genuineness of the consent. Many writers argue that either the characteristics of one of the parties to the relationship (a gullible student) or the structure of the relationship (a powerful professor importuning a powerless student) mean that even a clear "yes" is not what it seems. This argument is most likely to be made about faculty-student sex, but it might also be made about other relationships in which there is an imbalance of power. Arguing that such a "yes" does not mean "yes" requires an account of what makes consent genuine.

Medical ethics literature contains significant discussion of the nature of genuinely informed consent. There are important analogies between the physician-patient relationship and the professor-student relationship for purposes of analyzing problems with consent: the potential vulnerability of the student or patient, the power structure of the relationship, and even possibly the major life-significance of the choice at issue. The medical analogy therefore, is an appropriate framework for analyzing consent in romantic relationships on campus.

Writers in medical ethics focus on a number of factors in deciding whether consent is genuine: the patient's level of understanding, the patient's preferences, the patient's ability to link understanding with preferences and give an account of why s/he decided as s/he did, possible impairment of the patient's decision-making capacities, and features of the circumstances that might be regarded as coercive.[4]

For consent to be informed, the patient's level of understanding must be such that she can give an account of the options available to her and what their likely consequences would be. A student considering entering a romantic relationship, by analogy, would need to know what her choices are (enter the relationship, do not enter the relationship, or possibly delay entering the relationship). She also would need to understand what the likely consequences are of each of these options: Is the professor married? Is the relationship likely to be a fling or a long-term affair? How will she feel if the relationship ends despite her wishes to continue it? Because it involves difficult-to-predict factors—how will the relationship develop? how will she feel if things go badly from her perspective? what will be the effects on her education?—levels of understanding are likely to be limited, especially for students who have not had previous serious romantic relationships.

A second factor important to informed consent is an understanding of preferences. For patients, this includes an understanding of which kinds of risks are more or less troublesome—for example, risks of loss of mobility or risks of pain. For someone considering a romantic relationship, many kinds of preferences might be relevant: preferences for a long- or short-term relationship, for a relationship that is primarily sexual or that is satisfying in other ways, or for a given balance between a relationship and a career. In some respects, it is unrealistic to expect such preferences to be mapped out clearly in advance: To an important extent, what one wants in life is developed along the way. At the same time, to the extent that a student has less clear preferences about the direction of her life, she is less congruent with the model of rational choice that underlies informed consent in medicine. For young undergraduates particularly, there are difficult questions about what autonomy means in a context of growing up. Colleges are places where people explore relationships, learn to make and reject overtures, try out different partners, and even find mates. To conclude that because her preferences are relatively unformed, an undergraduate does not have the capacity to consent would be to short-circuit much that is socially important on campus. On the other hand, to assume that younger students are rational consumers of romantic relationships in the way they might be rational consumers of products would be too simplistic. A tentative conclusion to draw here is that where students are less mature and have less self-knowledge of likely outcomes or how their preferences will be affected, there is more reason to be cautious about whether other aspects of the relationship also are problematic.

A third concern raised in medical ethics about consent is whether the patient is able to process information to realize satisfaction of his or her preferences. For example, suppose that a patient understands that a given diagnostic procedure (such as a spinal tap) will establish whether she suffers from a readily treatable condition (such as meningitis), expresses that she does not want to die, but refuses the procedure for no accountable reason (religion, fear of pain or needles, and so on). We might be inclined to question whether her refusal was genuine or whether some other factors, as yet unarticulated, were in play. Perhaps her understanding of the medical indications for the procedure was flawed, or perhaps she was angry at the medical professionals involved in her care, or perhaps she was suffering from an undiagnosed depression. Rather than accepting the refusal immediately, medical professionals would search for the as-yet unidentified grounds for the refusal. In the end, of course, defenders of autonomy would respect the patient's refusal, but only after being especially careful to understand whether it was the product of other problematic factors. The academic analogy would be a student who has expressed goals that have not changed, realizes that a particular romantic relationship puts all of those goals at risk (including goals for relationships), and yet persists in the relationship without giving any further explanation (even "love conquers all"). Perhaps love does conquer all, but perhaps other unidentified factors are also at work that would make it questionable as to whether the student is fully processing the information that she has.

In medicine, another of the problematic factors about consent is impairment of the patient's decision-making capacities as a result of illness. Temporary physical factors such as medication or fatigue can impair decision-making capacities. Treatable depression could alter decision making, as could other forms of mental illness, such as schizophrenia. It is not unlikely that college students would be fatigued or depressed. If they were medical patients making a momentous decision to refuse care, medical professionals would likely ascertain whether the students suffered from treatable conditions of this kind and at least offer the opportunity for therapy. This is not to say that college students should be offered treatment for depression before they enter romantic relationships with faculty. It is to say that attention to the possibility that a student may have impaired decision-making capacities is at least another reason for caution about across-the-board acceptance of all romantic relationships involving faculty and students.

Another set of problematic factors in medicine is the coercive aspects of the patient's situation. The overwhelming nature of illness can make patients particularly vulnerable and is a reason for caution in making important decisions. Students too may feel overwhelmed by the life-decisions they face about fields of study, jobs, or careers. Another aspect of patient vulnerability is being torn from familiar surroundings and familiar systems of support; patients in hospitals or nursing homes may suffer particularly from the effects of dislocation. Students also may be dislocated; an undergraduate, living away from home for the first time, faces new responsibilities and decisions without familiar landmarks. The comparative powerlessness of patients in medical institutions is another noteworthy concern; feminist bioethics writers point out the disparities in information, understanding, and dependency that affect a patient's medical decision making.[5] Although they are not physically dependent in the way patients are, students are powerless vis-à vis faculty in some ways analogous to the powerlessness of patients vis-à-vis physicians. There are imbalances in information between students and faculty. Faculty can manipulate information, for example, about the nature or importance of courses or fields of study. Faculty who have the power to evaluate students literally can make or break careers. Although colleges are not institutions in the same way hospitals are,[6] they may feel like them sometimes; particularly at small, residental campuses, students' lives may be spent in a confined setting for long periods. There even may be analogies between economic coercion in medicine and in education. Medical expenses may be more catastrophic, less predictable, and less voluntary than educational expenses, but educational expenses in today's world are comparatively huge. A student who fears that continued scholarship support or job recommendations are dependent on the good opinion of faculty may feel just as vulnerable as a patient who faces major medical expenses.

None of these five factors—understanding, preferences, reasoning ability, physical or mental condition, or circumstances—are sufficient grounds for concluding that faculty-student relationships cannot be consensual. They are all reasons for caution, however. When they are combined, as they are most likely to be in the case of an undergraduate at a traditional small college, with having a relationship with a professor who has supervisory authority, then the case for prohibition is strongest.

CONCLUSION

Consensual relationships on campus should be permitted when they do not threaten the educational or opportunity mission of the campus. However, there are three basic reasons for concern about consensual sexual relationships on campus: educational quality, educational opportunity, and the quality of consent. All are particularly weighty where a student is under the direct supervision of a faculty member. In such cases, therefore, consensual relationships should be prohibited. This would mean the prohibition of consensual relationships while a student is in the faculty member's class; while the faculty member has responsibility for the student in an extramural program (such as a study-abroad program); and while the faculty member serves on a supervisory committee, awards committee, or as a program director.

Some of these prohibitions will be relatively short-lived and hence minimally burdensome on relationships; quarters or semesters do end eventually. Others, such as Ph.D. supervision, are typically lengthy and may place significant burdens on relationships. Others, even though short-lived, may be unavoidable, as when a spouse in a program needs to take a required course taught by her spouse. Because of these burdens, universities should strive to help the people in the relationship make alternative arrangements so that one party is not supervising the other, such as appointing a new committee for a graduate student, reassigning evaluative functions, or even granting a special exception for a student to take a required course pass-fail if there is simply no other choice.

The university should also prohibit such relationships in other types of campus sexual relationships, involving those in supervisory positions over their partners. Faculty should not be able to vote on the tenure or promotion of those with whom they are romantically involved. Nor should employment supervisors be involved with those whose work they directly evaluate. These prohibitions are typically in force in nonacademic employment relationships, because of the potential for unfairness. As with faculty-student relationships, universities should strive to arrange alternatives in these cases; tenure decisions can be made in the absence of the department member with a conflict, and workplace lines of evaluation can sometimes be reconfigured.

Finally, other consensual relationships on campus should be permitted. Personal relationships are important, and such relationships do not threaten the educational or the opportunity mission of the academy. Caution is appropriate, particularly where there are imbalances in power, as with a faculty member and an undergraduate not in the faculty member's class or a student whom the faculty member mentors. When there are such imbalances, there may be reason for concern about the quality of the consent, and relationships that are not genuinely consensual are impermissible harassment on this basis. Those in the more powerful positions who are able to recognize these risks, should enter into such relationships with particular caution. Many colleges and universities approach this problem with policies cautioning that in the case of a complaint, the presumption will be that the relationship was not consensual (part II, chapter 17, Wellesley College policy). Chapter 7 considers these issues of policy design.

7

+

Sexual Harassment
Policies and Procedures

I begin this chapter by inviting the reader to write her—or his—own story. If you are a student, imagine that you suddenly find yourself in a quite disturbing situation. One of your professors, you believe, has been making advances to you. At first it was just that the professor looked at you a lot in class and praised your work to you as you were leaving the room. Then he—or she—invited you to coffee. You were confused by the invitation, but excited too, and went along. Under the table, his (or her) knees brushed against you. You were not sure that it was intentional and you were afraid that it was all your imagination. But tonight he—or she—called you up and asked you out. Your refusal was met with an impressively impolite epithet. Final exams are several weeks away, and you are afraid. What do you do, whom do you turn to, where do you go? How do you feel; do you think the whole thing was somehow your fault, maybe for going out to coffee? Do you know what resources are available on your campus to help you deal with your concerns? Do you perceive these resources as likely to be helpful or have you heard bad things about them? Do you tell your friends or family what happened?

If you are a faculty member, imagine that you have just been accused of sexual harassment. A student in one of your classes has gone to your university's antidiscrimination officer, complaining that you ogled her—or him—in class, flattered her—or him—excessively, took her—or him—to coffee, called her—or him—up for a date, and reacted extremely offensively to the refusal. It is true that you admired the student, praised the work, and extended the invitation to coffee. You did so because you believed the student has a great deal of potential but seriously underestimates her—or his—abilities. But you did not call to ask the student out and you cannot understand why the student is saying you did. How will you reply to the accusations? What resources can you call on to help you? Does your university offer any supportive services for you, or are you left on your own? Do you think you need a lawyer, would you know whom to call, and do you have the money to pay for one? Does your university provide you with any legal help? What do you anticipate will happen? Do you expect your spouse, children, and friends to know about the student's accusations?

If you are neither a student nor a faculty member, imagine you are a sympathetic friend of the university, perhaps a parent of a student, a devoted alum, or a loyal member of the local community. How do you think the university should handle each situation? What approaches would you admire, and what would make you feel that the university had not done well by its students, its faculty, or its community? Could the university have done anything to prevent what may turn out to be a very uncomfortable situation for everyone involved?

In designing a set of procedures for dealing with sexual harassment complaints, institutions of higher education should take several goals into account. The first is reducing the incidence of harassment through education, prevention, and deterrence. The second is striving to be fair to both complainants and alleged perpetrators. A disciplinary process is fair if it limits as much as possible its mistakes: the frequency of unwarranted complaints that are found to have merit and the frequency of warranted complaints that are found to be unjustified. A serious consideration in designing policies that are procedurally fair is to determine whether it is worse to err on the side of false positives or of false negatives. The third goal is limiting the wear and tear on those involved in the procedures: the complainant, who may find that she has put her sexual and academic history at risk; the accused, whose career and family may be on the line; other faculty and students, whose time and energies may be consumed in a wrenching process; and the university, whose reputation may be tarnished if it handles the situation inappropriately. The fourth goal is remedial: supporting a student whose ability and opportunity to learn may have been seriously compromised, or making it up to a faculty member who has been unjustly accused.

Sexual harassment complaints cause enormous emotional pain for all involved, and that makes the problem of designing procedures all the more difficult. This chapter begins by considering the deterrence and fairness goals of policy design. It then examines the tough issues of confidentiality for both accuser and accused in a sexual harassment complaint. It ends by discussing briefly the problem of appropriate remedies from the point of view of whether they should be chiefly individual, chiefly institutional, or a mixture of each.

GOALS OF A PROCESS: PREVENTION AND DETERRENCE OR PUNISHMENT?

A primary goal of sexual harassment policy should be to reduce the incidence of harassment, thereby furthering the knowledge and opportunity goals of the academy. In criminal law, advocates of deterrence give punishment pride of place as a strategy. Policy designs are favored that attempt to prevent repeat offenses by locking up offenders or discourage new offenses by punishment that is certain, swift, and severe. Just as in criminal law, it is debatable whether punitive strategies are likely to be the most effective method for reducing the incidence of sexual harassment on campus.

Nonetheless, a fair amount of the rhetoric about sexual harassment invokes punitive policies. Whether these discussions are motivated principally by efforts to reduce the incidence of harassment or by the retributivist view that harassers deserve punishment, however, is hard to know. Consider these examples from Dziech and Weiner:

> Informal mediation should always be attempted. It saves time, energy and money and helps to avoid the greater anxiety and embarrassment of formal grievances. . . .
>   Although informal mediation is the most frequent way of addressing sexual harassment problems, its limitations cannot be overlooked. Ironically, successful informal mediation deceives the campus community into not knowing or acknowledging that there are harassment problems. Files are not kept, public knowledge is minimal, and sanctions for an offender are limited. . . .
>   Even model prevention and grievance policies will fail if an institution refuses to punish harassment. . . .
>   A grievance that finds fault with faculty behavior should never end in token sanctions or meaningless slaps on the wrist. Compromise and vacillation defeat all of a college's good intentions by implying to victims and offenders that no one is really committed to stopping sexual harassment.[1]

These passages suggest both a commitment to deterrence and a commitment to punishment that is as severe as the wrongfulness of the conduct. In criminal law, a long-standing debate exists between retributivist and utilitarian views about whether punishment can be justified when no deterrent effects are likely, and whether punishment can be justified for its deterrent value even when the punishment exceeds what is deserved. These disagreements arise when one justification extends beyond the reach of another, or in situations of direct conflict, in which one justification might undermine the other. Does the possibility of the death penalty, for example, undermine the certainty of serious punishment for homicide, because it makes juries less willing to convict?[2] Do very severe punishments for all degrees of drunk driving decrease the likelihood of getting convictions for any drunk driving offenses?[3]

In campus sexual harassment cases, it seems plausible that an emphasis on the severity of punishment might undermine preventive goals. Reporting rates for sexual harassment on campus are notoriously low, typically no more than a handful of cases per year on most campuses, certainly far below even the most conservative incidence rates discussed in chapter 2.[4] No doubt there are many explanations for the low rates, including potential complainants' fears they will end up being treated as offenders, an issue discussed later in this chapter. Another possibility is that complainants believe that their concerns simply will be whitewashed. Yet another explanation may be that third parties are less likely to report offenses by colleagues if they believe that the offender will be punished too severely. This last factor particularly suggests caution about a highly punitive paradigm. In contrast to these reactions, the beliefs of complainants that their reports will be downplayed may cut both ways. On the one hand, if a punishment is not severe enough, it may seem like the harassment was not considered to be a very important action. On the other hand, if the punishment is harsh, then it seems like harassment is considered very important, and only severe cases should be pursued, discouraging people from coming forward with milder complaints not deserving such harsh punishment.

Although it does not correspond on every point, the problem of substance abuse by professionals may be an instructive parallel to the problem of designing policies to prevent campus sexual harassment. Despite estimates of abuse rates as high as 10 percent, professional societies such as medical or bar associations have confronted persistently low reporting rates. Even colleagues aware of the risks were reluctant to report a fellow professional if their report could be career-threatening. Diversionary programs, under which a professional can continue to practice if there is compliance with a treatment plan, have proved more successful at promoting colleagues to report substance abuse, thereby reducing the incidence of risky behavior.[5] For some critics, the disanalogies between such professional treatment programs and the problem of sexual harassment on campus may be highly significant.

With sexual harassment, there is an identified victim who may feel unjustly treated unless the offender is punished. In professional diversionary programs, there is no victim calling for justice; the idea is to encourage or to compel the professional to seek treatment before a patient or a client is injured, rather than to punish the offender for the unprofessional behavior. At least some sexual offenders, the critic might argue, have high rates of recidivism,[6] so they need punishment to discourage this behavior. And, although at cross purposes with the explanation that sexual offenders have high recidivism rates because they are mentally ill, some critics of applying the diversionary analogy to sexual harassers argue that they deserve punishment rather than treatment or education precisely because they are able to control their harmful behavior.

The discussion of this analogy shows the importance of differentiating kinds of harassment: those that are more rapelike and warrant punishment (particularly the forms of harassment discussed in chapter 4) and those that should continue to be treated on a civil law or administrative basis (perhaps at least first offenses of the types in chapters 5 and 6). May and Soule argue that it does a disservice to sexual harassment policy to classify all forms of harassment together, although they would classify a broader range of offenses, including gender harassment, as more like rape.[7] I argue that the design of harassment policy should not be guided by a "one-size-fits-all model" but should provide punitive or supportive services depending on the different circumstances.

A variety of supportive services may prove helpful for preventing sexual harassment. The University of Iowa policies, for example, suggest educational programs for faculty members or staff identified as having inadvertently engaged in behavior that makes others uncomfortable (part II, chapter 17). Education of victims and potential victims is perhaps equally important as a preventive, including help in identifying harassment and in responding when it occurs. Harassment counselors suggest that a direct response to the harasser, to the effect that this is unwanted behavior, may be very effective, not least because it is embarrassing. Mary Rowe reports good results from a three-part letter from the victim to the harasser, detailing the facts as the victim sees them, the victim's feelings about the harassment, and what the victim would like to see happen.[8] And several writers suggest damage remedies for the victim, including the possibility of tuition payments, in addition to or in lieu of punishment of the offender. Despite the poor record of punishment as a preventive strategy, however, some critics regard these supportive strategies as both too lenient to harassers and as unfairly burdensome to victims, issues of fairness that are the central topic of the next section. The relative roles of punishment and supportive strategies are considered further in the final section of this chapter.

FAIRNESS

Fairness is a second major problem in the design of disciplinary procedures. Procedures are fair if they do not produce an unjust pattern of either false negatives—judgments that there has not been harassment when there has—or false positives—judgments that there has been harassment when there has not been. Design of any adjudicative procedure is a problem of imperfect procedural justice.[9] In the abstract the right result would be a determination that there has been harassment in all and only those cases in which there has been harassment. Unfortunately, if it were possible to pick out exactly these cases, it would not be necessary to resort to a procedure at all. Moreover, a trade off is likely between procedural simplicity and accuracy: The more accurate the procedure, the more complex, time-consuming, and burdensome it may be.

In dealing with the uncertainties involved in constructing fair procedures, a primary problem is deciding whether to err on the side of false positives or false negatives. Is it more important to protect those reporting genuine incidents of harassment from judgments that the reports were nonmeritorious, or to protect those against whom complaints of harassment were lodged from erroneous "convictions"? It is easy to view this as a choice between protecting potential victims or potential victimizers, but this may be too simple. Certainly, reporters of harassment are far more likely to be powerless than those against whom harassment is reported. This difference alone might lead some to the conclusion that false negatives are worse than false positives: Better to harm an innocent with power (say, a faculty member) than an innocent who is powerless, (say, a student). The innocent with power may have more resources to call on in recovering from the damage. Or it may seem more egalitarian to risk harming the more powerful than to risk harming the already less powerful. On an individual basis, however, there may be no obvious way to choose between the errors. Both are painful: a student who rightly feels compromised, aggrieved, and unsupported because her valid complaint has been found to lack merit, and an accused who faces job discipline and a damaged reputation despite having done nothing wrong. Both errors may have major, ongoing life consequences. Neither error is in any obvious way voluntarily incurred, although there may be close cases here. For example, a faculty member may end up as the subject of an unjustified harassment complaint because he is rude to students and engages in gendered behavior that is quite close to the line of permissibility. Or a student bringing a complaint may make careless claims that cast doubt on her credibility, perhaps trying to paint too devastating a picture or to downplay the significance of her own actions although she is entirely right about the central charges.

Probably the most powerful way to defend a preference for erring on the side of false positives is to argue that there is a sense in which all those in a position of power—potential victimizers, as it were—bear some responsibility for an ongoing campus climate in which harassment flourishes. Many university statements about sexual harassment reflect the judgment that it is the obligation of the administration and faculty to create a campus climate that discourages harassment. This statement of Cornell's president is an example: "Beyond the [sexual harassment] policy itself and its enforcement, there remains a question of institutional culture. Each of us, by example, should make clear to those around us our rejection of sexual harassment in all its forms."[10] Collective responsibility thus argues for the claim that innocent victims are more genuinely innocent than alleged-but-innocent victimizers, who at least should play a role in reducing the frequency of harassment.[11] In addition, it might be argued that there are more "close cases" on the alleged victimizer's side than on the alleged victim's side—that is, more cases in which conduct that is not quite harassment is nonetheless troubling than cases in which reports are made of behavior that is not harassment but was misunderstood.

Nonetheless, it is worth remembering that a determination to err on the side of false positives would go absolutely against the standard assumptions of criminal law. The guarantees of due process rest on the foundation that it is better to let a guilty person go free (a false negative) than to convict an innocent person (a false positive). The corollary of erring on the side of false positives might, therefore, be a move away from the criminal law paradigm in campus sexual harassment cases, even where discipline might otherwise be thought appropriate, and a move toward educational (for faculty) and supportive (for students) approaches.[12]

Problems of evidence are a particularly good illustration of fairness concerns in designing sexual harassment procedures. As with many other sexual offenses, sexual harassment charges frequently rest on the word of the alleged victim against the word of the alleged perpetrator. Historically, rape law dealt with this problem with a series of rules that favored defendants. First, the requirement of corroborative evidence, such as bruises or semen, disadvantaged victims when no such evidence was to be found. Second, the requirement of a "fresh complaint," a complaint made almost immediately after the alleged attack, was thought to prevent alleged victims from making up their stories after the fact but disadvantaged victims who were too embarrassed or too terrified or too upset to come forth quickly. Third, the requirement of resistance to demonstrate unwillingness, discussed in chapter 3, burdened women to act, despite perceived danger, or forfeit their complaint. And fourth, evidentiary rules that presumed the relevance of the woman's past sexual history apparently left women on trial as much as men. These rules combined to create a regime that protected defendants except in the clearest cases of "real rape," violence against a stranger.[13] In most jurisdictions, this regime has been altered, at least with respect to formal rules if not with respect to actual practice.[14] Evidence of a woman's past sexual history, for example, typically is admissible only if it bears directly on the allegation at issue. In rape law, these changes in the rules of evidence have been coupled with the delineation of lesser sexual offenses, such as assault or negligent imposition. Here too, loosening the protections against false positives has been coupled with the introduction of new options calling for less severe punishment.

In universities, adjudicative procedures typically are far less formal than the due process structures of a courtroom. Rights of adjudication, such as the rules of evidence or the right to counsel, frequently are not guaranteed. Many policies encourage informal methods of resolution as an initial step, with the possibility of more formal methods when discipline is contemplated. The hope is that informal methods such as discussion or mediation will lead to a solution to the dispute that is satisfactory to everyone involved. The advantages of informal processes include limited emotional wear and tear on the parties involved, low costs, and speedy resolution. Even when more formal processes are invoked, they may well look like alternative forms of dispute resolution such as mediation rather than like adjudication. Some universities lodge the responsibility for handling complaints with the local administrative unit, such as a department chair, except in cases involving significant disciplinary measures.[15] Disciplinary hearings may be conducted before a body made up of peer faculty members or administrators that is called into session on an episodic basis for single cases only. The rules of evidence may not be applied. Lawyers may be excluded from the process, with the parties involved allowed counselors only.

This informal kind of process has the accommodationist advantages of alternative dispute resolution. Without the more formal and adversarial structure of a court, negotiated settlements may be achieved in a more expeditious manner. However, informality also has disadvantages. Although methods of alternative dispute resolution—ADR—have gained great popularity as replacements for formal adversarial adjudication, they are not without dissenters. In a seminal critique, Owen Fiss argued that where there is inequality between the parties, the ADR movement risks silencing the voices of the powerless.[16] These risks are magnified in cases when the dispute-resolver has links to the more powerful party, as might well be the case when a department chair attempts to reconcile a dispute between a student and a colleague. Imagine a student who has brought a complaint about a faculty member and then finds herself in a "discussion" with the faculty member and the department chair. It is not easy for such a student to stand up for what she believes to be her rights when arrayed against her are apparently reasonable people who have authority and who agree with one another. Even though she typically has rights to a formal process or rights of appeal if she is not satisfied with the resolution, these rights may seem overwhelmingly daunting to exercise in the face of closed ranks of authority. Informal processes, then, risk being less than fair to the alleged victim of harassment.

At least a partial solution to this concern seems to be to remove even informal dispute resolution from the immediate context, at least to some extent. One way to achieve such perspective is to assign to any complainant a counselor, whose role throughout the process would be to help the complainant understand what she wants from the process, what she can reasonably expect, and how to stand up for herself. Another way to achieve perspective is to require *review* of all complaints and their resolution at a senior administrative level; this review would allow patterns to be observed and results from different areas to be compared. Another solution to making informal processes more fair is to assign informal dispute resolution to trained mediators who would have the skill and experience in encouraging each party to clarify and articulate what they want in resolving the harassment complaint. Although university policies frequently have such options, they do not encourage them, which contributes to the risk of compromising fairness to the alleged victim.

Informal processes also have been criticized as increasing the risks of false positives, however. Without such protections as the rules of evidence, harassment reports are less carefully scrutinized and can be based on hearsay or innuendo. Because informal processes could therefore compromise fairness to the accused, it may be more appropriate to emphasize education and support as a preventive for harassment rather than discipline.

Thus, campus processes for resolving sexual harassment complaints face problems of fairness for both sides. Relaxing due process protections with the aim of reducing the incidence of harassment risks fairness to the accused, so this speaks against a highly punitive paradigm. At the same time, if more informal procedures such as mediation are inclined to compromise fairness to the victim, this suggests providing the accused with supportive services and possibly remedies as restitution.

CONFIDENTIALITY FOR ACCUSER AND ACCUSED

Providing confidentiality for both accuser and accused is a difficult but unavoidable aspect of the design of procedures for handling sexual harassment complaints. The accuser may find her life on trial if her credibility is questioned. If a harassment complaint becomes public knowledge, the accused may face gossip, loss of reputation, and damage to his career.

Guaranteeing confidentiality for the complainant may be an important step in encouraging victims to report sexual harassment. Without such a guarantee, potential complainants may fear the risk of embarrassing public revelations about her sexuality or reprisal from the accused, who may continue to be in a position of power that can affect the educational or employment future of his accuser. Because reprisals may be indirect and difficult to identify, colleges may not be able to guarantee complainants that they will be protected from harm. Direct reprisals such as assigning a failing grade or demoting the complainant are fairly easy to identify and correct, but even these actions may be open for dispute. The faculty member or employer may allege deficiencies in the quality of the complainant's work or may charge that the harassment complaint was brought in retaliation for the poor evaluation. More subtle or indirect reprisals may be even more difficult to observe and prove. A faculty member accused of harassment may, for example, make comments to colleagues that undermine the personal and academic credibility of an accusing student without the student ever knowing what has happened. The results may be lower grades or less favorable letters of recommendation from other faculty members for no apparent reason. These serious effects to an accuser's reputation speak for offering a mechanism that guarantees confidential complaints. Opening access to a counselor or a complaint officer, without the complaint becoming known either to the alleged harasser or to anyone else in the university community, is an important first step in encouraging reports of harassment.

Once a confidential complaint has been made, moreover, harassment officers ought to be able to conduct a preliminary investigation without revealing the identity of the student. Such a preliminary investigation is necessary for the officer to be able to form a tentative judgment as to whether the complaint has substance. On the basis of such an investigation, the officer will be able to advise the student about whether the complaint should be brought forward or dropped. Because these judgments require experience, and because inquiries will need to be conducted with circumspection, universities should encourage the development of professional staff to handle harassment complaints, because their investigations require experienced judgment and tact. Preliminary inquiries should be made following harassment complaints to determine whether the complaint has substance and should be continued and should be conducted without violating constraints of confidentiality. It is possible to conduct preliminary inquiries without revealing the identity of the alleged harasser by asking coworkers or fellow students who have been named as possible witnesses whether they have ever observed incidents of the type alleged, without naming the alleged perpetrator. Such a line of questioning would not be, for example, "Did you ever observe Professor X call women students by sexist epithet Y"? But, "Have you ever observed professors in department Z call women students by sexist epithet Y"? Inquiries also should be conducted in a manner that avoids revealing the identity of the complainant. If the alleged harasser is approached as part of the inquiry, however, it may be difficult to provide information about the complaint while preventing the accused from guessing its source.

If there is any likelihood that the source will be revealed, the complainant should grant permission before the inquiries are made, except when the officer judges that a complaint is so serious it should be investigated even without the complainant's permission.

If the complaint goes beyond the stage of a preliminary investigation, the alleged harasser will need to be told the substance of the harassment complaint and the identity of the complainant. Without such information, the accused will not have a fair chance to respond to the charges against him. Denying the accused such a chance to respond is wrong both because it increases the risks of false positives and because it fails to respect the accused as a person by not allowing him to answer the charges against him. If the complainant refuses to allow the alleged harasser to be told of her charges, no disciplinary proceedings should take place.

The information in dropped harassment complaints need not be forgotten entirely, however. The institution, in the interests of prevention, could still choose to keep records of the alleged harassment, so long as they are divorced from adverse consequences for the alleged harasser.[17] These records might be useful in identifying patterns if subsequent allegations of harassment are lodged against this same person. They also might be useful in deciding where to target educational programs. For example, if a department is the subject of several harassment complaints within a relatively short period, the institution could target that department for education about sexual harassment. These efforts to identify patterns and the need for education, however, should be kept scrupulously separate from individual records to avoid possible unfairness in individual criticism or discipline. The institution also might choose to offer remediation to the complainant, even if her complaint does not go forward in a disciplinary process. Such remediation might at a minimum include supportive services such as counseling but could also include other benefits such as those discussed in the following section.

In particularly serious cases, the institution also might decide to pursue the complaint despite the complainant's wish that her identity not be revealed. This choice should be based on a judgment that intervention is desirable to protect other students from likely harassment. If the university chooses this course, it owes the complainant a special obligation of support and care to prevent retaliation, because her privacy is being put at risk for the overall institutional good.

Another aspect of confidentiality in these cases is the relevance of making public the private lives of the parties involved. Perhaps the complainant has a history of ill-founded harassment complaints. Perhaps her diaries are revealing of the legitimacy of her charges.[18] Perhaps her medical records indicate something about the likely reliability of her allegations. Under rules of evidence in court, such information would need to meet very strict standards of relevance. Although university disciplinary proceedings are less formal, it raises serious questions of fairness to the complainant to bring in evidence about other aspects of her life—say, past sexual history—without careful scrutiny of its bearing on the likely reliability of her charges. It is also unfair to allow the defendant access to her records without her knowledge and opportunity to contest their availability. This last point is especially important, because universities may have access to a student's academic records as well as her medical records if she has sought treatment at a student health service or a university-run facility. This was a problem in one particularly outrageous case, in which a university obtained a complaining student's health records (she had been treated at the university hospital), without her consent and without any review by the court, in the effort to put her credibility into question.[19]

A third confidentiality issue is whether the institution should make public the existence of the complaint and its ultimate disposition. Because the mere fact of a complaint can have serious reputational consequences, complaints should not be made public by the institution unless they have reached the formal hearing stage or a decision has been made that the complaint had merit (including through a settlement). To be sure, the institution cannot prevent the complainant herself—or her friends—from speaking publicly about the complaint. It is unfair to the alleged harasser, however, to allow information about the complaint to come from institutional sources, even if the complaint is shown to have no verification, because of the increased credibility of the charge this may convey. Formalization of the complaint requires at least a judgment that it should not be dismissed at a preliminary stage, and the formal hearing process itself should provide the alleged harasser with protection against unfair reports of the process and its outcome.

A final confidentiality concern is whether harassment complaints should be reported to other institutions contemplating hiring an accused harasser. A recent article in *The Chronicle of Higher Education*, the journal of the American Association of University Professors, contended that universities are all too ready to pass known offenders on to other institutions without revealing their problematic histories.[20] It is unfair to the accused to convey information about complaints that have been judged not to be meritorious. To relate such complaints may allow false positives to have damning consequences for careers. At the same time, to prevent future harassment, it is important to let other institutions know about harassment charges that have been sustained. Moreover, institutions should not dodge the responsibility to be honest about members of their community by agreeing to drop harassment charges and remaining silent in exchange for the harasser's going elsewhere.

REMEDIES: INSTITUTIONAL OR INDIVIDUAL

One result of a sexual harassment complaint may be the imposition of discipline on an adjudged harasser. Although punishment is certainly an important means for protecting the institution against predatory behavior and deterring potential harassers, primary emphasis on punitive remedies may be misguided. If procedures for handling complaints are relatively informal, or if overly punitive judgments actually discourage reporting, institutions may find that giving punitive remedies pride of place jeopardizes both fairness and the goal of reduced incidence. Accordingly, I recommend that institutions consider seriously at least two other remedial approaches: education about harassment and supportive services for alleged victims.

Required education about what harassment is, what its consequences are, and how to recognize and prevent it can be a useful way of reducing harassment levels. General programs offered to all university employees may have some benefits but are likely to be diffuse. Instead, colleges and universities should consider more focused educational strategies, targeting units that have had allegations of harassment for serious educational efforts. Such departments might be required, for example, to participate in a seminar about harassment and to institute practices, such as publishing syllabi that are designed to reduce misunderstandings. The *Cohen* case, discussed in chapter 3, resulted in a victory for Dean Cohen because his behavior was perceived to be a disciplinary problem. Yet educational requirements could have been placed on that department without any imposition of discipline, with perhaps similar results. Because such requirements do not impose punishment on particular staff members, they need not follow a finding of actual offense. Another strategy for identifying units in need of harassment education is the exit interview; graduating seniors, for example, can be asked as part of a review of their education whether they ever experienced harassment. One particularly interesting, however positive, response to the problem of possible underreporting is the University of Pennsylvania's commitment to periodic exit interviews with departing students, faculty, and staff to determine whether they have experienced harassment and whether there is a need for further university efforts on the issue.[21] Anonymous course evaluations are another potential source of data about student perceptions and the impact of staff behavior on educational opportunity.

The second remedy suggested recently by several commentators is funding supportive services or providing other benefits for the possible victim. Ellen Frankel Paul, a libertarian, has argued that tort remedies are a way to realize respect for the victim.[22] Diana Meyers has argued from a feminist perspective that scholarships for offended students are a desirable remedy for campus hate speech.[23] Of course, for such remedies actually to be awarded in a tort suit, there would need to be a finding of wrongdoing and responsibility on the part of the institution. Institutions may choose to award benefits that go beyond the scope of available tort remedies, however. Because the costs of such remedies are shared rather than imposed on a particular person, it is not unfair to award them in the absence of a finding of harassment. The institution might decide, in the interests of supporting equality for its students, to fund supportive services for those experiencing difficulty with al-leged harassment, even if their complaints have not reached a final adjudi-cation of merit. These services can be defended as part of the shared costs of providing equal educational opportunity, just as investments in good cam-pus lighting promote access to night classes.

CONCLUSION

Sexual harassment is a significant problem on today's college campuses. When it occurs, it impairs educational quality and opportunity. Reporting rates suggest, however, that typical procedures in place on contemporary campuses have not been very successful in addressing the issue. This chapter has argued that universities should explore alternatives to disciplinary para-digms as a way to reduce the frequency of harassment and mitigate its effects, relying on punishment only for more serious cases. Education is a critical means to equal opportunity, and universities owe their students no less.

Part II

Part II

8

Sexual Harassment of Working Women: A Case of Sex Discrimination

Catharine A. MacKinnon

FOREWORD

Sexual harassment of working women has been one of the most pervasive but carefully ignored features of our national life. As women's liberation makes progress, the facts are beginning to come into the open and the profound implications for our society are beginning to be understood. We have even reached a point where the law may start to do something about the problem. Up to the present time, however, no comprehensive treatment of the social and legal issues has been available.

Catharine MacKinnon's study of sexual harassment in the working place makes a unique contribution at several levels. First of all it provides a skillful analysis of the legal questions that are posed in the emerging effort to use the law to support women who seek to challenge the patterns and practices of sexual harassment. The questions are novel and in many respects complex. Is sexual harassment, when it occurs in connection with operations of government, a violation of the Equal Protection Clause of the Constitution? Is it a "discrimination" in employment because of "sex," forbidden by Title VII of the Civil Rights Act of 1964 and similar legislation? When a woman leaves her job because of sexual harassment, is she quitting for "personal" reasons or is she entitled to unemployment compensation? To what extent is an employer responsible for the actions of his employees who engage in sexual harassment?

The answers given by the courts thus far, in the few cases that have presented these issues, have been hesitant, inconsistent, and ill-informed. By setting the problem in the context of the inferior position of women in the labor market, by providing a full factual account of the nature and extent of sexual harassment, by showing how sexual harassment grows out of and reinforces the traditional social roles of men and women in our society, and by "fitting [this] experience to legal contours," MacKinnon makes a convincing case that sexual harassment does constitute unlawful discrimination within the meaning of the Equal Protection Clause and the relevant statutes. The legal foundations are thus established for a major effort to bring the force of law to bear upon an uncivilized practice that has long been silently sanctioned. How successful a litigation campaign might be is a open question. It could have a substantial impact on the status of women in the United States.

Second, MacKinnon undertakes to give a new dimension to the Equal Protection Clause. In standard equal protection theory, when a law or official practice treats one category of persons differently from another, the courts examine the difference to determine whether there are adequate reasons for making the distinction. In the case of race classifications, the courts insist that the government demonstrate "compelling" reasons for any difference in treatment and, except for the Japanese detention during World War II, have never found such reasons to exist. In other types of cases the courts are satisfied if any "rational" reason or "substantial" reason can be found. The result has been that, in cases where a difference in treatment is based on sex, the courts have frequently held the different treatment justified. Moreover, in all types of cases, laws and regulations affirmatively designed to overcome the past effects of inequality have run into trouble on the ground that they themselves make invidious distinctions. The outcome has been that in many respects equal protection law, while it has prohibited substantial overt discrimination, has not succeeded in achieving actual equality between the groups involved.

MacKinnon argues that the focus in equal protection law should not be on the "differences," or whether the differences are "arbitrary" rather than "rational," but upon the basic issue of "inequality." In other words the courts should consider whether the treatment by the law results in systematic "disadvantagement" because of group status. Thus, in the area of sex discrimination, the "only question for litigation is whether the policy or practice in question integrally contributes to the maintenance of an underclass or a deprived position because of gender status."

Such an approach deserves serious consideration. It would force the courts to take into account the actual effect of claimed discriminatory laws and practices, rather than find distinctions rational because they reflected existing social conditions that in turn embodied the result of the very discrimination against which protection was sought. Furthermore, it would direct attention to the group nature of the problems of equality in our society. Under our system of law it is the individual who is entitled to relief, but ultimately the disparities between citizens that the law seeks to eliminate through the Equal Protection Clause are "disadvantagements" as the member of a group. In addition, an "inequality" approach would more readily support the type of affirmative action that, as experience has shown by now, is essential to the achievement of real, as distinct from formal, equality.

There are problems with MacKinnon's view of the legal path to equality between the sexes. The concept of "inequality" or "disadvantagement" must be translated into more specific legal doctrine. And MacKinnon envisages, in part at least, the achievement of a dual system of rights, in which equality for women would not necessarily be measured by the prevailing standards of equality now imposed by the white male. But these may be only challenges to overcome, not necessarily flaws in her conceptual scheme.

On a third level MacKinnon offers us, or at least us males, important information about a dark side of our society, a sensitive insight into the plight of those on the receiving end of sexual harassment, and an eloquent statement of her vision of equality between the sexes. A Supreme Court that can decide that an employment disability plan covering every form of disability except pregnancy does not discriminate against women plainly has need of education on these matters. So do many others. MacKinnon's portrayal in depth of a pernicious social problem, and the light it throws upon the nature of our society, is not the least of the contributions made by this book.

One final word. Although the book is addressed in the first instance to a legal problem, it is not for lawyers alone. The law of sex discrimination is not so esoteric that, at least on the ultimate issues, it cannot be understood and appraised by lay persons. More important, in dealing with the legal questions MacKinnon necessarily moves into the economic, social, and political considerations that underlie the legal problem. It quickly becomes, therefore, a book for everyone.

Thomas I. Emerson
New Haven, Connecticut

INTRODUCTION

Intimate violation of women by men is sufficiently pervasive in American society as to be nearly invisible. Contained by internalized and structural forms of power, it has been nearly inaudible. Conjoined with men's control over women's material survival, as in the home or on the job, or over women's learning and educational advancement in school, it has become institutionalized. Women employed in the paid labor force, typically hired "as women," dependent upon their income and lacking job alternatives, are particularly vulnerable to intimate violation in the form of sexual abuse at work. In addition to being victims of the practice, working women have been subject to the social failure to recognize sexual harassment as an abuse at all. Tacitly, it has been both acceptable and taboo; acceptable for men to do, taboo for women to confront, even to themselves. But the systematic silence enforced by employment sanctions is beginning to be broken. The daily impact upon women's economic status and work opportunities, not to mention psychic health and self-esteem, is beginning to be explored, documented, and, increasingly, resisted.

Sexual harassment, most broadly defined, refers to the unwanted imposition of sexual requirements in the context of a relationship of unequal power. Central to the concept is the use of power derived from one social sphere to lever benefits or impose deprivations in another. The major dynamic is best expressed as the reciprocal enforcement of two inequalities. When one is sexual, the other material, the cumulative sanction is particularly potent. American society legitimizes male sexual dominance of women and employer's control of workers, although both forms of dominance have limits and exceptions. Sexual harassment of women in employment is particularly clear when male superiors on the job coercively initiate unwanted sexual advances to women employees; sexual pressures by male coworkers and customers, when condoned or encouraged by employers, might also be included. Lack of reciprocal feeling on the woman's part may be expressed by rejection or show of disinclination. After this, the advances may be repeated or intensified; often employment retaliation ensues. The material coercion behind the advances may remain implicit in the employer's position to apply it. Or it may be explicitly communicated through, for example, firing for sexual noncompliance or retention conditioned upon continued sexual compliance.

Sexual harassment may occur as a single encounter or as a series of incidents at work. It may place a sexual condition upon employment opportunities at a clearly defined threshold, such as hiring, retention, or advancement; or it may occur as a pervasive or continuing condition of the work environment. Extending along a continuum of severity and unwantedness, and depending upon the employment circumstances, examples include verbal sexual suggestions or jokes, constant leering or ogling, brushing against your body "accidentally," a friendly pat, squeeze or pinch or arm against you, catching you alone for a quick kiss, the indecent proposition backed by the threat of losing your job, and forced sexual relations.

Complex forms include the persistent innuendo and the continuing threat that is never consummated either sexually or economically. The most straightforward example is "put out or get out."

Typically, employers, husbands, judges, and the victims themselves have understood and dismissed such incidents as trivial, isolated, and "personal," or as universal "natural" or "biological" behaviors. This book interprets sexual harassment in the context of women's work and sex roles, in which women as a group are seen to occupy a structurally inferior as well as distinct place. Sexual harassment is argued to derive its meaning and detrimental impact upon women not from personality or biology, but from this *social* context. The defining dimensions of this social context are employer-employee relations (given women's position in the labor force) and the relationship between the sexes in American society as a whole, of which sexual relations are one expression.

If sexual harassment is a product of social factors, it might be expected to be a common occurrence. Preliminary indications, although tentative, suggest that it is pervasive, affecting in some form perhaps as many as seven out of ten women at some time in their work lives. Yet sexual harassment of women in employment has provided explicit grounds for legal action in only a handful of cases. Why has so apparently massive a social problem surfaced so seldom within the legal system? The reasons are probably not limited to the lack of legitimized or sympathetic channels for complaint short of the courts, or to women's learned reticence, enforced through fear of reprisals, although these would seem deterrent enough. It is probably not because the problem has been adequately handled socially. That there has not been *even one* reported case until very recently implicates the receptivity of the legal system.

Applicable legal concepts, with the social relations they reify, have tended to turn women's differences from men at once into special virtues and special restraints. In effect, if not intent, the law has conceptualized women workers either in terms of their "humanity," which has meant characteristics women share with men, or in terms of their womanhood, which has meant their uniqueness. These two standards have been mutually exclusive. When women have been defined "as women" their human needs have often been ignored. An example is "protective" laws that, in shielding women's femininity from work stress, often excluded women from desperately needed jobs or job benefits. Alternatively, when women have been analyzed as "human," their particular needs as women have often been ignored. An example is employment insurance plans that cover virtually every work disability (including many unique to men) except pregnancy. In a long-ignored analysis that can be applied to the legal conceptualizations of women both "as human" and "as woman," the sociologist George Simmel observed:

> Man's position of power does not only assure his relative superiority over the woman, but it assures that his standards become generalized as generically human standards that are to govern the behavior of men and women alike. . . . Almost all discussions of women dealt only with what they are in relation to men in terms of real, ideal, or value criteria. Nobody asks what they are for themselves.

On the whole, the legal doctrine of "sex discrimination" as interpreted by the courts has implicitly used such standards and criteria. In the analysis to follow, legal interpretations that give concrete meaning to the sex discrimination prohibition are reconsidered in their theoretical underpinnings, both for their potential in prohibiting sexual harassment and for their limitations, as the issue of sexual harassment reveals them.

The legal argument advanced by this book is that sexual harassment of women at work is sex discrimination in employment. The argument proceeds first by locating sexual harassment empirically in the context of women's work, showing that the structure of the work world women occupy makes them systematically vulnerable to this form of abuse. Sexual harassment is seen to be one dynamic that reinforces and expresses women's traditional and inferior role in the labor force. Next, reports of sexual harassment are analyzed, with a focus on the dimensions of the experience as women undergo it. This is followed by an account of those few legal cases that have raised the problem of sexual harassment at work. Once the problem has been defined within its material context and as experienced, and the legal attempts to address it have been initially explored, the central legal question can be confronted: Is sexual harassment sex discrimination?

Two distinct concepts of discrimination, which I term the "differences" approach and the "inequality" approach, emerge as approaches to answering this question. These conceptions are not strictly legal doctrines in the sense that judges recognize them as alternative views on the meaning of discrimination. Rather, they are the result of an attempt to think systematically about the broader concepts that underlie the logic and results of the discrimination cases as a whole, with particular attention to discrimination law's most highly developed application: the cases on race. Applied to sex, the two approaches flow from two underlying visions of the reality of sex in American society. The first approach envisions the sexes socially as well as biologically *different* from one another, but calls impermissible or "arbitrary" those distinctions or classifications that are found preconceived and/or inaccurate. The second approach understands the sexes to be not simply socially differentiated but socially *unequal.* In the broader view, all practices that subordinate women to men are prohibited. The differences approach, in its sensitivity to disparity and similarity, can be a useful corrective to sexism; both women and men can be damaged by sexism, although usually it is women who are. The inequality approach, by contrast, sees women's situation as a structural problem of enforced inferiority that needs to be radically altered.

The view that discrimination consists in arbitrary differentiation dominates legal doctrine and scholarly thinking on the subject, reaching an epiphany in the Supreme Court's majority opinion in *Gilbert v. General Electric* (1977). General Electric excluded only pregnancy and pregnancy-related disabilities from risks covered under an employee disability insurance plan. Had the case been approached with an awareness of the consequences of pregnancy and motherhood in the social inequality of the sexes, the Court would have found such a rule discriminatory. More narrowly, only women are excluded from insurance coverage against a detriment in employment due to temporary disability, creating unequal employment security on the basis of sex. Taking the differences approach, however, the Court thought that, although all pregnant persons are women, because pregnancy is unique (but not universal) to women, excluding it from coverage was not a distinction "based on sex," hence not discriminatory. Because women actually had *different* disabilities from men, it was not discriminatory to fail to insure them. By contrast, the result (although not every feature of the reasoning) in a 1978 case, *City of Los Angeles v. Manhart,* illustrates the inequality approach. There, the Supreme Court found that requiring women to make larger contributions to their retirement plan was discriminatory, in spite of the proved sex difference that women on the average outlive men. A real difference between the sexes was not allowed to obscure or excuse socially unequal consequences.

Implicit in the distinction in approach are different conceptions of reasonable comparability: Must women and men be able to be compared on the variable in question? Further, exactly what the variable in question is defined to be is decided by the approach that is taken. Under the differences approach, if the context is defined so that the sexes cannot be reasonably compared, discrimination cannot be seen to be sex-based. By contrast, the inequality approach comprehends that women and men may, due to sex or sexism, present noncomparabilities. In this view, lack of comparability is not a permissible basis for socially perpetuating women's disadvantages.

In terms of the social context discussed, and under the legal doctrines that context has produced, sexual harassment is argued in this book to be not simply abusive, humiliating, oppressive, and exploitative, but also to be sex discrimination in employment. Specifically, this is argued under Title VII of the Civil Rights Act of 1964, as amended, and the Equal Protection Clause of the Fourteenth Amendment. In relevant part, Title VII states:

a) It shall be an unlawful employment practice for an employer—
   1) to fail or refuse to hire or to discharge any individual, or otherwise to discriminate against any individual with respect to his compensation, terms, conditions, or privileges of employment because of such individual's . . . sex . . ; or
   2) to limit, segregate, or classify his employees or applicants for employment in any way which would deprive or tend to deprive any individual of employment opportunities or otherwise adversely affect his status as an employee, because of such individual's . . . sex.

The Equal Protection Clause of the Fourteenth Amendment to the Constitution guarantees that no state shall "deny to any person within its jurisdiction the equal protection of the laws." Sexual harassment is argued to be sex discrimination under these sections according to both the inequality approach, which is favored, and the differences approach, which is criticized.

Both arguments can be briefly stated. Under the inequality approach, sexual harassment is seen to disadvantage women as a gender, within the social context in which women's sexuality and material survival have been constructed and joined, to women's detriment. Under the differences approach, sexual harassment is sex discrimination *per se* because the practice differentially injures one gender-defined group in a sphere—sexuality in employment—in which the treatment of women and men can be compared. Sexuality is universal to women, but not unique to them. All women possess female sexuality, so the attribute in question is a gender characteristic. But men also posses sexuality and could be sexually harassed. When they are not, and women are, unequal treatment by gender is shown. If only men are sexually harassed, that is also arbitrary treatment based on sex, hence sex discrimination. If both sexes are, under this argument the treatment would probably not be considered gender-based, hence not sex discriminatory. Thus, sexual harassment of working women is treatment impermissibly based on sex under both approaches.

Sexual harassment is also discrimination in employment. Current cases are analyzed in which courts have found sexual harassment "personal," "biological," "not a policy," and thus (implicitly) not employment discrimination as well as not based on sex. These objections are found uncompelling, mutually inconsistent, without weight in analogous areas of law, and ideologically sexist. Although some of the cases that rely on these formulations have been reversed on appeal, most of these assertions, which represent deep and broadly held social views on women's sexuality, have not been squarely controverted by the courts and continue to arise in litigation. The Supreme Court has yet to hear its first sexual harassment case.

Opposing sexual harassment of women at work through the legal system deserves evaluation from a social standpoint. Sexual harassment is addressed in this book in terms of employment, and women's employment status in terms of sexual harassment, not because work is the only place women are sexually harassed nor because sexual harassment is women's only problem on the job. Legally, women are not arguably entitled, for example, to a marriage free of sexual harassment any more than to one free of rape, nor are women legally guaranteed the freedom to walk down the street or into a court of law without sexual innuendo. In employment, the government promises more.

Work is critical to women's survival and independence. Sexual harassment exemplifies and promotes employment practices that disadvantage women in work (especially occupational segregation) and sexual practices that intimately degrade and objectify women. In this broader perspective, sexual harassment at work undercuts woman's potential for social equality in two interpenetrated ways: by using her employment position to coerce her sexually, while using her sexual position to coerce her economically. Legal recognition that sexual harassment is sex discrimination in employment would help women break the bond between material survival and sexual exploitation. It would support and legitimize women's economic equality and sexual self-determination at a point at which the two are linked.

SEXUAL HARASSMENT: THE EXPERIENCE

. . . I envision a two-way process of interaction between the relevant legal concepts and women's experience. The strictures of the concept of sex discrimination will ultimately constrain those aspects of women's oppression that will be legally recognized as discriminatory. At the same time, women's experiences, expressed in their own way, can push to expand that concept. Such an approach not only enriches the law. It begins to shape it so that what *really* happens to women, not some male vision of what happens to women, is at the core of the legal prohibition. Women's lived-through experience, in as whole and truthful a fashion as can be approximated at this point, should begin to provide the starting point and context out of which is constructed the narrower forms of abuse that will be made illegal on their behalf. Now that a few women have the tools to address the legal system on its own terms, the law can begin to address women's experience on women's own terms.

Although the precise extent and contours of sexual harassment await further and more exacting investigation, preliminary research indicates that the problem is extremely widespread. Certainly it is more common than almost anyone thought. In the pioneering survey by Working Women United Institute, out of a sample of fifty-five food service workers and one hundred women who attended a meeting on sexual harassment, from five to seven of every ten women reported experiencing sexual harassment in some form at some time in their work lives. Ninety-two percent of the total sample thought it a serious problem. In a study of all women employed at the United Nation, 49 percent said that sexual pressure currently existed on their jobs. During the first eight months of 1976, the Division of Human Rights of the State of New York received approximately forty-five complaints from women alleging sexual harassment on the job. Of nine thousand women who responded voluntarily to a questionnaire in *Redbook Magazine,* "How do you handle sex on the job?" nine out of ten reported experiences of sexual harassment. Of course, those who experience the problem may be most likely to respond. Nevertheless, before this survey, it would have been difficult to convince a person of ordinary skepticism that 8,100 American women existed who would report experiencing sexual harassment at work.

Using the *Redbook* questionnaire, a naval officer found 81 percent of a sample of women on a navy base and in a nearby town reported employment-related sexual harassment in some form. These frequency figures must, of course, be cautiously regarded. But even extrapolating conservatively, given that nine out of ten American women work outside the home some time in their lives and that in April 1974, 45 percent of American women sixteen and over, or 35 million women, were employed in the labor force, it is clear that a lot of women are potentially affected. As the problem begins to appear structural rather than individual, *Redbook*'s conclusion that "the problem is not epidemic; it is pandemic—an everyday, everywhere occurrence" does not seem incredible.

One need not show that sexual harassment is commonplace in order to argue that it is severe for those afflicted, or even that it is sex discrimination. However, if one shows that sexual harassment in employment systematically occurs between the persons and under the conditions that an analysis of it as discrimination suggests—that is, as a function of sex as gender—one undercuts the view that it occurs because of some unique chemistry between particular (or aberrant) individuals. That sexual harassment does occur to a large and diverse population of women supports an analysis that it occurs *because* of their group characteristic, that is, sex. Such a showing supports an analysis of the abuse as structural, and as such, worth legal attention as sex discrimination, not just as unfairness between two individuals, which might better be approached through private law.

If the problem is so common, one might ask why it has not been commonly analyzed or protested. Lack of public information, social awareness, and formal data probably reflects less its exceptionality than its specific pathology. Sexual subjects are generally sensitive and considered private; women feel embarrassed, demeaned, and intimidated by these incidents.

They feel afraid, despairing, utterly alone, and complicit. This is not the sort of experience one discusses readily. Even more to the point, sexual advances are often accompanied by threats of retaliation if exposed. Revealing these pressures enough to protest them thus risks the very employment consequences that sanctioned the advances in the first place.

It is not surprising either that women would not complain of an experience for which there has been no name. Until 1976, lacking a term to express it, sexual harassment was literally unspeakable, which made a generalized, shared, and social definition of it inaccessible. . . .

Apparently, sexual harassment can be both a sexist way to express racism and a racist way to express sexism. However, black women also report sexual harassment by black men and white women complain of sexual harassment by black male superiors and coworkers. One complaint for slander and outrageous conduct accused the defendants of making statements including the following:

> warning customers about plaintiff's alleged desire to "get in his pants," pointing out that plaintiff had large breasts, stating "Anything over a handful is wasted," calling plaintiff "Momma Fuller" and "Big Momma," referring to her breasts, "Doesn't she have nice (or large) breasts?" "Watch out, she's very horny. She hasn't gotten any lately" "Have you ever seen a black man's penis?" "Do you know how large a black man's penis is?" "Have you ever slept with a black man?" "Do you want to stop the car and screw in the middle of the street?"

One might consider whether white women more readily perceive themselves as *sexually* degraded, or anticipate a supportive response when they complain, when they are sexually harassed by a black man than by a white man. Alternatively, some white women confide that they have consciously resisted reporting severe sexual harassment by black men to authorities because they feel the response would be supportive for racist reasons. Although racism is deeply involved in sexual harassment, the element common to these incidents is that the perpetrators are male, the victims female. Few women are in a position to harass men sexually, since they do not control men's employment destinies at work, and female sexual initiative is culturally repressed in this society.

As these experiences suggest, the specific injury of sexual harassment arises from the nexus between a sexual demand and the workplace. Anatomized, the situations can be seen to include a sexual incident or advance, some form of compliance or rejection, and some employment consequence. Sometimes these elements are telescoped, sometimes greatly attenuated, sometimes absent. All are variable: the type of incident or advance, the form of response, and the kind and degree of damage attributable to it.

The critical issues in assessing sexual harassment as a legal cause of action —the issues that need to be explored in light of women's experiences—

center on the definition of and the relationship among three events: the advance, the response, and the employment consequence. Critical questions arise in conceptualizing all three. Where is the line between a sexual advance and a friendly gesture? How actively must the issue be forced? If a woman complies, should the legal consequences be different than if she refuses? Given the attendant risks, how explicitly must a woman reject? Might quitting be treated the same as firing under certain circumstances? To get legal relief, must a job benefit be shown to be merited independent of a sexual bargain, or is the situation an injury in itself? When a perpetrator insists that a series of touchings were not meant to be sexual, but the victim experienced them as unambiguously sexual, assuming both are equally credible, whose interpretation controls when the victim's employment status is damaged? . . . In addressing these questions, it is important to divide matters of persuasion from issues of fact, and both of these from issues that go to the core of the legal concept of the discrimination. The first distinguishes the good from the less good case; the second sets a standard of proof; the third draws a line between a legal claim and no claim at all.

Women's experiences of sexual harassment can be divided into two forms that merge at the edges and in the world. The first I term the *quid pro quo,* in which sexual compliance is exchanged, or proposed to be exchanged, for an employment opportunity. The second arises when sexual harassment is a persistent *condition of work.* This distinction highlights different facets of the problem as women live through it and suggests slightly different legal requirements. In both types, the sexual demand is often but an extension of a gender-defined work role. The victim is employed, hence treated, "as a woman." In the quid pro quo, the woman must comply sexually or forfeit an employment opportunity. The quid pro quo arises most powerfully within the context of horizontal segregation, in which women are employed in feminized jobs, such as office work, as a part of jobs vertically stratified by sex, with men holding the power to hire and fire women. In a job that is defined according to gender, noncompliance with all of the job's requirements, which may at the boss's whim come to include sexual tolerance or activity, operatively "disqualifies" a woman for the job. In sexual harassment as a condition of work, the exchange of sex for employment opportunities is less direct. The major question is whether the *advances themselves* constitute an injury in employment. . . .

"The other side" of sexual harassment is commonly thought to be raised by [the] situation in which women who comply with sexual conditions are advantaged in employment over men or over women who refuse. Despite the indications that few benefits redound to the woman who accedes, much folklore exists about the woman who "slept her way to the top" or the academic professional woman who "got her degree on her back." These aphorisms suggest that women who are not qualified for their jobs or promotions acquire them instead by sexual means. Do these stories raise serious difficulties for a conceptualization of sexual harassment as integral to women's employment disadvantagement?

Since so few women get to the top at all, it cannot be very common for them to get there by sexual means. Yet undoubtedly some individuals, whether by calculation or in the face of discrimination and lack of recognition of their qualifications, must have followed this course. A mix of these elements is suggested in the following (undocumented) observation: "By using sex, women were able to diminish the social distance between important, rich or powerful men and themselves, and to obtain desirable goods such as economic security and social status through marriage, or a desirable job or promotion through sexual relations with an influential man." Although the author of this statement qualifies it substantially in a footnote, she concludes: "There are, however, even at present a few outstanding examples of professional women, businesswomen, and artists whose occupational success is largely due to a powerful male with whom they have a long-standing and open relationship." This portrays a relationship that appears more like a consensual one than like unwanted sex acquiesced in for career advancement, although it is admittedly difficult to tell the difference.

As discussed earlier, women consistently occupy the lowest-status, lowest-paying jobs, much lower than men of the same education and experience. Given this, it is difficult to argue that women in general receive advantages even remotely comparable with the sexual harassment to which they are subjected. This, after all, is the implication of the supposed "other side": some women are hurt by the practice, it is said, but then look at all the women who benefit from it. Initially, it seems worth asking, as a hypothetical parallel, whether if some blacks are advantaged just because they are black, that is a reason why blacks who are disadvantaged because they are black should continue to be. Next, from the available data on sex discrimination, it cannot be deduced that women in general (and certainly not in individual cases) derive undeserved job opportunities from sexual compliance or by any other means. On the contrary, it would be difficult to show that cooperating women derive advantages commensurate even with the disadvantage of being female. Of course, it is impossible to estimate how much worse women's position might be without the possible contribution of unwanted sex to their side of the bargain. Overall, however, the statistics on discrimination suggest that no fulfillment of any requirement, sexual demands included, results in job status for which women are qualified, much less undeserved advancement.

Presuming for the argument that these stories have some truth, one might look at women who "succeed" this way as having extricated themselves from

a situation of sexual harassment. Rather than deriving unfair advantages because of their sex, perhaps they had to meet unfair requirements because of
their sex. In this perspective, the woman who "slept her way to the top" may
have been the woman who would not have been hired or promoted, regardless of qualifications, without fulfilling sexual conditions, conditions
equally qualified men do not have to fulfill. Moreover, for every woman who
"got her degree on her back," there were men who offered rewards, supervision, and attention to her development only at a sexual price. To the extent
they are true, then, these stories document a point seldom made: Men with
the power to affect women's careers allow sexual factors to make a difference. So the threats are serious: Those who do not comply are disadvantaged in favor of those who do. (It is also seldom considered that a woman
might be an attractive sexual object to her superior for the same reasons that
qualify her for the position.)

Further, there may be compelling explanations for these stories other than
their truth. How many men find it unbearable that a woman out-qualifies
them in an even competition? Perhaps they assuage their egos by propagat-
ing rumors that the woman used her sexuality—something presumptively
unavailable to men—to outdistance them. These stories may exemplify a
well-documented inability of both sexes to see women in any but sexual
terms. Willingness to believe the stories may illustrate the pervasive assumption that, since a career is so intrinsically inappropriate for a woman,
her sexuality must define her role in this context, as well as in all others. This
dovetails with the prior assumption that if a woman's sexuality is present at
all, she must be receiving unfair consideration.

Certainly it is important to establish in individual cases whether a woman
is complaining about a failed attempt cynically to use sex to get ahead or a
bona fide situation of sex imposed as a career requirement. But to believe
that instances raised in this situation symmetrically outweigh the injury that
women as a whole suffer from sexual harassment ignores the evidence and
provides a convenient excuse not to take the problem seriously. . . .

SEXUAL HARASSMENT CASES

The underlying sense seems to be that even though the incident occurred on
the job, between persons who are working, and in a relationship hierarchi-
cally defined by the work situation, and although the job is thereby made unbearable and/or the incident has resulted in loss of job opportunities, somehow the incident has nothing to do with work. This is clearly a matter of
point of view. For the perpetrator, it may be a diversion; the victim undoubtedly *wishes* it had nothing to do with work. . . .

By analogy to race, the fact that a sexual relation between a woman and
a man is felt to be personal does not exempt it from helping to perpetuate

women's subordinate place in the workplace and in society as a whole. The barriers to recognition of its social structural character are merely very high. Many men go home every night to a person they fully consider themselves to be relating to "as an individual," unconscious of how their feelings, attitudes, and treatment of her might contribute to her subordination and to that of women as a whole. When whites say that they relate to blacks "as people," meaning "without regard to race"—a covert insult in itself to blacks who are affirmatively proud of their racial heritage and do not see it as something to be done "without"—they may mask sheer unconsciousness of the participation of racist social factors in comprising what "a person" means. Race as much as sex comprises part of what a person is "as a person." Physical closeness and daily contact seem to lend the appearance of individuation to relationships, a factor that obscures the group character of social identity and reinforces oppressive institutions at the very moment when it most appears that they are being transcended. It may be that at the very moment treatment appears most individualized one has most *become* the person one is socially determined to be. The social factors that shape that personhood are, at that moment, the most deeply hidden, hence the most determinative.

To view work relations between women and men this way focuses attention on the operation of socially defined sex roles even in the closest personal relations, relations in which people are accustomed to thinking of themselves as most "themselves," hence most free. For women, as these cases suggest, the reverse often seems to be the case: The measure of the closeness is often the measure of the oppression and the greatest denial of self. The ideological and legal function of considering these matters "personal," as opposed to "sex-based," "reasonable," or "employment-related," is to isolate, individuate, invalidate, and stigmatize women's experience in order to maintain sexual oppression on the job beyond the reach of the law. Once the "personal" is seen to conform to a hierarchical social pattern, it is no more unique to, and without meaning beyond, each individual than are race relations. The "personal" life here protected, and the "natural" law vindicated, is nothing other than men's traditional prerogative of keeping sexual incursions on women beyond scrutiny or change. These most "private" of relations, instead of providing a sphere for particularity and uniqueness, appear in this perspective distressingly stereotypical, as each man and woman, in their own particular way, reproduce in these most personal interactions the structure of dominance and submission that characterizes the entire socioeconomic system.

Natural/Biological

With a tone of "you can't change *that*," the cases rejecting sexual harassment claims repeatedly excuse the incidents as "biological" or "natural." In the

Miller case, Judge Williams, denying relief, stated with astonishing equanimity and/or candor: "The attraction of males to females and females to males is a natural sex phenomenon and it is probable that this attraction plays at least a subtle part in most personnel decisions." One wonders what this factor has to do with merit and whether subtle racial revulsion is equally permissible. The brief for Bausch & Lomb was similarly explicit in its appeal to nature to exonerate the perpetrator: "Obviously, certain biological differences exist between male and female. . . . [I]t would appear that in the foreseeable future that the attraction of males to females and females to males will not soon disappear." The *Tomkins* district court also referred to "this natural sex attraction," stating, in a breathtaking but indecisive midsentence reversal, "while sexual desire animated the parties, or at least one of them. . . ."

On the level of superficial contradiction, these statements at least concede that the sexual advances derive from a basis generic to women and men, as opposed to being purely specific (or "personal") to the individuals involved, as was simultaneously asserted. The only question then is whether this generic basis is accurately termed biological or whether sexual harassment is more open to criticism as a social phenomenon. In the biological view, sexual expression seems presumed to derive from a biological need or genital drive or to be deeply rooted in a natural order that connects biological differences with expressions of mutual attraction. The idea is that biology cannot be questioned or changed, and is legitimate, while society can be, and may be "artificial." Perhaps this presumption underlies the clear doctrinal necessity, if sexual harassment is to be considered sex discrimination under existing conceptions, to establish sexual harassment as less a question of "sexuality" than of gender status: an implicit legal presupposition that sexuality is buried in nature, while gender status is at least in part a social construct. In the above quotations, in an attempt to justify legal nonintervention, sexual harassment is implicitly argued to be an inevitable and integral part of the naturally given, not socially contingent or potentially changeable, sexual relations between women and men.

On closer scrutiny, these presumptions about sex have little to do with the occurrence of sexual harassment. Women posses a physical sex drive equal to or greater than that of men, yet do not systematically harass men sexually. Some men, who have nothing wring with them sexually, seem able to control their behavior. Not all women experience sexual attraction to all men, nor all men to all women. These factors suggest that something beyond pure biology is implicated. Usually, the last thing wanted in these incidents is species reproduction, which removes any connection with a natural drive in that direction. Moreover, not everything deemed natural by defining all sexual behavior as biological is thereby made socially acceptable. If economically coerced intercourse is biological, rape must be also, but it is not legally allowed for that reason.

The image of codetermination in sexual matters by men and women is scrupulously maintained in these cases. But for the unwilling woman, no "attraction" is involved, and little power. Even if the "attractiveness of the sexes for one another" were inevitable, that would not make its expression indiscriminate. Calling sex "natural" means here, in effect, that women are to be allowed no choice of with whom and under what conditions to have sexual relations. In these cases, we are dealing with a male who is allegedly exercising his power as an employer, his power over a woman's material survival, and his sexual prerogatives as a man, to subject a woman sexually. One would have to argue that sexual power is by nature asymmetrical, and hence that it is biological for males to threaten, force, blackmail, coerce, subject, exploit, and oppress women sexually, to conclude that sexual harassment is natural.

More likely, it is only under conditions of women's social inequality (conditions which Congress responded to by the passage of Title VII and other legislation) that sexual harassment is presented as a social inevitability mystified as a natural one. In this view, it is only under conditions in which men systematically hold superior positions to women and are not only willing but able to abuse their position with impunity, and in which women have so few practical alternatives, that so natural an occurrence persists. This is not to deny the existence of social and biological differences, but to question whether the economic subordination of women by sexual means is an inevitable consequence of those differences. Arguably, we are here confronting an inequality in social power rationalized as a biological difference, specifically with a society that rigidly defines role opportunities in terms of sex, and then sanctifies those roles by attributing to them a basis in nature. This is as true for the fact that women are inferiors on the job as it is for the sexual relations that male superiors coercively initiate.

9

✛

The Lecherous Professor

Billie Dziech and Linda Weiner

Popular fiction . . . perpetuates the lecherous stereotypes. Jacob Horner, John Barth's protagonist in *The End of the Road,* described his opening day of classes:

> Indeed! One hundred spelling words dictated rapidly enough to keep their heads down, and I, perched high on my desk, could diagnose to my heart's content every bump of femininity in the room (praised be American grade schools, where little girls learn to sit up front!). Then, perhaps, having ogled my fill, I could get on with the business of the course. For as a man must grow used to the furniture before he can settle down to read in his room, this plenitude of girlish appurtenances had first to be assimilated before anyone could concentrate attention on the sober prescriptions of English grammar.
>
> Four times I repeated the ritual pronouncements—at eight and nine in the morning and at two and three in the afternoon. Between the two sessions I

Billie Dziech and Linda Weiner's account of the scope and gravity of the problem of sexual harassment on university campuses nearly created a scandal. Their work is particularly noteworthy for powerfully detailed descriptions of sexual predation and the impact on the lives and futures of students. From *The Lecherous Professor* by Billie Dziech and Linda Weiner. Copyright © by Billie Dziech and Linda Weiner. Reprinted with permission of Beacon Press, 1990.

146

lounged in my office with a magnificent erection, wallowing in my position, and watched with proprietary eye the parade of young things passing my door. I had nothing at all to do but spin indolent daydreams of absolute authority—Neurotic, Caligular authority of the sort that summons up officefuls of undergraduate girls, hot and submissive—leering professorial dreams!

Horner's adventures may sell books, but they miss the point about everyday life in higher education. The truth is that most faculty probably lack the time and energy required for "leering professorial dreams." Literary characters can afford the luxury of "magnificent erection(s)," whereas real-life college professors spend their working hours juggling time between classes, meetings, research, writing, and professional conferences. Those who fit the Jacob Horner stereotype are the exception, not the rule, but lecherous professors repeat their offenses on multiple victims and do so much damage that they claim more attention than professors who simply do their jobs.

A crucial concern for both students and academicians is learning to recognize the characteristics that differentiate the lecherous professor from his colleagues. There are no infallible predictors for recognizing sexual harassment. The most pernicious behavior can occur exclusive of "giveaways," or isolated actions can be misinterpreted as sinister when they are simply examples of clumsy professional or social style. However, a tentative list of warning signs might include the following:

- *Staring, leering, ogling* These behaviors may be surreptitious or very obvious. In any case, college faculty should possess knowledge of social decorum, and must avoid such activities.
- *Frequently commenting on personal appearance of the student* In the academic setting, most professors refrain from discussing the apparel and physical traits of their students.
- *Touching out of context* Every physical gesture should be appropriate to the occasion, setting, and need and character of the individual student. Professional educators may legitimately be expected to possess the ability to make such determinations.
- *Excessive flattery and praise of the student* This behavior, exhibited with others present, is especially seductive to students with low self-esteem or high aspirations. By convincing a student that she is intellectually and/or physically exceptional, the lecherous professor gains psychological access to her.
- *Deliberately avoiding or seeking encounters with the student in front of colleagues* Depending on the type of harasser, he may either attempt to hide from or to perform for colleagues in interactions with the student. The key is that in either case his behavior with the student changes when he is being observed.

- *Injecting a "male versus female" tone into discussions with students or colleagues* A frequent behavior of verbal harassers, this conduct signals a generally disparaging attitude toward women. Its initial effect is to make them feel outsiders in the academic environment, but it may also be an indicator of other potential forms of abuse.
- *Persistently emphasizing sexuality in all contexts* Pervasive, inordinate emphasis on sex can occur in class or outside. For the lecherous professor, sexuality becomes, in effect, the prism through which all topics are focused. Students, male and female, can usually detect this behavior readily, and such professors often acquire a reputation for "being fixated on sex" in papers, tests, and discussions.

Such behaviors can serve as signals to the student. Another key to understanding the lecherous professor is assessing the setting or context in which he works. There are both public and private harassers, and they act in very different fashions. The public harasser engages in observable, flagrant posturing toward women. He is the most likely to intimidate or seek control through sexist remarks and advances that may be offensive but are essentially free from sanctions. Students sometimes refer to him as "hands," "touch-feely," or "mouth." Colleagues describe him as "patronizing," "always performing," "convinced of his own cuteness." He frequently costumes himself by extreme dressing up or down and seldom employs standard academic vocabulary—except to punctuate a witticism. He is articulate, glib, sarcastic and/or funny. His general image is that of a casual "good guy" or an imposing man of the world.

The public harasser appears always available, always approachable. He spends enormous amounts of time with students—in his office, in the halls during breaks, in the student union or at a nearby bar when the day or week ends. His informality is a welcome contrast to the authoritarian style of most of his colleagues. The more perceptive of them detect but hesitate to question his intentions. This was the position of a male philosophy professor:

> I'm really not particularly comfortable with _____'s style. Perhaps because it's so different from mine and so unlike what we were taught to emulate in graduate school. I do feel a sense of unease when I see him several times a week huddled with a group of young women over coffee in the Union. I have other colleagues who are just as concerned about students and spend equal amounts of time with them, but they don't seem to need to flaunt those relationships before others.

The high profile of the public harasser is his defense. It deters observers or victims from protesting when he touches too often or cracks one joke too many. Even male students hesitate to criticize public harassers. A sophomore at a college in Michigan explained:

Sure, I was afraid to say anything to anyone about Mr. _____. They all laughed every time he made some stupid remark. You would have thought he was a burlesque comedian or something. What I really couldn't get, what really floored me was why the girls laughed at him too. He was supposed to be teaching psychology, and there he was making these gross remarks that should have embarrassed them half to death (they sure as hell embarrassed me) and they just kept on laughing all year.

When an individual's remarks to and about women or his physical contact with them appears open, he can easily contend, "I have nothing to hide. There's nothing malevolent in my intentions. Everything I say or do is right out there for everyone to see." The difficulty is that an institution's ability to restrain a public harasser depends on the level of awareness of those within the environment. Some "see" malevolent intentions and others do not, but the harasser's reputation as communicative, friendly, and open provides a sure defense. Thus he is free to perform and be observed but not challenged or chastised for his behavior.

The style and intent of the private harasser are directly opposite. He may be the more genuinely "lecherous" of the two, for he uses his authority to gain private access to the student. Unlike his counterpart, he deliberately avoids notoriety. He not only seeks but depends on privacy because he requires a domain in which there are no witnesses to his behavior. He is the harasser of greatest interest to the public and the media, the one who demands sexual favors of students, the one most readily cast in the image of despoiler of innocence and molester of youth.

His personal and professional styles lend credence to the epithets. The private harasser often adheres to academic stereotypes. He usually dresses conservatively. His language and demeanor are generally formal, perhaps even intimidating, to the student. Because he appears so circumspect, he is the last to be suspected by colleagues. The Levi-clad professor who sits casually before the class seems more culpable than the imposing man with the resonant voice who stands behind the lectern.

The lectern symbolizes the private harasser's teaching style. Characteristically removed and aloof, he lectures while the class listens. Just as the public harasser uses his openness to move the student to compliance, the private offender employs authority to lure her into acquiescence. The ability to control the setting gives him special access to the women under his power. He can seduce them into his private domain with a simple oral or written directive. "Please see me" or "I would like a conference with you" are familiar demands.

But, few are prepared for the deception that occurs when the professor closes the office door and sheds the professorial for the male role. Whether he begins with overt sexual advances or the more subtle verbal approach ("My wife doesn't love me anymore," "Young women like you are so lovely"), his sudden role change causes the student surprise and confusion. Her role submissiveness, female self-doubt, and shock combine with the privacy of the interaction to provide a cover for the harasser. When there are no witnesses and the student experiences extreme disorientation, there are seldom sexual harassment grievances.

Another way of understanding sexual harassers is to describe the roles they most commonly assume:

- *The Counselor-Helper* This type of professor uses the guise of nurturer and caretaker to gain access to the student. If she feels lonely and anonymous on campus, she may be flattered or consoled by his interest. He invites her confidence and uses information about her private life to discover her vulnerabilities, commitments, and attitudes about men and sex. Then he can tailor his "line" to her specific need. One professor, after encouraging a student's anguished account of rejection by a boyfriend, replied earnestly, "I'd never treat you like that." To her, it was a terribly moving assertion. To the witness to the incident, it was far less compelling because she had observed the professor making the statement to at least three other female students from whom he later sought sexual favors.

    The counselor-helper may act as a go-between in male-female relationships of students. This behavior, described by one ombudsman as "pimping," encourages the student to see the professor as a broker or gatekeeper in her relationship with a significant male. The professor's intent can be to derive vicarious sexual pleasure from thus involving himself or to use the male as a foil to increase his own stature in the eyes of the female. One administrator describes this as "seduction with an agent." An accomplished harasser in one university was fond of acting as go-between and then reporting to the female that he had advised her boyfriend, "She's a real woman. Are you prepared to satisfy her?" The motive was to win the seduction when the student became attracted to the professor's image of her as experienced and voluptuous.

- *The Confidante* This individual approaches the student not as a superior who can help her but as an equal and friend. Sharing is an essential element in their interaction. He may invite her confidences, but he also offers his own. In an attempt to impress or win sympathy from the student, he may relate or invent stories about his private and professional life. Placed in this role, the student often feels that he values and trusts her, so she becomes an involuntary confidante. Without genuine mutual agreement, the relationship is moved into an intimate domain from which she may find it difficult to extricate herself.

    Another method a harasser may employ is creating indebtedness through gestures of friendship. Offers from a professor to lend the student books, money, notes, a place to study or providing her with free tickets or rides may signal an attempt to make her feel obligated.

- *The Intellectual Seducer* Called "mind fucking" or "intellectual intercourse" by some, this kind of seduction results from the professor's ability to impress students with his skill and knowledge. He may use class content to gain access to personal information about the student. Self-disclosure on the part of the student is often invited in disciplines like psychology, sociology, philosophy, and literature where personal values, beliefs, and experiences are easily related to course content. At one college, students told of being required to write about their sex fantasies. Such information may be used to identify areas of vulnerability and/or accessibility in the student. A psychology professor bragged to a colleague about requiring students to take personality inventories. He told them they demonstrated uses of the test, but his real motivation was to gain personal information about respondents in whom he was interested.

  A professor's avocations may also be engaging or dangerous. A common example is the faculty member who uses his knowledge of books or movies to move the student into discussions of erotic topics. Another is that of the professor who hypnotizes students outside the classroom. While some use hypnosis appropriately, it can be dangerous when done by a sexual harasser. Finally, there is the case of the art professor who employs female students as nude models for private studio work.

- *The Opportunist* This person takes advantage of the physical setting and unusual or occasional circumstances to obscure his inappropriate behavior and to gain intimacy with students. He may rely on equipment or subject matter to gain physical access to the student. A serious problem in clinical, laboratory, counseling, performance, and vocational-technical setting, this behavior is often described by students as stealing "cheap feels." The lecherous professor discovers ways to touch the student by using proximity to equipment as an excuse or by employing parts of her body in class demonstrations. One student complained that her woodwind professor persisted in touching her breasts while telling her he was illustrating the movements of her diaphragm; another that her nursing instructor "felt [her] up" while using her body to demonstrate physical disabilities in patients. . . .

[A common question] in sexual harassment workshops is, "How can I talk to a professor without judging the truth or falsity of a student's complaint?" Following are some possible approaches:

- The administrator can and should, in a positive tone, alert the faculty member to any complaint made against him. A dean or department head can make a nonjudgmental observation: "I want you to know that there has been a complaint about your behavior toward women students, a perception of inappropriate comments or action. You might want to think about how that perception can be avoided." There is no blaming, no assertion of guilt in such a statement. No action is threatened or taken; the faculty member is simply alerted and can respond or not. Intrusions and threats are distinguishable from positive interventions and expressions of professional concern. The administrator needs to have confidence that his or her faculty can tell the difference.

- If a student's complaint is very serious or is part of a history of such charges, the approach must be more direct. The faculty member should be informed about disciplinary actions that may be taken. The illegality and inappropriateness of such behavior should be clearly mentioned. The conversation can be deliberate without being determinant: "Have you considered the professional consequences if this student files a formal grievance? Are you aware that it could result in . . . ?"

- The dean or department head should rely on his or her own professionalism. Other judgments of a faculty member need not be "tainted" if a sexual harassment complaint is addressed. The minds of deans and department heads are filled with all sorts of impressions—a drunken scene at a faculty party, a pass at the dean's wife, financial problems, medical difficulties, late grades, a student grievance over a grade. Administrators know the difference between their personal reactions or suspicions and what they should include in their official judgments of professional competence. Sexual harassment charges are no different. They can be treated with the same objectivity, discretion, and judiciousness that characterize other administrative perceptions.

- Attention should be given to the possibility that members of racial, religious, or national minorities tend to be suspect in organizations. While nothing excuses harassing behavior, it is worthwhile to remember that some individuals are move vulnerable to scrutiny than others.

- The administrator should recognize that both the student and the faculty member deserve support, professional treatment, objective assessment of the problem, and decisive judgment. Administrators who accept responsibility for the actions of their faculty and the well-being of their students do not wait for gossip to erupt into formal grievances and adverse publicity. That is not what leadership, impartiality, or professional propriety are about. What they *do* imply is that those in authority must be willing to act and lead.

CONCLUSION

The resolution of sexual harassment will come when it is made the concern and responsibility of everyone who is associated with the institution. If the climate on campus is to change, the men and women who work there must lead the way.

In *The Leaning Ivory Tower,* Warren Bennis' observations about higher education are correct:

> Our inability to transcend the dangerous notion that we don't wash our dirty linen in public verges on the schizophrenic. It implies not only that dissent is bad but that our public institutions are made up not of men but of saints, who never engage in vulgar and offensive activities. . . . In fact, organizations are vulgar, sweaty, plebeian; if they are to be viable, they must create an institutional environment where a fool can be called a fool and all actions and motivations are duly and closely scrutinized for the inevitable human flaws and failures. In a democracy, meanness, dullness, and corruption are always amply represented. They are not entitled to protection from the same rude challenges that such qualities must face in the "real" world. When banal politeness is assigned a higher value than accountability or truthfulness, the result is an Orwellian world where the symbols of speech are manipulated to create false realities.

"Banal politeness" and "false realities" cannot disguise the truth about most administrators and faculty members. At base, they are adept "people-watchers," a highly self-conscious lot, politically and professionally sensitive to others. This explains the unwritten codes governing their behaviors. There is, for example, no formal supervision in the typical college classroom. Yet the faculty member who intends to keep his job meets classes regularly, evaluates students objectively, prepares class presentations, refrains from denigrating colleagues, avoids appearing bigoted or racist. It is time to add to that list "refrains from sexist behaviors."

Higher education needs what Margaret Mead termed "new taboos" in her 1978 article "A Proposal: We Need Taboos on Sex at Work":

> What should we—what can we—do about sexual harassment on the job? . . . As I see it, it isn't more laws that we need now, but new taboos. . . .
>
> When we examine how any society works, it becomes clear that it is precisely the basic taboos—the deeply and intensely felt prohibitions against "unthinkable" behavior—that keep the social system in balance. . . .
>
> The complaints, the legal remedies and the support institutions developed by women are all part of the response to the new conception of women's rights.

But I believe we need something much more pervasive, a climate of opinion that includes men as well as women, and that will affect not only adult relations and behavior on the job but also the expectations about the adult world that guide our children's progress into that world.

What we need, in fact, are new taboos, that are appropriate to the new society we are struggling to create—taboos that will operate within the work setting as once they operated within the household. Neither men nor women should expect that sex can be used either to victimize women who need to keep their jobs or to keep women from advancement or to help men advance their own careers. A taboo enjoins.

Taboos enjoin. They make demands. They establish that some forms of behavior are "unthinkable." Creating a taboo on the campus means that male professors must establish new male norms. Male faculty will have to let each other know that the campus is not a locker room, that sexual harassment does not prove virility, that abusing professional authority to exact sexual favors makes a man not more but less masculine. Women faculty who have accepted or ignored harassment of their students must cease being passive and accommodating in their male-dominated campus world.

College professors must be willing to say directly to sexual harassers what they already say behind their backs. If there is such a thing as collegiality, faculty should feel free, even obligated, to deal personally with the issue. The notion that academic protocol prohibits someone from warning another of threats to his reputation is distorted. A colleague feels concern for a co-worker, or he does not. If he suspects that the individual is unjustly accused, then he must alert him for his own protection. A teacher either feels concern for students and the reputation of the institution, or not. If there is the suspicion that a charge against a colleague is accurate, the responsibility is to inform the colleague so that he may alter his behavior.

Because so many academicians—both male and female—have allowed harassment to become a private rather than a professional consideration, they have been inarticulate and naive in their discussions. Sexual harassment has been a titillating closet issue because professionals have confused their personal conflicts about male-female relationships with an institutional concern. When academics learn to recognize sexual harassment as abusive behavior—an aberrant manifestation of a need for power, prestige, recognition, or acceptance—they can discuss it rationally, as they would any other problem in their institutions.

The taboo has implications for students as well. Like faculty, they do not like to assume personal responsibility for the campus environment. But the people most affected by the problem must take the lead in remedying it. If students were to take a more aggressive stand, sexual harassers would be far less likely to act and to go unpunished. Women who have experienced harassment and yet allow a handful of peers to complain for an entire group take the easy way out. Student newspapers that do in-depth reporting on campus athletics and editorializing on federal economic programs shirk their responsibilities if they ignore sexual harassment on their own campuses. The roles that individual students and their organizations can and should assume are at present controversial. But one point is clear—when they have involved themselves, students have made a difference. For groups without power, there is always safety and visibility in numbers.

The unique characteristic of higher education, which sets it apart from and, to many, above other institutions in society is its ability to analyze and understand complexity. The pursuit of knowledge—whether in scientific, social, technological, or humanistic realms—is undertaken with exquisite concern for detail, innuendo, subtlety, and implication. Sophisticated inquiry is what higher education does better than any other institution, not because of its ivory-tower purity but because of the intrinsic pride academics have in acquiring understanding and communicating it to others.

But forced to deal with sexual harassment, higher education has behaved as if it is incapable of sophisticated inquiry and must rely instead on second-grade approaches to determine what is knowable and believable. Confronted with cases of harassment, the same minds that move gracefully through dazzling theoretical issues revert to an eighteenth-century dunking-stool standard of truth. This lapse cannot be explained as inability to apply complex rationality to the housekeeping issues of higher education. The explanation, instead, is that cultural patterns of society hold firmer sway than intellectual method, that sexism and stereotyping overcome sophisticated rationality.

It is possible to apply academe's own rigorous standards of inquiry to understanding sexual harassment. The very act of analyzing the problem should lead naturally to an intellectual and psychological breakthrough for institutions, administrators, faculty, and students. To learn is not to wallow in self-recrimination over past failures and negligence. Genuine education means change; it involves understanding the past in order to design a better future.

In the late 1960s the image of the campus as a sanctuary where fresh-faced youngsters strolled tree-lined paths between the chapel and library vanished forever. With the dissolution of the myth went the fiction of the benign, fatherly professor. Neither was a great loss. Fantasies about real places and real people are never as compelling as the truth. The truth about higher education is that it is struggling to discover as well as to preserve an identity in a world that it did not anticipate and for which it is, in many ways, ill prepared.

The campus is not inhabited by omniscient deities; it never was. Its people are no more or less flawed than the rest of us.

The campus is a mirror held up to our society, and in it all are reflected. If it succeeds in curing itself of sexual harassment, higher education will prove that human beings and the institutions they create, while far from perfect, are nevertheless capable of coping with their limitations. If it should fail, no amount of rationalization will restore its lost myth or compensate for its harsh reality.

10

+

Sexual Harassment: Offers and Coercion

Nancy Tuana

Sexual harassment has as its central meaning the coercion of sexual activ-ity. Charges of sexual harassment are most generally raised when an em-ployee or student feels that his or her employer, supervisor, or instructor has used his or her institutional authority over them to coerce sexual favors from them. However, current analysis of coercion reject the possibility of offers being coercive. Such analysis thus call into question the status of attempts to procure sexual favors by offers of rewards. Are we to classify such actions as cases of sexual harassment?

Nancy Tuana argues that offers can be coercive if they make the student's situation worse than it otherwise would have been without the offer. She counters the suggestion that attractive of-fers—for example, of fellowships in exchange for sex—are advantages rather than problematic forms of harassment. From "Sexual Harassment in Academe: Issues of Power and Coercion," by Nancy Tuana, *College Teaching* 33:53–63 (1983). Copyright © 1983 by Nancy Tuana. Reprinted with permission of the author.

THE CASE AGAINST COERCIVE OFFERS

The main attack on the possibility of coercive offers was developed by Michael Bayles who argued that only actions that involve threats can be viewed as coercive. By claiming that offers do not involve threats, he was able to conclude that offers cannot be coercive. His attempt to illustrate this position is directly applicable to the issue of sexual harassment. In his rejection of Virginia Held's position that inducements can be coercive, Bayles offers the following example to illustrate his position:

> Assume there is a mediocre woman graduate student who would not receive an assistantship. Suppose the department chairman offers her one if she goes to bed with him, and she does so. In what sense has the graduate student acted against her will? She apparently preferred having an assistantship and sleeping with the chairman to not sleeping with him and not having an assistantship. So it would appear that she did what she wanted in the situation. Held may mean that the woman acted against her will in that she would rather have had the assistantship and not slept with the chairman; that is, there was a consequence of her choice which she found undesirable. But the fact that a choice has an undesirable consequence does not make it against one's will. One may prefer to have clean teeth without having to brush them; nonetheless, one is not acting against one's will when one brushes them.

From this analysis, Bayles would have us conclude that offers to students by instructors (or by extrapolation, to employees by employers) do not involve sexual harassment if sexual harassment is viewed as involving coercion. In fact, Bayles would have us believe that in such situations, students and employees experience no impairment of their freedom of choice.

Such an analysis of offers or rewards in return for sexual favors does not fit well with the experiences of students and employees who have been in such situations. A classification of the results of a 1978 study of sexual harassment at the University of California at Berkeley, in which students who felt that they had been harassed were asked to describe that harassment, includes sexual bribery as one of the self-reported types of sexual harassment. A number of students, in reporting the events they perceived to constitute harassment, described grade offers in exchange for affairs. A survey conducted at the University of California at Santa Barbara in 1981, which consisted of student reactions to a series of vignettes, revealed that the inclusion, within such a vignette, of the instructor indicating that sexual cooperation would improve the student's grade dramatically, increased the sexual harassment rating of that vignette. In fact, the survey revealed that the addition of sexual bribery to a vignette increased the sexual harassment rating of a vignette more that did the addition of a warning by the instructor that the student's success in the class could be affected if he or she did not consent to sexual activity with the instructor.

Thus we see a clear tension between philosophical analyse that reject the possibility of coercive offers and the experiences of students and employees. In order to reconcile the tension between these two positions, it would be helpful to look at the standard analysis of coercion.

THE STANDARD ANALYSIS OF COERCION

According to the accepted analysis of coercion, there are six criteria that must be satisfied to classify an action as coercive. The analysis of a person, X, having coerced another person, Y, to do an action, A, would be the following:

1. X intends that Y do A
2. X further intends to harm Y if Y does not do A
3. X threatens Y with harm if Y does not do A
4. Y does A
5. Y would have done otherwise had Y so chosen
6. Y would have chosen otherwise had Y not been threatened by X.

Given this analysis of coercion, it becomes clear why one might reject the possibility of offers being coercive. If we examine the illustration given above, we can see that Bayles is claiming that the offer merely makes the action of sex with the chair more desirable or less undesirable to the student than it had been prior to the offer, or makes available a choice not previously available to the student. Such an offer then, according to this analysis, presents no harm to the recipient. It would seem to follow from this that if in order for there to be coercion, there must be a person (or group of people) who threatens to harm the coerced individual and intends to so harm her or him, then it would appear that offers could not be coercive. In order for an action to be threatening, that act must make a victim's choice situation less desirable or more undesirable, and this is done either by adding some undesirable consequence to, or removing a desirable consequence from, one of the victim's alternative choices, which will result in harm to him or her if he or she refuses to act as is desired. Bayles claims that the offer made by the chair made the student's choice situation more desirable by providing her the option of an assistantship that would not otherwise have been available. If sexual harassment is defined as involving coercion, one could use the analysis above to deny that solicitation of sexual favors by promise of rewards falls under the category of sexual harassment.

It is my contention that the attempt to procure sexual contact through the promise of rewards can be and often is coercive when the person who makes the offer is in a position of authority over the person to whom he or she makes the offer. I believe that the above illustration could be classified as coercive even though there is no threat to harm the student and the chair has no intention of harming the student should she refuse. I will therefore show that the standard analysis of coercion is not complete, for it omits a very important and common type of coercion.

OFFERS AND COERCION

Let us look again at the above illustration of solicitation of sexual favors. Bayles spends no time considering the context in which the offer was made nor does he consider the beliefs or reactions of the student to whom the offer was made. I will show that this is a significant omission that, when rectified, will demonstrate the possibility of coercive offers.

In this case the person who has made the offer is the chairperson of the department. The chairperson of this department has a variety of powers, including the ability to offer or refuse assistantships. Given typical department politics it would be fair to assume that the chairperson also has the power to make other very important decisions that could affect the career of this graduate student, such as assigning the members of her dissertation committee, deciding on the jobs for which she will receive a departmental recommendation, and the like. In other words, the chair has the power to make it very difficult for this student to receive her degree and to succeed in her career. We have to add to this the fact that this graduate student is "mediocre." What this means is that if the chairperson wishes to, he would have a less difficult time getting this student dropped out of the program than he would if she had been a star student. Given her record, there are probably no instructors who are willing to support her case should she complain, for it would be difficult to make a case for her given her less than excellent record. Also, as all of us who have been a part of academia know, the decisions of retention or expulsion in borderline cases are difficult and anything but objective. It would be very easy for the chairperson of a department to recommend against retention when the student's record is reviewed, using her mediocre performance as the sole reason for this recommendation, and probably not raise anyone's suspicions in so doing. Had the student an excellent record it would be more difficult for the chairperson to recommend against retention without casting suspicion on his motives. But given her mediocre record, should she protest such an action or claim that it was the result of her refusal to grant sexual favors, most people would tend to discredit her complaint as "sour grapes." Now let us assume that the student believes all of this.

In addition to the above beliefs about the power of the chairperson of one's department, given that the chairperson has offered this student a position better than she deserves in return for sexual favors, she now knows that the chairperson of her department feels neither morally nor legally obliged to promote fairly. The very fact that the chairperson was willing to give her a position for which she did not qualify is good reason to believe that he might be the type of person who would be willing to abuse a student who displeases him. So the student now knows that the chairperson is the type of person who is willing to misuse his power to obtain what he wants, and thus has good reason to believe that this misuse of power might extend to penalizing a student who gets in the way of his wants.

An additional aspect of this situation that must be taken into consideration is the nature of the action being requested by the chair and the social attitudes surrounding such an action. We live in a culture in which people are often very sensitive about another person's response to their request for sexual contact. People generally have very fragile egos concerning rejections of sexual advances. A very common response to a refusal of a sexual proposition is to feel hurt and upset. Furthermore, many people who experience such hurt then develop the desire to retaliate. The graduate student will be well aware of this and will probably start thinking about all the instances she has heard of in which instructors retaliated against students who refused their sexual advances by misusing their authority to hurt the student.

So the graduate student accepts the chairperson's offer. Notice that Bayles' explanation is that she did so because "she apparently preferred having an assistantship and sleeping with the chairman to not sleeping with him and not having an assistantship." If that was all there was to the situation (the student was quite willing to have sex with the chairperson in oder to acquire the assistantship), then I would be willing to say that there was no coercion and that the situation involved no sexual harassment, though I would want to fault the chairperson for immoral and unprofessional conduct. But it is not acceptable to assume that this explanation will fit all cases. I would like to suggest another plausible scenario, which happens quite frequently, which does involve coercion and should be classified as sexual harassment.

Given the context of the situation as I have spelled it out in the above paragraphs, the student finds herself in a situation where she is very vulnerable to being harmed by the chairperson, well knowing that there is a very good chance that if she rejects his proposition, he will be upset enough to want to hurt her in turn. The student has no desire to have any sexual contact with the chairperson, and she does not think that getting the assistantship is a good reason for having the sexual contact. However, being aware of the power of the chairperson and the vulnerability of her position in the department, she fears that a refusal of the offer will upset and anger the chairperson, making him want to retaliate. Furthermore, she believes that such retaliation could result in her being failed out of the program, thus ending her hopes of an academic career. Because of her fear of such harm, the student accepts the offer.

If we were to analyze this case based on the above model, where X is the chair, Y the student, and A the act of sexual involvement, the result would be the following:

1. X intends that Y do A
2. Y does A
3. Y would have done otherwise had Y so chosen
4. Y would have done otherwise had he or she not feared that Y would harm him or her if he or she did not do A.

It is important to notice that this analysis is significantly different from the standard analysis of coercion. There is no initial intention to harm on the chairperson's part, nor does the student think that the chair has the intention to harm her when the chair makes the offer. Also there is no threat made by the chairperson, nor does the student think that the chairperson has threatened her. One cannot thus object that the case that I am describing is a case of a mixed offer and threat where the student is offered an inducement for submitting to the sexual involvement, and threatened with a harm if she refuses. I have no doubt that such situations do occur, but such an analysis does not fit the above situation in that it is not the case, nor does the student believe that it is the case, that the chair has the *intention* to threaten the student with harm, or to harm the student should she refuse *when the offer is made*.

Despite the absence of a threat or any intention to harm on the part of the chair, what makes this action coercive and thus a case of sexual harassment is that the student's choice situation is made less desirable or more undesirable because of her fear of harm if she refuses to act as is desired. What is significantly different about this case, and what the standard analysis of coercion misses completely, is that a person can reasonably believe that her refusal of an offer, like the one above, would result in a situation in which she would be harmed. As I am describing it, the above situation is one in which the student believes that there is a very high probability that her rejection of the offer will *cause* the chairman to have the desire to harm her. So the situation is one in which the threat of harm that the student fears is not made prior to or at the time of the offer, but will *come into existence* as a result of her refusal. One thing that is overlooked on the standard analysis of coercion is a person's reaction to having his or her offer rejected. Some offers are so loaded that a refusal may cause a desire to retaliate. In the words of a lawyer who was a junior member of a law firm, regarding the sexual proposition of one of the senior members of that firm:

> . . . I also recognized I was in a compromising and extremely dangerous position. I definitely didn't want to have an affair with Mr. Scott . . . however, Mr. Scott's ego was on the line. Terribly frightened of offending him and possibly

ruining my chances for success in the firm, I knew I was treading on thin ice . . . Mr. Scott had a reputation for extreme ruthlessness when crossed.

What my depiction of the "offer" scenario illustrates is that in certain situations, a student's situation after an offer can be worse than it was before the offer. Accounts that consider offers noncoercive deny that even unwelcome offers are coercive, ". . . for one would not have done or chosen otherwise had they not been made. Nor are they turned into threats, for they do not make any of the alternative choices less desirable or more undesirable." I have, on the contrary, shown that this need not be the case. In the present situation, if the student consents to a sexual involvement in order to avoid the harm in which she thinks a refusal will result, *then the offer does modify her choice.* The offer also makes alternative choices less desirable, for the student reasonably believes that the choice of rejecting the offer will result in harm that she would not have experienced had the offer never been made. Hence, I conclude that the above described situation is an offer situation involving coercion, and is the type of situation that we would want to classify as sexual harassment.

What I have shown is that the standard analysis of coercion is inadequate in that it omits sufficient reference to the context, the situation in which the action is performed. Once this omission is remedied, it can be shown that offers can be coercive whenever the background context is such that it is reasonable for the victim to believe that her refusal to accept the offer will result in harm.

11

Sexual Harassment as Sex Discrimination: A Defective Paradigm

Ellen Frankel Paul

ANOMALIES

Sexual Harassment as Sex Discrimination

One should not place much credence on the absence of legislative intent. If sexual harassment logically belongs within the broader category of Title VII sex discrimination, then judges and commentators should be commended—not faulted—for making an astute connection. This inclusion, however, seems an uneasy one at best. The subsumption of sexual harassment under Title VII's ban on sex discrimination in employment, though now accepted by courts as self-evident, merits further consideration. The pioneers for a Title VII sexual harassment cause of action, Catharine A. MacKinnon principal among them, conceptualized sexual harassment as a wrong to

Ellen Frankel Paul argues that sexual harassment should not be viewed as a form of sex discrimination. She objects to what she sees as the essentialism of Catharine MacKinnon's view of women as victims, as well as to the understanding of sexual harassment as a social harm. Instead, she sees sexual harassment as a dignitary harm to an individual victim. She urges the development of a tort remedy for damages when the rights of an individual victim have been violated. From "Sexual Harassment as Sex Discrimination," by Ellen Frankel Paul, *Yale Law and Policy Review* 8: 333–65 (1990) Copyright © 1990 by *Yale Law and Policy Review* and Ellen Frankel Paul. Reprinted with permission of *Yale Law and Policy Review*.

women as members of an oppressed and legally protected group. This section will reexamine these arguments and question the assumptions behind the inclusion of sexual harassment under Title VII.

The early partisans used sexual harassment as a metaphor for the position of women in our male-dominated, capitalistic (i.e., exploitative) society, and thus tended to view virtually all women as victims. These partisans, often substantiating their claims with highly questionable statistical studies, regard sexual harassment, like rape, as a reification of male perfidy. While undeniably serving a useful and necessary function in raising people's consciousness about offensive behavior, these pioneers, as is the wont of pioneers in most things, overstated their case.

MacKinnon's argument for sexual harassment as a metaphor for capitalism is a case in point. For MacKinnon, sexual harassment is "in essence a group injury" that women suffer because they are women, regardless of their unique qualities, and that men perpetrate because they enjoy economic power over women. She writes:

> Sexual harassment perpetuates the interlocked structure by which women have been kept sexually in thrall to men and at the bottom of the labor market. Two forces of American society converge: men's control over women's sexuality and capital's control over employees' work lives. Women historically have been required to exchange sexual services for material survival, in one form or another. Prostitution and marriage as well as sexual harassment in different ways institutionalize this arrangement.

Stated more truculently, "Economic power is to sexual harassment as physical force is to rape."

According to MacKinnon, women's roles in society are defined largely by their sexuality. She therefore finds spurious the argument advanced in an early case that sexual harassment is a matter of sexuality rather than gender, and thus does not qualify as sex discrimination. "Sexual harassment," she argues, "makes of women's sexuality a badge of female servitude." She thus considers it ludicrous to contend that a woman fired for refusing to have sex with her supervisor is discharged for that refusal rather than for being a woman. If particular women, whom men find attractive, are especially likely to trigger sexual harassment, this does not defeat the argument that the harassment is essentially sex-based, and thus sex discrimination. In MacKinnon's analysis, attractiveness is a "sex-plus" criterion that merely serves to select some as victims and exempt others. Moreover, since women tend to be the victims of sexual harassment, only women and not men must choose between tolerating the harassment or suffering the consequences. MacKinnon concludes that sexual harassment is discrimination in employment—it has an impact both on employment decisions and on the general atmosphere of the workplace—and a "condition of work" within the meaning of Title VII.

MacKinnon's argument comes freighted with excess ideological baggage. Casting women in the guise of helpless victims, economically dependent on men and thus pawns to men's sexual desires, does little to bolster women's self-image or to inspire them to breach male bastions. It casts women in a deterministic nexus of economic powerlessness and physical weakness that, curiously, gives them no recourse but to throw themselves on the mercy of male judges enforcing legislation enacted by a male Congress. the argument seems vulnerable as well to a reductio ad absurdum in which males, as well as females, could be viewed as the victims of roles impressed on them by the same capitalist system that allegedly circumscribes women's choices: They are forced always to maintain an aura of invincibility and machismo; to shoulder responsibility for dependent women and children; to be enslaved to economic necessity for most of their adult lives; and to die early for their efforts.

"Victimology" serves no purpose other than the propagandistic. MacKinnon's argument, however, bereft of this ideological excrescence, does raise two points that merit scrutiny: Sexual harassment is essentially a group injury, and sexual harassment is sex discrimination within the scope of Title VII.

The "group injury" contention is questionable both on Title VII and theoretical grounds. Disparate treatment lawsuits under Title VII typically raise issues of discrimination in the policies of corporations or in the practices of key personnel that adversely affect particular plaintiffs simply because they fall within a protected group. Rather than being judged on individual merit in the hiring or promotion process, individuals are treated differently, and worse, than others simply because of their race, color, religion, sex, or national origin. The standard *McDonnell Douglas* evidentiary scheme assumes situations where the claimant is denied a job or job benefit due to the bare fact of the claimant's membership in a disadvantaged group. Employers attempting to defend their practices and to rebut a plaintiff's prima facie case of discrimination often will raise issues bearing on the uniqueness of the particular person. Employers may argue, for example, that their refusal to hire or to promote was the result not of a discriminatory animus against this person but of a legitimate business judgment that she was not the most qualified candidate.

Does sexual harassment conform to this disparate treatment paradigm? The typical quid pro quo sexual harassment plaintiff complains about behavior (i.e., practices) that a particular supervisor directs at her. The complaint is never about a general policy of the employer; indeed, what employer would be so foolish as to issue a policy encouraging its supervisors to extort sexual favors for job benefits? Thus, the typical quid pro quo incident needs to be compared to the typical disparate treatment/practices incident. In the former, a supervisor demands sexual favors in return for job benefits because of sexual desire, and he selects his target because he finds her sexually attractive. In the latter, the supervisor refuses to hire, to promote, or to reward a female employee as he would a comparable male, because he has an animus of some sort against women.

What is missing from the former and is present in the latter is an essential attribute of discrimination: that is, that any member of the scorned group will trigger the response of the person who practices discrimination. Nazis despised all Jews, not just those with certain attributes; South African apartheid is directed at all Blacks, not just those with certain features; Jim Crow laws were aimed at all Blacks. Discrimination, concededly, is difficult to define, but one of its essential attributes is that it fastens on all members of the group to be scorned (or devalued by a negative stereotype). Thus, something essentially different from discrimination in this classic sense seems to be occurring in quid pro quo sexual harassment. Attempting to overcome this difference, as MacKinnon tries, with the device of "sex-plus," does not eliminate the fact that the discriminator scorns or devalues all members of a group, while the sexual harasser targets only someone whom he finds attractive. While it is undoubtedly true that many practitioners of sexual harassment are recidivists, their targets are not just any female simply because she is female.

Hostile environment plaintiffs complain of offensive overtures, comments, or gestures of a sexual nature directed at them by supervisors or coworkers. While they sometimes allege that other women in the workplace also are abused, behavior that reaches the threshold of pervasiveness and seriousness for Title VII purposes is limited to discrete individuals. Admittedly, this becomes a bit murky in factories, for example, where only one or two women have breached a formerly male enclave; if they suffer harassment, then all women suffer harassment. These unique (or what philosophers call the "lifeboat") cases are not paradigmatic; typically, many women work together and only one or some may suffer flagrantly intolerable treatment.

As late as 1985, Judge Bork voiced a similar criticism of the sexual harassment paradigm. He favored the line of argument taken in the earliest sexual harassment cases: "Congress was not thinking of individual harassment at all but of discrimination in conditions of employment because of gender," when it enacted Title VII. He found it peculiar that the Court of Appeals for the District of Columbia had stated twice before that Title VII does not prohibit sexual harassment by a bisexual supervisor if he demanded sexual favors of both males and females. In Judge Bork's view, the classification of sexual advances as discrimination was awkward. While he considered harassment to be reprehensible, he noted that "Title VII was passed to outlaw discriminatory behavior and not simply behavior of which we strongly disapprove."

Indeed, the bisexual supervisor does raise a perplexing doctrinal anomaly. The identical offense is sex discrimination under Title VII when perpetrated by a man against a woman, by a man against a man, by a woman against a woman, or by a woman against a man; yet, if a bisexual of either sex preys equally upon men and women, he (or she) is beyond the reach of Title VII. The law is supposed to look to acts, whether criminal or tortious, to determine culpability and not to the individual characteristics of the perpetrators: that is precisely what is meant by the rule of law. Yet, if sexual harassment is sexual discrimination under Title VII, why are some perpetrators insulated? A savvy harasser need only note this anomaly and become an equal opportunity harasser.

Taking the point one step further, it also seems peculiar to call sexual harassment of a male by a male, or a female by a female, sex discrimination. In these scenarios a male (or a female) is selecting a member of his (or her) own sex (i.e., his or her own group on the group-injury model) for harassment. How can this be discrimination? Discrimination, as this article has defined it, is harming someone or denying someone a benefit because that person is a member of a group that the discriminator despises. What the harasser is really doing is preferring or selecting some one member of his gender for sexual attention, however unwelcome that attention may be to its object. He certainly does not despise the entire group, nor does he wish to harm its members, since he is a member himself and finds others of the group sexually attractive. Virtually all Title VII suits deal with intergroup discrimination, and not, as here, with complaints within a group. Homosexual sexual harassment—viewed as in some sense a preference phenomenon in which the harasser prefers, first, his own sex, and then a particular member—raises the larger issue of whether it makes sense to characterize the archetypical case of male to female harassment as discrimination, rather than as a preference, albeit misguided and objectionable.

Individual acts of sex discrimination fall into the following pattern: A refuses to do X for B because B is a member of group Y (where X stands for hire, promote, etc., and Y stands for blacks, women, etc.) Sexual harassment of the classic, quid pro quo type does not fit this pattern, but another: A refuses to do X for B unless B provides A with sexual favors. In sexual harassment, it is not simply the "bare fact" of B's existence as a Y that triggers A's oppressive conduct, but B's unwillingness to do something, namely to provide sexual favors. Thus, sexual harassment seems to be hitched uneasily to Title VII's sex discrimination cart. One need not be convinced entirely of this disanalogy to realize that there may be a more doctrinally felicitous means of remedying sexual harassment than the present jury-rigged arrangement. . . .

Intimate Private Relations or Sexual Harassment

Some sexual overtures in the workplace are perfectly legitimate. It is often difficult, if not impossible, to predict beforehand whether an invitation for intimacy is going to be welcome or not. Mixed signals, gamesmanship (or gameswomanship), and changes of heart are features of male-female relations. Office romances are commonplace, especially now that women increasingly populate the workforce. Frustrated, would-be, jilted, and jealous lovers all have been known to behave in the ways that plaintiffs complain of in sexual harassment suits. Thus, sexual harassment stands as a correlate to legitimate behavior of a private and sexual nature that could be initiated in the workplace.

Commentators have wrestled with the problem of distinguishing sexual harassment from legitimate sexual overtures, but their efforts have not been particularly successful. Susan Dodds, in proposing a behavioral account, writes that, "There is something intrinsically different about the two kinds of activity." She urges that one ought to be alert to risks and seek appropriate evidence from the other person's behavior when making sexual offers. Her argument, however, is circular: If actions typical of a sexual harasser define sexual harassment, then how does one determine in the first instance what these actions are? Hughes and May offer a more concrete distinction between coercive and "sincere" sexual offers: The latter promise benefits that are not a condition of employment success. Given the difficulty of separating "sincere" offers from coercive offers in the business environment, the authors recommend that one err on the side of avoiding potentially harassing conduct; one should refrain from making any overtures at work if one is in a relationship of unequal power. This recommendation might be feasible in a world populated by asexual creatures, but it is of limited use in drawing a bright line between harmless office flirtations and sexual harassment.

Nancy Brown points to another difficulty in the task of line-drawing. Men and women diverge in their perceptions of what constitutes acceptable behavior and what slips over the line into harassment. A man accused of sexual harassment typically either denies that the event occurred or admits to the conduct but claims that it was harmless and that the woman misinterpreted his intent. When the offensive behavior is of the hostile environment sort—e.g., sexual overtures without explicit threats of reprisal, lewd comments, language laden with sexual innuendos, sexual jokes—men may believe sincerely that their conduct falls within the bounds of generally acceptable male deportment.

Concerns such as these have prompted some commentators to suggest that the courts ought to adopt an objective victim standard in assessing cases of sexual harassment, particularly those of the hostile environment genre: "The standard would assess behavior from the viewpoint of the ordinary reasonable person in the particular employment setting of the plaintiff." This proposal would respond to the problems of distinguishing acceptable from unacceptable behavior.

In addition to these epistemological questions there is another problem: What about workplace environments that have been and still are infused with sexual banter and crude language that is inoffensive to male workers but disconcerting to their new female associates? As the district judge observed in *Rabidue v. Osceola Refining Co.*:

> [T]he standard for determining sex harassment would be different depending upon the work environment. Indeed, it cannot seriously be disputed that in some work environments, humor and language are rough hewn and vulgar. Sexual jokes, sexual conversation and girlie magazines may abound. Title VII was not meant to—or can—change this . . . [Title VII was not designed] to bring about magical transformation in the social mores of American workers.

The court recommended applying an objective test of the "average female employee" in order to assess whether a working environment is "offensive." Yet, as the quotation above indicates, even under an "objective" standard, judges will have to make close judgment calls about when they think women ought to be offended and when not. Thus, an objective victim standard cannot eliminate entirely the need for discretion on the part of judges. They must determine when behavior constitutes actionable sexual harassment and when it is only a harm without any available legal remedy.

IS THERE A BETTER WAY?

In recent years, some plaintiffs have appended tort claims to their Title VII suits, and federal courts have excised pendent jurisdiction to hear these state, common law grievances. Torts that have accompanied Title VII sexual harassment claims include wrongful discharge, invasion of the right to privacy, interference with contract, intentional assault and battery, interference with a contractual relationship, and intentional infliction of emotional distress. Given the problems in the sexual-harassment-as-sexual-discrimination theory indicated earlier, a tort may have two advantages: (1) it offers greater doctrinal coherence; and (2) it offers plaintiffs compensatory and punitive damages, which are currently unavailable under Title VII.

Some commentators oppose tort remedies for sexual harassment because they consider the problem societal—not personal. Not surprisingly, Catharine A. MacKinnon spearheaded this resistance. "[B]y treating the incidents as if they are outrages particular to an individual woman," she wrote, "rather than integral to her social status as a woman worker, the personal approach on the legal level fails to analyze the relevant dimensions of the problem." Another commentator agrees, arguing that under tort law sexual harassment would be viewed merely as an affront to a person's dignity. Such an approach would overlook the primary affront, that "sexual harassment injures a discrete and identifiable group by subjecting its victims to demeaning treatment and relegating them to inferior status in the workplace."

These objections, once again, highlight the differences between a group-discrimination approach and an individualist approach that stresses the victim's rights to privacy, to freedom from physical assault or the threat of it, and to freedom from the infliction of severe emotional distress. An individual-rights perspective calls for vindicating these rights, while a group-rights approach subsumes the victim's rights under a diffuse claim of affront to all of womankind. This group-rights approach, if carried to its logical extreme, would make each of us a victim of every criminal act—every robbery, assault, murder—thus vitiating the rights of the actual victim.

By contrast, a tort approach would remain true to an individual-rights perspective by focusing on the individual harm to the victim and the individual liability of the harasser. The tort approach would also place all similar behavior under the same theoretical umbrella. Sexually offensive behavior occurs in settings other than the workplace—in universities, housing, and ordinary social situations of all sorts. When such behavior becomes egregious, plaintiffs should have a remedy, and a tort would allow courts to treat all sexual harassment alike. Moreover, a new state tort of sexual harassment, created by judicial construction or legislative craftsmanship, would be preferable to the doctrinal and theoretical confusion that the sexual-harassment-as-sexual-discrimination theory has engendered. Rather than focusing sexual harassment to lie on the Procrustean bed of Title VII disparate-treatment sexual discrimination, a new tort could be crafted to the dimensions of the victims.

A tort of sexual harassment could be patterned after the tort of intentional infliction of emotional distress, which in most states parallels Section 46 of the Restatement (Second) of Torts. "[M]ere insults, indignities, threats, annoyances, petty oppression, or other trivialities" will not suffice to generate liability, for plaintiffs must be "hardened to a certain amount of rough language" and the occasional inconsiderate or unkind remark.

Liability has been found only where the conduct has been so outrageous in character, and so extreme in degree, as to go beyond all possible bounds of decency, and to be regarded as atrocious, and utterly intolerable in a civilized community. Generally, the case is one in which the recitation of the facts to an average member of the community would arouse his resentment against the actor, and lead him to exclaim, "Outrageous."

Emotional distress must be "so severe that no reasonable man could be expected to endure it." To trigger liability, the "extreme and outrageous" conduct must be committed either intentionally or recklessly; the perpetrator is then responsible for any emotional distress or bodily harm that may result. Thus, as one district judge put it, the tort has three elements: the conduct must be extreme and outrageous; it must be done intentionally or recklessly; and it must cause severe emotional distress.

A tort of sexual harassment, patterned on the tort of intentional infliction of emotional distress, would look something like this:

1. Sexual harassment is comprised of
   a. unwelcome sexual propositions incorporating overt or implicit threats of reprisal, and/or
   b. other sexual overtures or conduct so persistent and offensive that a reasonable person when apprised of the conduct would find it extreme and outrageous.
2. To be held liable, the harasser must have acted either intentionally or recklessly and the victim must have suffered, thereby, economic detriment and /or extreme emotional distress.
3. In the employment context,
   a. the employer is liable when the plaintiff had notified an appropriate officer of the company (not himself the alleged harasser) of the offensive conduct, and the employer failed to take good faith action forestall future incidents;
   b. The employer is liable, also, when he should have known of the offending incident(s) (that is, when he failed to provide an appropriate complaint mechanism).

Element (1) defines sexual harassment to include both the quid pro quo and the hostile environment types. The new tort would use a reasonable person standard for hostile environment claims, which would prevent ultrasensitive plaintiffs from prevailing on evidence of conduct that is generally acceptable, although not particularly desirable, in the prevailing social milieu. The requirement in (1)(b) that the conduct be "persistent and offensive" would eliminate suits based on casual or incidental insults; it would be difficult for offensive language, dirty jokes, or displays of pictures of naked women to rise above this threshold. A threshold is desirable, for it curtails frivolous suits and dissuades those who encourage virtually all women to view themselves as victims. To see all women as victims of sexual harassment is, in effect, to see none. As one commentator wrote: "[E]ach insult or sexist remark should not create a cause of action. . . . Suffice it to say that a small degree of thick skin is probably required, on the part of everyone."

Element (2) holds the harasser liable if he (or she) acts intentionally or recklessly. In quid pro quo cases, a court should infer such motivation or lack of care from the act itself; in hostile environment cases, the court should infer it if the act breaches the "extreme and outrageous" threshold. Also, the victim must show that she (or he) has sustained verifiable harm. The final element, (3), attempts to remedy the various theoretical problems with employer liability in the sexual harassment arena raised earlier. Employers would be liable under (3)(a) if, once given notice, they failed to take reasonable measures to insure that the outrageous conduct would not be repeated. The employer can escape liability if it makes good faith efforts, since no one can predict the proper deterrent for every harasser. Placing the onus on the victim to notify her employer may seem harsh, but it has a side benefit: The notification requirement tells women to take responsibility for their own lives and not to fall into a "helpless victim syndrome." Naturally, if the employer has neither an officer charged with receiving such complaints nor a review process, the company is more likely to be held liable; under such circumstances, (3)(b) holds the employer to a constructive knowledge standard.

The new scheme would encourage companies to provide an effective mechanism for dealing with sexual harassment. A few large compensatory and even punitive damage awards would send a louder message than EEOC conciliation sessions or a few small awards of back pay after years of litigation. And in contrast to Tile VII, the new tort would place the onus for sexual harassment squarely on the perpetrator. It thus would send a clear, unmixed message that such conduct is unacceptable in our society and that those who practice such behavior will suffer the full consequences. Finally, the new tort, which emanates from the individual-rights perspective, would encourage victims to object vigorously to acts of sexual harassment to their employers and, if this fails to remedy the problem, to vindicate their rights in court.

CONCLUSION

Including sexual harassment claims under the ban on sex discrimination in Title VII of the Civil Rights Act of 1964 is problematic for several principal reasons. No legislative history warrants such an interpretation. Sexual harassment differs in fundamental ways from disparate treatment sex discrimination. Strict employer liability for sexual harassment perpetrated by supervisory employees is inequitable because it punishes one of the victims (the employer) rather than placing the responsibility on the perpetrator. Finally, sexual harassment is sometimes difficult to distinguish from acceptable sexual overtures.

Years of judicial interpretation have transformed Title VII. In the process it has strayed from its original philosophical moorings in the vindication of individual rights and in the goal of a color-blind society. The victims and perpetrators of sexual harassment are discrete, identifiable individuals. Unless a group-injury model of sexual harassment (with all of its ideological ramifications) is defensible—and this article has argued it is not—the courts, by accepting such suits as cognizable under Title VII, have unwittingly imported philosophical assumptions from a radical agenda that characterizes all women as victims and all men as oppressors.

These defects in Title VII call out for an alternative. Tort law could offer a more propitious remedy for unwelcome sexual impositions in the workplace (and elsewhere). The new tort of sexual harassment proposed in this article has several advantages over the present Title VII doctrinal muddle: (1) it is theoretically consistent, always a good thing in itself; (2) it gets the federal courts out of what is essentially a personal matter between individuals; (3) it provides more compelling incentives to employers to both discourage such conduct and discipline transgressors; (4) it places fault where fault truly lies—with the perpetrator—rather than with the employer; (5) it discourages frivolous suits and compensates more completely true victims of outrageous conduct; (6) it signals to women, the usual victims of sexual harassment, that they should take responsibility for their lives by bringing complaints to the attention of their employers; (7) it names the offense appropriately as sexual harassment rather than as sex discrimination, an awkward appellation at best; and, finally, (8) it handles like conduct alike regardless of its social setting.

12

A Feminist Definition of
Sexual Harassment

Anita M. Superson

INTRODUCTION

By far the most pervasive form of discrimination against women is sexual harassment (SH). Women in every walk of life are subject to it, and I would venture to say, on a daily basis. Even though the law is changing to the benefit of victims of SH, the fact that SH is still so pervasive shows that there is too much tolerance of it, and that victims do not have sufficient legal recourse to be protected.

The main source for this problem is that the way SH is defined by various Titles and other sources does not adequately reflect the social nature of SH, or the harm it causes all women. As a result, SH comes to be defined in sub-

Anita M. Superson defends the view that sexual harassment is a form of domination of women by men. She argues that harassment represents not merely bad conduct on the part of a particular man to a particular woman, it represents an attack on all women. Whether behavior is properly viewed as harassing is not a matter of the subjective intentions of the harasser or the subjective reactions of the harassee. From "A Feminist Definition of Sexual Harassment" by Anita M. Superson. *Journal of Social Philosophy* 24:46–64 (1993). Copyright © 1993 by *Journal of Social Philosophy*. Reprinted with permission of Blackwell Publishers.

jective ways. One upshot is that when subjective definitions infuse the case law on SH, the more subtle but equally harmful forms of SH do not get counted as SH and thus not afforded legal protection.

My primary aim in this chapter is to offer an objective definition of SH that accounts for the group harm all forms of SH have in common. Though my aim is to offer a moral definition of SH, I offer it in hopes that it will effect changes in the law. It is only by defining SH in a way that covers all of its forms and gets at the heart of the problem that legal protection can be given to all victims in all circumstances.

I take this chapter to be programmatic. Obviously problems may exist in applying the definition to cases that arise for litigation. In a larger project a lot more could be said to meet those objections. My goal is merely to defend my definition against the definitions currently appealed to by the courts in order to show how it is more promising for victims of SH.

I define SH in the following way:

> any behavior (verbal or physical) caused by a person, A, in the dominant class directed at another, B, in the subjugated class, that expresses and perpetuates the attitude that B or members of B's sex is/are inferior because of their sex, thereby causing harm to either B and /or members of B's sex. . . .

THE SOCIAL NATURE OF SEXUAL HARASSMENT

Sexual harassment, a form of sexism, is about domination, in particular, the domination of the group of men over the group of women. Domination involves control or power that can be seen in the economic, political, and social spheres of society. Sexual harassment is not simply an assertion of power, for power can be used in beneficial ways. The power men have over women has been wielded in ways that oppress women. The power expressed in SH is oppression, power used wrongly.

Sexual harassment is integrally related to sex roles. It reveals the belief that a person is to be relegated to certain roles on the basis of her sex, including not only women's being sex objects, but also their being caretakers, mothers, nurturers, sympathizers, etc. In general, the sex roles women are relegated to are associated with the body (v. mind) and emotions (v. reason).

When A sexually harasses B, the comment or behavior is really directed at the group of all women, not just a particular woman, a point often missed by the courts. After all, many derogatory behaviors are issued at women the harasser does not even know (e.g., scanning a stranger's body). Even when the harasser knows his victim, the behavior is directed at the particular woman because she happens to be "available" at the time, though its message is for all women. For instance, a catcall says not (merely) that the perpetrator likes a woman's body but that he thinks women are at least primarily sex objects and he—because of the power he holds by being in the dominant group—gets to rate them according to how much pleasure they give him. The professor who refers to his female students as "chicks" makes a statement that women are intellectually inferior to men as they can be likened to nonrational animals, perhaps even soft, cuddly ones that are to serve as the objects of (men's) pleasure. Physicians who use Playboy centerfolds in medical schools to "spice up their lectures" send the message that women lack the competence to make it in a "man's world" and should perform the "softer tasks" associated with bearing and raising children.

These and other examples make it clear that SH is not about dislike for a certain person; instead, it expresses a person's beliefs about women as a group on the basis of their sex, namely, that they are primarily emotional and bodily beings. Some theorists—Catharine MacKinnon, John Hughes and Larry May—have recognized the social nature of SH. Hughes and May claim that women are a disadvantaged group because (1) they are a social group having a distinct identity and existence apart from their individual identities, (2) they occupy a subordinate position in American society, and (3) their political power is severely circumscribed. They continue:

> Once it is established that women qualify for special disadvantaged group status, all practices tending to stigmatize women as a group, or which contribute to the maintenance of their subordinate social status, would become legally suspect.

This last point, I believe, should be central to the definition of SH.

Because SH has as its target the group of all women, this group suffers harm as a result of the behavior. Indeed, when any one woman is in any way sexually harassed, all women are harmed. The group harm SH causes is different from the harm suffered by particular women as individuals: It is often more vague in nature as it is not easily causally tied to any particular incident of harassment. The group harm has to do primarily with the fact that the behavior reflects and reinforces sexist attitudes that women are inferior to men and that they do and ought to occupy certain sex roles. For example, comments and behavior that relegate women to the role of sex objects reinforce the belief that women *are* sex objects and that they *ought to* occupy this sex role. Similarly, when a female professor's cogent comments at department colloquia are met with frowns and rolled eyes from her colleagues, this behavior reflects and reinforces the view that women are not fit to occupy positions men arrogate to themselves.

The harm women suffer as a group from any single instance of SH is significant. It takes many forms. A Kantian analysis would show what is wrong with being solely a sex object. Though there is nothing wrong with being a caretaker or a nurturer, etc., *per se*, it is sexist—and so wrong—to assign such roles to women. In addition, it is wrong to assign a person to a role she may not want to occupy. Basically women are not allowed to decide for themselves which roles they are to occupy, but this gets decided for them, no matter what they do. Even if some women occupy important positions in society that men traditionally occupy, they are still viewed as being sex objects, caretakers, etc., since all women are thought to be more "bodily" and emotional than men. This is a denial of women's autonomy, and degrading to them. It also contributes to women's oppression. The belief that women must occupy certain sex roles is both a cause and an effect of their oppression. It is a cause because women are believed to be more suited for certain roles given their association with body and emotions. It is an effect because once they occupy these roles and are victims of oppression, the belief that they *must* occupy these sex roles is reinforced.

Women are harmed by SH in yet another way. The belief that they are sex objects, caretakers, etc., gets reflected in social and political practices in ways that are unfair to women. It has undoubtedly meant many lost opportunities that are readily available to men. Women are not likely to be hired for jobs that require them to act in ways other than the ways the sex roles dictate, and if they are, what is expected of them is different from what is expected of men. Mothers are not paid for their work, and caretakers are not paid well in comparison to jobs traditionally held by men. Lack of economic reward is paralleled by lack of respect and appreciation for those occupying such roles. Certain rights granted men are likely not to be granted women (e.g., the right to bodily self-determination, and marriage rights).

Another harm SH causes all women is that the particular form sex stereotyping takes promotes two myths: (1) that male behavior is normally and naturally predatory, and (2) that females naturally (because they are taken to be primarily bodily and emotional) and even willingly acquiesce despite the appearance of protest. Because the behavior perpetuated by these myths is taken to be normal, it is not seen as sexist, and in turn is not counted as SH.

The first myth is that men have stronger sexual desires than women, and harassment is just a natural venting of these desires that men are unable to control. The truth is, first, that women are socialized *not* to vent their sexual desires in the way men do, but this does not mean these desires are weaker or less prevalent. Masters and Johnson have "decisively established that women's sexual requirements are no less potent or urgent than those of men." But second, SH has nothing to do with men's sexual desires, nor is it about seduction; instead, it is about oppression of women. Indeed, harassment generally does not lead to sexual satisfaction, but it often gives the harasser a sense of power.

The second myth is that women either welcome, ask for, or deserve the harassing treatment. . . . The idea that women welcome "advances" from men is seen in men's view of the way women dress. If a woman dresses "provocatively" by men's standards, she is said to welcome or even deserve the treatment she gets. One explanation harassing professors give for their behavior is that they are bombarded daily with the temptation of physically desirable young women who dress in what they take to be revealing ways. When the case becomes public, numerous questions arise about the attractiveness of the victim, as if she were to blame for being attractive and the consequences thereof. Catcallers often try to justify their behavior by claiming that the victim should expect such behavior, given her tight-fitting dress or shorts, low-cut top, high heels, etc. This way of thinking infests discussions of rape in attempts to establish that women want to be raped, and it is mistaken in that context, too. The myth that women welcome or encourage harassment is designed "to keep women in their place" as men see it. The truth of the matter is that the perpetrator alone is at fault.

Both myths harm all women as they sanction SH by shifting the burden on the victim and all members of her sex: Women must either go out of their way to avoid "natural" male behavior, or establish conclusively that they did not in any way want the behavior. Instead of the behavior being seen as sexist, it is seen as women's problem to rectify.

Last, but certainly not least, women suffer group harm from SH because they come to be stereotyped as victims. Many men see SH as something they can do to women, and in many cases, get away with. Women come to see themselves as victims, and come to believe that the roles they *can* occupy are only the sex roles men have designated for them. Obviously these harms are quite serious for women, so the elimination of all forms of SH is warranted.

I have spoken so far as if it is only men who can sexually harass women, and I am now in a position to defend this controversial view. When a women engages in the very same behavior harassing men engage in, the underlying message implicit in male-to-female harassment is missing. For example, when a women scans a man's body, she might be considering him to be a sex object, but all the views about domination and being regulated to certain sex roles are absent. She cannot remind the man that he is inferior because of his sex, since given the way things are in society, he is not. In general, women cannot harm or degrade or dominate men *as a group*, for it is impossible to send the message that one dominates (and so cause group harm) if one does not dominate. Of course, if the sexist roles predominant in our society were reversed, women *could* sexually harass men. The way things are, any bothersome behavior a woman engages in, even though it may be of a sexual nature, does not constitute SH because it lacks the social impact present in male-to-female harassment. Tort law would be sufficient to protect against this behavior, since it is unproblematic in these cases that tort law fails to recognized group harm.

SUBJECTIVE V. OBJECTIVE DEFINITIONS
OF SEXUAL HARASSMENT

Most definitions of "sexual harassment" make reference to the behavior's being "unwelcome" or "annoying" to the victim. *Black's Law Dictionary* defines "harassment" as a term used "to describe words, gestures and actions which tend to annoy, alarm and abuse (verbally) another person." *The American Heritage Dictionary* defines "harass" as "to disturb or irritate persistently," and states further that "[h]arass implies systematic persecution by besetting with annoyances, threats, or demands." The EEOC *Guidelines* state that behavior constituting SH is identified as "unwelcome sexual advances, request for sexual favors, and other verbal or physical conduct of a sexual nature." In their philosophical account of SH, Hughes and May define "harassment" as "a class of annoying or unwelcome acts undertaken by one person (or group of persons) against another person (or group of persons)." And Rosemarie Tong takes the feminists' definition of noncoercive SH to be that which "denotes sexual misconduct that merely annoys or offends the person to whom it is directed."

The criterion of "unwelcomeness" or "annoyance" is reflected in the way the courts have handled cases of SH, as in *Lipsett, Swenick,* and *Meritor,* though in the latter case the court said that the voluntariness of the victim's submission to the defendant's sexual conduct did not mean that she welcomed the conduct. The criterion of unwelcomeness or annoyance present in these subjective accounts of harassment puts the burden on the victim to establish that she was sexually harassed. There is no doubt that many women *are* bothered by this behavior, often with serious side-effects including anything from anger, fear, and guilt, to lowered self-esteem and decreased feelings of competence and confidence, to anxiety disorders, alcohol and drug abuse, coronary disturbances, and gastro-intestinal disorders.

Though it is true that many women are bothered by the behavior at issue, I think it is seriously mistaken to say that whether the victim is bothered determines whether the behavior constitutes SH. This is so for several reasons.

First, we would have to establish that the victim was bothered by it, either by the victim's complaints, or by examining the victim's response to the behavior. The fact of the matter is that many women are quite hesitant to report being harassed, for a number of reasons. Primary among them is that they fear negative consequences from reporting the conduct. As is often the case, harassment comes from a person in a position of institutional power, whether he be a supervisor, a company president, a member of a dissertation committee, the chair of the department, and so on. Unfortunately for many women, as a review of the case law reveals, their fears are warranted. Women have been fired, their jobs have been made miserable forcing them to quit, professors have handed out unfair low grades, and so on. Worries about such consequences means that complaints are not filed, or are filed years after the incident, as in the *Anita Hill v. Clarence Thomas* case. But this should not be taken to imply that the victim was not harassed.

Moreover, women are hesitant to report harassment because they do not want anything to happen to the perpetrator, but just want the behavior to stop. Women do not complain because they do not want to deal with the perpetrator's reaction when faced with the charge. He might claim that he was "only trying to be friendly." Women are fully aware that perpetrators can often clear themselves quite easily, especially in tort law cases where the perpetrator's intentions are directly relevant to whether he is guilty. And most incidents of SH occur without any witnesses—many perpetrators plan it this way. It then becomes the harasser's word against the victim's. To complicate matters, many women are insecure and doubt themselves. Women's insecurity is capitalized upon by harassers whose behavior is in the least bit ambiguous. Clever harassers who fear they might get caught or be reported often attempt to get on the good side of their victim in order to confuse her about the behavior, as well as to have a defense ready in case a charge is made. Harassers might offer special teaching assignments to their graduate students, special help with exams and publications, promotions, generous raises, and the like. Of course, this is all irrelevant to whether he harasses, but the point is that it makes the victim less likely to complain. On top of all this, women's credibility is very often questioned (unfairly) when they bring forth a charge. They are taken to be "hypersensitive." There is an attitude among judges and others that women must "develop a thick skin." Thus, the blame is shifted off the perpetrator and onto the victim. Given this, if a woman thinks she will get no positive response—or, indeed, will get a negative one—from complaining, she is unlikely to do so.

Further, some women do not recognize harassment for what it is, and so will not complain. Sometimes this is because they are not aware of their own oppression, or actually seem to endorse sexist stereotypes. I recall a young woman who received many catcalls on the streets of Daytona Beach, Florida, during spring break, and who was quite proud that her body could draw such attention. Given that women are socialized into believing their bodies are the most important feature of themselves, it is no surprise that a fair number of them are complacent about harassing behavior directed at them. Sandra Bartky provides an interesting analysis of why every woman is not a feminist, and I think it holds even for women who understand the issue. Since for many women having a body felt to be "feminine" is crucial to their identity and to their sense of self "as a sexually desiring and desirable subject," feminism "may well be apprehended by a woman as something that threatens her with desexualization, if not outright annihilation." The many women who resist becoming feminists are not likely to perceive harassing behavior as bothersome. It would be incorrect to conclude that the behavior is not harassment on the grounds that such victims are not bothered. What we have is a no-win situation for victims: If the behavior bothers a woman she often has good reason not to complain, and if it does not bother her, she will not complain. Either way, the perpetrator wins. So we cannot judge whether woman are bothered by the behavior on the basis of whether *they* say they are bothered.

Moreover, women's behavior is not an accurate indicator of whether they are bothered. More often than not, women try to ignore the perpetrator's behavior in an attempt not to give the impression they are encouraging it. They often cover up their true feelings so that the perpetrator does not have the satisfaction that his harassing worked. Since women are taught to smile and put up with this behavior, they might actually appear to enjoy it to some extent. Often they have no choice but to continue interaction with the perpetrator, making it very difficult to assert themselves. Women often make up excuses for not "giving in" instead of telling the perpetrator to stop. The fact that their behavior does not indicate they are bothered should not be used to show they were not bothered. In reality, women are fearful of defending themselves in the face of men's power and physical strength. Given the fact that the courts have decided that a lot of this behavior should just be tolerated, it is no wonder that women try to make the best of their situation.

It would be wrong to take a woman's behavior to be a sign that she is bothered also because doing so implies the behavior is permissible if she does not seem to care. This allow the *perpetrator* to be the judge of whether a woman is harassed, which is unjustifiable given the confusion among men about whether their behavior is bothersome or flattering. Sexual harassment should be treated no differently than crimes where harm to the victim is assessed in some objective way, independent of the perpetrator's beliefs. To give men this power in the case of harassment is to perpetuate sexism from all angles.

An *objective* view of SH avoids the problems inherent in a subjective view. According to the objective view defended here, what is decisive in determining whether behavior constitutes SH is not whether the victim is bothered, but whether the behavior is an instance of a practice that expresses and perpetuates the attitude that the victim and members of her sex are inferior because of their sex.

13

Sexual Harassment
and the University

Robert L. Holmes

S exual harassment is a serious and insufficiently recognized problem for universities. But while virtually everyone can agree that sexual harassment is wrong, there is little agreement as to what precisely it is. Here one finds a proliferating array of definitions. They include the following:

> Sexual harassment, most broadly defined, refers to the unwanted imposition of sexual requirements in the context of a relationship of unequal power.
>
> Sexual harassment is the use of words, gestures, bodily actions or other means of verbal and nonverbal communication to insult, degrade, humiliate, or otherwise dehumanize women.
>
> . . . sexual harassment is defined as any action occurring within the workplace whereby women are treated as objects of the male sexual prerogative.
>
> Unwelcome sexual advances, requests for sexual favors, and other verbal or physical conduct of a sexual nature constitute sexual harassment when . . . such

Robert L. Holmes argues that sexual harassment should be viewed as unwanted sexual attention. Although it may sometimes have the consequence of being discriminatory, the principal reason why it is wrong, Holmes maintains, is that it is an invasion of privacy. From "Sexual Harassment and the University," *The Monist* 79: 499–518 (1996). Copyright © 1996 by *The Monist*. Reprinted with permission of *The Monist*.

conduct has the purpose or effect of unreasonably interfering with an individual's work performance or creating an intimidating, hostile, or offensive working environment.

Even a cursory review of such definitions reveals wide differences. Some represent sexual harassment as occurring only in the workplace; some understand it only in the context of unequal power; and some view it as directed solely against women. This seems to bear out the conclusion that "no definition of the many that exist is complete or acceptable to everyone."

I

Unclarity about what sexual harassment is, however, predictably results in confusion over what sorts of conduct constitute sexual harassment. As this is an obstacle to an effective engagement with the problem in the university, let us begin with the question of what sexual harassment is, adhering as closely as possible to ordinary language in proposing an answer to it.

Harassment in general is repeated unwanted behavior. It can be directed against persons or groups because of race, sex, religion, ethnicity, sexual preference, physical appearance, or virtually any other attributes, as well as be practiced by police, governments, and nations in a wide range of areas, including warfare. In all such cases it is *prima facie* wrong, and, arguably, presumptively wrong as well.

A single instance of unwanted behavior may also be wrong, but it doesn't constitute harassment. To be harassment it must be repeated or continuing. Nor do actions that exceed a certain threshold of severity constitute harassment, even if they are repeated. The United States harassed German submarines in World War II by continually tracking and trying to sink them. But the atomic bombing of Hiroshima wasn't harassment; it was of a different order of magnitude. In short, harassment is always a serious matter, but some forms of it are more serious than others. At one end of the scale, it may be no more than mildly bothersome; at the other end of the scale, terrifying or traumatizing.

In light of these considerations, let us define sexual harassment as follows:

SEXUAL HARASSMENT = def. repeated unwanted sexual attention.

"Unwanted" doesn't require that the behavior in question be harmful or even offensive, or that it result in economic or social deprivation. And sexual "attention" need not always signify any expectation or even hope of sexual involvement with the person harassed (so-called "street harassment"—such as by construction workers of women passersby—isn't usually accompanied by any such expectations). Nor need there be any intention on the part of the offender to harass his victim. That may be the furthest thing from the mind of one whose amorous importunings alienate the object of his affections.

At the same time, it is important that the adjective "sexual" be attached to "attention." For not every unwanted expression of friendly or even potentially romantic interest is sexual harassment—such as if a man invites a woman to lunch a couple of times to discuss their mutual interest in herbal medicine, and she declines because she doesn't want to have lunch with him. There are platonic friendships between men and women, as well as among gays and among lesbians, and not every unwelcome attempt to initiate such a friendship is sexual harassment. In other words, in understanding sexual harassment we must attend to the nature of the interest governing the offending behavior as well as to the effects of the behavior on the harassed. Not all nettlesome attention to a member of the opposite sex (or among homosexual members of the same sex) is sexually motivated. Such attention, if it persists, doesn't cease for that reason to be harassment, but it does fail for that reason to be sexual harassment.

The one qualification of this concerns harassing behavior that is overtly sexual but in fact expresses no sexual interest. A man might use sexual language solely for the purpose of demeaning women, where far from seeking any sexual involvement he may deliberately distancing himself from them. Here the governing interest isn't sexual but, most likely, misogynistic. While such behavior is more accurately characterized as *sex* (or gender) harassment than as sexual harassment, the ordinary use of the term "sexual harassment" provides some warrant for including it under that heading by virtue of the fact that the form the behavior takes makes it a candidate for sexual "attention." What isn't sexual harassment (despite the fact that some courts have so found it), is clearly unwanted—even egregiously offensive—behavior that neither reflects sexual interest nor represents sexual attention, even in the broad sense just characterized.

Where conduct expresses sexual and/or romantic interest the matter is often complicated. Whereas the behavior that constitutes most other forms of harassment is unwanted whenever it occurs (and, as with racial harassment, is usually engaged in precisely because it is unwanted), much of the behavior that constitutes sexual harassment is not. In fact, it is often encouraged and reciprocated. As a popular commentator on such matters writes: "Courtship is best conducted, and romantic interest indicated . . . by hints, suggestions and little actions. . . . That is why we have always had the gestures of interest—the lingering look, the hand laid on the other person's arm, the brushing together too often for it to seem an accident."

This creates considerable potential for misunderstanding. Persistent attention that is welcome from one person may be unwelcome from another. The lingering look may be perceived as a leer, the suggestion an innuendo. And behavior that is acceptable in one social context may be inappropriate in another. Inquiries about personal life that are the norm in a singles bar may be out of place in a professor's office. Extrapolation beyond social contexts, it has even been said that "[t]here is so much variation in human behavior cross cultures that behavior which may be sexual harassment in one need not be in another."

So while some behavior is almost certainly harassing whomever it is directed against, much of the behavior that constitutes sexual harassment its not. Whether it is harassing is relative to the person affected and sometimes to the broader social and cultural context. So whether an act is a case of sexual harassment cannot be inferred from an evaluatively neutral description of the behavior itself. It requires consideration of context, at least to the extent of establishing the governing interest of the behavior and how it is received. But it should be stressed that harassment isn't necessarily less serious just because it isn't *sexual* harassment, or less serious just because it may be misperceived as sexual harassment when it is not.

If the preceding is correct, sexual harassment doesn't, by definition, occur only in the context of unequal power; it isn't confined to the workplace (and by extension, the university); it doesn't extend to offensive nonsexual behavior; and it isn't experienced only by women. . . .

III

. . . Now, while sexual harassment can be practiced by sexists, it needn't be (meaning that sexists needn't practice sexual harassment, and that those who practice it needn't be sexists). And while it may be an expression of overt sexism, it needn't be. This suggests that sexual harassment might be partly constitutive of covert sexism even in circumstances in which it is not an expression of overt sexism. And it might contribute to sex discrimination even when it is not (in individual cases) an instance of sex discrimination; that is, when its practitioners don't target all women, but only those they find sexually attractive. In other words, sexual harassment could conceivably be so pervasive, and have such prejudicial effects, that even women who were not themselves targeted by it (say, in the workplace or the university) were nonetheless disadvantaged by it, through its creation of a hostile social environment for virtually all women. But whether it is that pervasive and has that effect is a factual issue, not one that can be resolved by definitional fiat or ideological dictate.

In any event, whether or not sexual harassment can be shown to be wrong by means of these largely consequentialist considerations, it can be seen to be wrong on one important deontological ground, that it is a violation of privacy. Privacy is freedom from intrusion into areas of one's life that one hasn't explicitly or implicitly opened to others. And sexual harassment, by virtue of being unwanted, is always such an intrusion. This makes it presumptively wrong, and virtually always actually wrong as well. If widely and systematically practiced it may also be an expression of overt or covert sexism, and contributory to sex discrimination, as well; even if it should not express sexism and contribute to sex discrimination, the fact that it violates privacy suffices to establish its presumptive wrongness.

IV

The tendency has been to extend to the university the same thinking—largely imported from the law—that has come to govern the workplace. This is in keeping with a growing tendency to view universities on an industrial model. But learning isn't a commercial product, and education isn't the delivery of a product. Education is the encouragement of learning, and the aim of the university should be to foster the conditions under which that can best take place.

A sufficient reason for the wrongness of sexual harassment in the university is that the harassment of any person or group for any reason—sexual, religious, ethnic, racial, etc.—jeopardizes the conditions under which learning can take place. It should, if only for that reason (and apart from the issue of privacy), not be engaged in. But there are other reasons why it is wrong in the university.

Besides being an invasion of privacy and often harmful to those victimized by it, sexual harassment of a student by a professor represents a betrayal of trust on the part of the professor. A community of learning, unlike the workplace, isn't—or ought not to be—governed by economic motives, in which a pervasive *quid pro quo* set of values obtain. In the workplace the employer tries to extract the best from his employees, not because it is to their benefit to do so, but because it profits him to do so. In the university the central concern should be the enrichment and empowerment of the learner to continue the process of intellectual growth in the ways he or she personally deems best. This requires confidence on the part of students that professors, their guides in this enterprise, won't exploit the trust placed in them for their won ends. To harass a student in any way, including sexually, is to violated that trust.

The university setting, of course, is a minefield of potential problems in honoring this trust. In this respect it differs from most workplaces. For the vast majority of university students are young, single, and (many of them) sexually active, facts that create both opportunities and temptations for amorous relations between professors and students. These cannot all be dismissed as cases of lecherous 50-year-old male professors and 18-year-old ingenues. There are also worldly 22-year-old women and 28-year-old assistant professors (or occasionally professors and graduate students of roughly the same age). And these are more difficult. While some analysis of sexual harassment start from the assumption that all intimated relations between professors and students should be prohibited, and that even consensual relations constitute misconduct, that is a separate issue, and would need consideration on its own. Persons on both sides of that issue could be in agreement on sexual harassment and the reasons for its wrongness, and for that reason we shall not attempt to resolve that issue.

For better or worse, romantic and sometimes sexual relationships develop throughout the university community. They occur between undergraduates and undergraduates, graduate students and undergraduates, faculty and graduate students, secretaries and students, faculty and secretaries, librarians and faculty, faculty and faculty, and sometimes between faculty and undergraduates. They have even been know to occur among administrators. This isn't to say that any or all of these are advisable or even conscionable. Only that they occur, and almost certainly will continue to do so. Sometimes they even result in marriages—occasionally even good ones. It is not unreasonable to assume that most of them begin with signals and subtle forms of behavior of the sorts referred to in the earlier quotation, and only later grow into more assertive and declaratory behavior. This means that the possibilities for misunderstanding abound. It also means that the possibilities for intimidation and coercion abound. Faculty should be particularly mindful of this when dealing with students, and graduate students (in their capacity as teaching assistants) should be mindful of it in their dealing with undergraduates.

In any event, much of the sexual harassment in the university occurs among students (or among professors, or among staff, or administrators, or between members of these various groups). Where there is no differential in power or authority, this constitutes peer harassment, and normally doesn't fit the model of *quid pro quo* harassment. This doesn't, however, affect its wrongness. For peer harassment is still an invasion of privacy and still jeopardizes the conditions under which learning can best take place.

Peer harassment does, however, focus the issue of the responsibilities and obligations of a university, for it raises the question of the extent to which the university should monitor the nonacademic behavior of students. At a time when universities have moved away from the conception of the university as in *loco parentis*, they must reconsider whether, or to what extent, they are to resume or expand that role—a decision complicated by the fact that threat of lawsuits under federal law may be a severe constraint on them.

Students are nearly all over eighteen, many of them over twenty-one, as well, and graduate students are virtually all over twenty-one. All things being equal, how they live and conduct their personal affairs is their business.

While individual faculty members may be sought out for advice or counsel concerning various personal problems, the university doesn't routinely involve itself in such matters, and probably shouldn't. If two students develop a relationship that turns sour, and one of them pursues the other (say, by phoning at all hours, or appearing unexpectedly at the door pleading for just one more chance), that is clearly harassment, arguably even sexual harassment, if one accepts our broad understanding of the concept to include romantic interest. But it is the kind of problem that adults are normally expected to cope with on their own.

When, however, harassment occurs in the setting provided for learning and the conducting of affairs relating thereto (such as in the classroom or the library or around a department), and/or when it interferes with the ability of the person harassed to function comfortably and effectively in that setting, it becomes a proper concern of the university. Steps should then be taken to see that it stops, and that it is understood by the offender (and others, if necessary) why it is wrong. What exactly these steps should be may vary from case to case. Where possible, it is probably best if the matter is resolved directly between the parties (say, by discussion, or if that isn't feasible, by a letter from the person harassed to the harasser detailing what behavior is objectionable and asking that it cease; or through the mediation of a third person, perhaps a fellow-student or faculty member). Victims of harassment may, however, feel unable to cope with the situation on their own, in which case the university should become directly involved. And if it should be unable to handle the situation informally, it should then proceed to implement fair and impartial judicial proceedings, followed by sanctions when warranted. That is, the goodwill and mutual respect of all members of the university community are best presumed until shown not to obtain, and it is best that the least damaging steps (to both parties) be taken that are consistent with a prompt and satisfactory resolution of the problem.

The preceding applies to cases in which sexual harassment has occurred and is known to have occurred. Often these conditions aren't met. There may be cases in which it is alleged to have occurred but hasn't, or in which it has occurred but no one but the principals involved knows it. Allowing for extraordinary cases of miscommunication, in which an offender doesn't realize that his behavior is unwanted, there may even be cases in which the victim is the only one who knows it has occurred. The problems then are compounded further. To handle all of them adequately would require shifting from the God's-eye point of view of the preceding (where, *ex hypothesi,* one person is known to be victim, the other victimizer) to the point of view of a third party trying to adjudicate conflicting claims, often without benefit of adequate evidence.

If sexual harassment is alleged and there are witnesses and supporting evidence, the university can assess testimony and evidence and reach the conclusion to which they point. If there are no witnesses and no independent evidence, it may be confronted with nothing more than the conflicting testimony of two equally respected students. Short of looking deep into their eyes as they tell their respective stories, there may be no way of knowing precisely what the truth is. And if that is unavailing, and if students, like everyone else, should be presumed innocent unless proven guilty, there may be no recourse but to suspend judgment. This may sometimes mean that a guilty person goes scot-free, in which case a victim of sexual harassment will undergo the added distress of seeing a miscarriage of justice. But it may also mean that an innocent person, unjustly accused, isn't himself victimized. Which of these is the case the university may be unable to tell. As unsatisfactory as that conclusion is, there may sometimes be no way to avoid it.

Be that as it may, a university can nonetheless take steps to see that the chances of a recurrence of whatever it was that led to the initial accusation be minimized. That is, even if it should not be possible to make a finding with regard to the truth or falsity of the charges in question, it is possible to safeguard the well-being of the accuser in the event the charges are in fact true. With a little good sense it should be possible to do this in ways that aren't detrimental to the accused if the accused should in fact be innocent. And it is important to do that as well. In short, a university's concern should extend equally to all of its students. If it is important that victims of sexual harassment not be doubly victimized by being made to feel guilty about having sought help or, worse yet, being made to feel they are themselves to blame, it is also important that innocent persons not be unjustly stigmatized as offenders. There probably aren't any rules that are very helpful in this regard, as the whole matter is a case of highly imperfect procedural justice.

The best safeguard against sexual harassment even occurring in the first place, or if it does occur, against its leading to unnecessarily harmful consequences, is to educate both students and faculty about what sexual harassment is and why it is wrong, and to foster a sense of community in which friendship, trust, caring, and mutual respect enable everyone to flourish intellectually in as relaxed and supportive an environment as possible. Faculty in particular can help to do this. They can be open and available as friends and counselors or mediators when problems arise. And they can promote understanding and reconciliation when conflicts occur. But it is something for which everyone shares responsibility. Students can foster these conditions as well. They can help create a climate in which problems like sexual harassment don't arise, or if they do arise, are handled in ways that don't leave any of the persons involved feeling isolated and adrift. In short, the good will that a sense of community can generate, through women and men working cooperatively on an equal and respectful basis, is more likely in the long run to be effective in ending sexual harassment than are threats and punishment.

14

Feminist Accused
of Sexual Harassment

Jane Gallop

FEMINIST ACCUSED OF SEXUAL HARASSMENT

My initial and formative experience of feminism was this entry into a milieu bubbling indiscriminately with ideas and lusts. *Feminism turned me on*, figuratively and literally: My body and my mind began firing, pulsing with energy, an energy that did not distinguish between mind and body. Feminism made me feel sexy and smart; feminism felt smart and very sexy. When I call myself a feminist, as I have for twenty-five years, I necessarily refer to that milieu where knowledge and sex bubble together, to that possible community, to that possibility for women.

Perhaps that is what makes me the kind of feminist who gets accused of sexual harassment.

Since being accused of harassment, I feel like my life has fallen into sensationalism. I've become a spectacle. Despite the urge to hide in shame, I've decided to speak from this sensational location. I'd like to make spectacle speak, to use spectacle to explore our assumptions about sexual harassment and feminism.

To do this, I have to tell what happened to me, tell how and why I was accused of harassment and what the investigation determined. But I won't be telling what happened chronologically; the story will appear broken into pieces and out of order. For spectacle to speak, it must be analyzed, broken down into its various components.

My purpose is not simply to tell my story but rather to use that story to understand what's going on with sexual harassment. The spectacle taught me a thing or two, and I'd like to try to explain what I've learned.

Feminist sexual harasser seems like a contradiction in terms. I find myself positioned at the center of this contradiction. Although the position has been personally quite comfortable, professionally I can see it as a rare vantage point, an opportunity to produce knowledge. I have long suspected that a contradiction in terms might present an occasion to confront and rethink the terms themselves.

As a feminist theorist of sexuality, I consider it my business to understand sexual harassment. And so I'd like to take advantage of my peculiar position as an accused harasser to provide a fresh feminist view of the issue. Theorizations of harassment generally focus on what is clearly the classic scenario: the male boss uses his professional clout to force himself upon a female subordinate—sleep with me or you'll lose your job, sleep with me and you'll get a raise, a promotion. Rather than refer to this classic case, I want to produce an understanding of sexual harassment based instead on the case of a feminist so accused.

The classic scenario is explicit and quid pro quo (demand for sex in exchange for professional support). The concept of harassment also includes more implicit forms, where the sexual demand or the professional threat is not stated but understood. Implicit sexual demands might ultimately include any charged talk or behavior; implicit professional threats could possibly cover the entire range of professional interaction. While these possibilities are potentially already limitless, the range of harassment is also expanding in other directions. Harassment need not be perpetrated by bosses; peers can harass, even subordinates. And gender can be a variable: Increasing numbers of cases involve a man claiming to have been harassed or a woman accused of harassment.

The classic scenario—easy to recognize and deplore as sexual harassment—expands its application in every direction. I want to ground my theorizing in a limit case precisely because I believe that there should be limits to this bloated general application. I hope that my example can expose the limitations of loose analogies and impede this rampant expansion of the concept of sexual harassment.

Feminism has a special relation to sexual harassment. One could in fact say that feminism invented sexual harassment. Not, of course, the behavior itself, which presumably has gone on as long as men have held power over women. But, until feminism named it, the behavior had no official existence. In the mid-seventies, feminism got women to compare notes on their difficulties in the workplace; it came out that women employees all too frequently had to cope with this sort of thing. Feminism named this behavior "sexual harassment" and proceeded to make it illegal.

Today the general public knows that sexual harassment consists of some form of unwanted sexual advances and that it is some sort of crime. Inevitably people assume that it is sex that makes harassment criminal. Feminism's interest in prosecuting harassment is then chalked up to feminism's supposed hostility to scx.

But, whatever the feelings of individual feminists, feminism is not in principle a movement against sexuality. It is, in principle and in fact, against the disadvantaging of women. Sexual harassment is a feminist issue not because it is sexual but because it disadvantages women. Because harassment makes it harder for women to earn a living, feminists declared it a form of discrimination against women. This framing was so persuasive that, within a few years, harassment was added to the legal definition of sex discrimination. Since discrimination on the basis of sex was already illegal, once harassment was included within the category of discrimination, it immediately became a crime. Sexual harassment is criminal not because it is sex but because it is discrimination.

When I was charged with sexual harassment, the accusations were made on official university forms that bore the heading "COMPLAINT OF DISCRIMINATION." Under that heading, the students filed formal complaints against me, checking the box marked "Sexual Harassment." This form includes twelve such boxes, each pertaining to a type of discrimination (race or color, sex, national origin, etc.). The form itself makes it clear that harassment is treated as a subspecies of the general wrong, discrimination.

After reviewing the evidence and interviewing the witnesses, the university officer who investigated the charges against me was convinced that I had not in fact discriminated—not against women, not against men, not on the basis of sexual orientation, not on any basis whatsoever. She believed that my pedagogical practices had been, as she put it, applied in a consistent manner. Yet she nonetheless thought I probably was guilty of sexual harassment.

When it is possible to conceive of sexual harassment without discrimination, then sexual harassment becomes a crime of sexuality rather than of discrimination. There is, in fact, a recent national trend toward findings of sexual harassment where there is no discrimination. This represents a significant departure from the feminist formulation of harassment.

Although the shock value of my case resides in the supposition that it is impossible to be both a feminist and a harasser, the spectacle fascinates because it suggests the possibility that a feminist *could* be a sexual harasser—which would mean that either feminism or sexual harassment (maybe even both) are not what we assumed they were. A feminist sexual harasser is no longer a contradiction in terms; rather, it is the sign of an issue drifting from its feminist frame.

I was construed a sexual harasser because I sexualize the atmosphere in which I work. When sexual harassment is defined as the introduction of sex into professional relations, it becomes quite possible to be both a feminist and a sexual harasser.

The classic harassment scenario clearly involves both discrimination against women and sexualization of professional relations. Because people always refer to that classic case, it has been assumed that sexualizing the workplace is automatically disadvantageous to women. But if we base our thinking in the more exotic possibility of a feminist sexualizer, these two aspects of harassment no longer fit so neatly together. And sexualizing is not necessarily to women's disadvantage.

It is no coincidence that I happen to be both a feminist and someone whose professional relations are sexualized. It is because of the sort of feminist I am that I do not respect the line between the intellectual and the sexual. Central to my commitment as a feminist teacher is the wish to transmit the experience that brought me as a young woman out of romantic paralysis and into the power of desire and knowledge, to bring the women I teach to their own power, to ignite them as feminism ignited me when I was a student.

The chill winds of the current climate threaten to extinguish what feminism lit for me. What felt liberating to me as a student is today considered dangerous to my students. Today's antiharassment activism is, of course, a legacy of seventies feminism. But the antisexual direction of the current trend makes us forget how women's liberation turned us on. The present climate makes it easy to forget and thus crucial to remember. And so, at the risk of sounding as old as I am, I want to tell you again what feminism on campus felt like back when I was a student.

In 1971, there was a weekend-long feminist event on campus, lots of workshops and seminars, that combined teaching the issues and reorganizing us for activism. As part of this event, Saturday night there was a dance—women only, featuring a women's rock band (the first I'd ever seen).

Outraged at the idea of a women-only dance, male students came to crash the party. A large group of us women threw ourselves against the door. It was a thrill keeping men out, feeling the power of our combined weight, heaping our bodies together in this symbolic enactment of feminist solidarity. And then, after the men gave up, we decided to celebrate our triumph, our women-only space by taking off our shirts and dancing bare-breasted.

Our breasts were political. In those days feminists were said to burn bras. Restricting and constraining movement, bras provided a metaphor for women's bonds. We didn't wear bras. We stripped off our shirts in triumphant defiance of the men we had kept out. With no men around to ogle our breasts, we were as free as men to take off our shirts in public; so we were asserting equal rights. But our breasts were not just political.

I remember Becca that night, a gorgeous young woman a year or so older than me. She had been one of the first to the door, expertly throwing her long, rangy body against the would-be intruders. And she was the first to take off her shirt and start dancing, revealing the most beautiful breasts I had ever seen. We all danced together in a heap, intoxicated with the joy and energy of our young feminism. The bacchanalian frenzy did not in the least cloud my focus on Becca's breasts. I was dancing with those beautiful breasts, dancing all the harder because I so wanted to touch those breasts. . . .

CONSENSUAL AMOROUS RELATIONS

Just last week, I was gossiping with a friend of mine about the department she teaches in. My friend, who is a feminist, confessed that she supported a junior colleague "even though he is a sexual harasser." Being pretty sensitive about the issue, I confronted her: "Is he really a sexual harasser, or does he just date students?"

She only meant that he dated students. Thanks to an administrative stint, my friend is very familiar with academic policy. Her casual use of the term "sexual harasser" was not aberrant but, in fact, represents a new sense of sexual harassment operative in the academy today.

Nowadays, most campus sexual-harassment policies include a section on "consensual relations" between teachers and students. These range from outright prohibitions of teacher-student relationships to warnings that a consensual relationship will not protect the teacher from the student's claims of harassment. Although the range suggests some uncertainty about the status of consensual relations, *their very inclusion within harassment policies* indicates that consensual relations are themselves considered a type of sexual harassment.

Sexual harassment has always been defined as *unwanted* sexual attention. But with this expansion into the realm of consensual relations, the concept can now encompass sexual attention that is reciprocated and very much welcome. This reconfigures the notion of harassment, suggesting that what is undesirable finally is not unwelcome attention but sexuality per se. Rather than some sexuality being harassing because of its unwanted nature, the inference is that sexuality is in and of itself harassment.

I have reason to be sensitive to this slippage in meaning. When I was accused of sexual harassment by two students, my relation to one of the complainants was deemed to be in violation of the university's policy on "consensual relations."

The two students charged me with classic quid pro quo sexual harassment. They both claimed that I had tried to get them to have sex with me and that, when they rejected me, I had retaliated by withdrawing professional support (in one case with negative evaluations of work, in the other with a refusal to write letters of recommendation). The university's affirmative-action office conducted a lengthy investigation that resulted in a pretty accurate picture of my relations with these students. I had not tried to sleep with them, and all my professional decisions regarding them seemed clearly based in recognizable and consistent professional standards. No evidence of either "sexual advances" or "retaliations" was to be found.

What the investigation did find was that I indulged in so-called sexual behavior that was generally matched by similar behavior directed toward me on the part of the students. Not only did they participate in sexual banter with me, but they were just as likely to initiate it as I was. With one of the students, this banter was itself so minimal that the case was dismissed. But because my relationship with the other complainant was much more elaborate, it was determined that this mutual relationship of flirtatious banter and frank sexual discussion violated the consensual-relations policy.

The woman who conducted the investigation thought that because I had a consensual "sexual relation" with a student, I should be considered guilty of sexual harassment. My lawyer argued that if this were a consensual relation, I was at most guilty of violating a university policy, not of breaking the federal law prohibiting harassment. While campus harassment policies increasingly encompass consensual relations, the laws that make harassment illegal not only do not concern themselves with such mutual relations, but would seem specifically to exclude them.

This confrontation between my lawyer and the university investigator (both specialists in the area of discrimination) demonstrates the gap opening of between a general understanding of harassment as unwanted sexual attention and this new sense of harassment operating in the academy today—which includes all teacher-student sexual relations, regardless of the student's desires.

After the investigation had been conducted, but before the findings were released, the university hired a lawyer from off-campus to head the affirmative-action office. It was she who wrote the final determination of my case. This lawyer found no probable cause to believe that I had sexually harassed anyone. But her determination does go on to find me guilty of violating university policy because I engaged with one of my students in a "consensual amorous relation."

The document explains the choice of "amorous" (a word that appears in the policy) as denoting a relation that was *"sexual" but did not involve sex acts*. Much less serious than quid pro quo harassment (trading professional support for sexual favors), less serious than hostile-environment harassment (discrimination by emphasis on sexuality), less serious even than consensual *sexual* relations, the precise finding of "consensual amorous relations" is, in fact, the slightest infraction comprised within the policy.

It was as if I had been accused of "first-degree harassment," and the charge had been reduced to something like "fourth-degree harassment." The distinction between sexual harassment and consensual relations becomes not a difference in kind but merely a difference in degree. The university found no evidence of compromised professional judgments, or of discrimination, unwanted sexual attention, or any sort of harassment; it found I wasn't even having sex with students. But the investigation revealed that I did not in fact respect the boundary between the sexual and the intellectual, between the professional and the personal. It was as if the university, seeing what kind of relations I did have with students, felt I must be *in some way* guilty and was able, through this wrinkle in the policy, to find me *slightly guilty of sexual harassment*.

The presumption on campuses today is that any sexual relation between a teacher and a student constitutes sexual harassment. One of our most esteemed universities explains: "What might appear to be consensual, even to the parties involved, may in fact not be so." The contrast here between "appearance" and "fact" suggests that so-called consensual-relations policies are *not in reality* about consensual relations, but about relations that are only *apparently* consensual. The policies assume that there is, in fact, no such thing as a consensual relation between a teacher and a student.

The policy of another major university elaborates: "The respect and trust accorded a professor by a student, as well as the power exercised by the professor in giving praise or blame, grades, recommendations, etc., greatly diminish the student's actual freedom of choice. Therefore, faculty are warned against even an apparently consenting relationship. The administration involved with a charge of sexual harassment shall be expected to be unsympathetic to a defense based upon consent when the facts establish that a professional power differential existed within the relationship."

Students do not have full freedom of choice; thus their consent is not true consent but merely the appearance of consent. The very existence of "a professional power differential" between the parties means a relationship will not be treated as consensual, regardless of whether consent was in fact granted. Because students cannot fully, freely, and truly consent, all teacher-student relations are presumed to be instances of sexual harassment.

As a teacher of feminist theory, I recognize this critique of consent. It is based on a radical feminist critique of heterosexuality. Students cannot "really" consent to sex with professors for the same reasons that women cannot "really" consent to sex with men. Feminists saw that economic arrangements make heterosexuality generally "compulsory" for women. In a society where women are economically disadvantaged, most women must depend on sexual relations with men (ranging from legal marriage to literal prostitution) for economic survival. If women need to have sex with men in order to survive, their consent to these sexual relations is not freely given.

There has been a good deal of confusion about what this critique of compulsory heterosexuality means. A few feminists have taken it to mean that no women *really want* to have sex with men. This then slides into the injunction that any woman who wants to be free *should not* have sex with men. Although only a very small number of feminists have ever taken this position, a lot of people have mistaken this extreme opinion for *the* feminist line. This confusion has resulted in widespread outrage at the idea that feminism would deny women the right to desire and enjoy men.

The feminist critique of compulsory heterosexuality was not meant to be a condemnation of heterosexuality per se but only of the way society forces men upon women without regard for our desire. Most feminists, in fact, understand this critique as an attempt to distinguish between socially coerced heterosexuality and women's actual desires for men. The crucial question is whether women are treated as mere sex objects or whether we are recognized as desiring subjects.

University administrators who piously intone against teacher-student sex, citing the student's impossibility to freely grant consent, would be shocked if they knew their position was based in a critique of the institution of marriage. And I don't think you could get them to agree to policies likewise prohibiting heterosexuality on the grounds that the power differential means a woman's consent is always to some extent coerced. Yet campuses around the country are formulating and enforcing policies that are the equivalent of the much-decried and seldom-embraced fringe feminist injunction against women sleeping with men.

As a feminist, I am well aware of the ways women are often compelled to sexual relations with men by forces that have nothing to do with our desire. And I see that students might be in a similar position with relation to teachers. But, as a feminist, I do not think the solution is to deny women or students the right to consent. Denying women the right to consent reinforces our status as objects rather than desiring subjects. That is why I believe the question of whether sexual advances are *wanted* is absolutely crucial.

Prohibition of consensual teacher-student relations is based on the assumption that when a student says yes she really means no. I cannot help but think that this proceeds from the same logic according to which when a woman says no she really means yes. The first assumption is protectionist; the second is the very logic of harassment. What harassment and protectionism have in common is precisely a refusal to credit women's desires. Common to both is the assumption that women do not know what we want, that someone else, in a position of greater knowledge and power, knows better.

I think back to that jubilant feminist dance I attended in 1971. Although sexual harassment was not a phrase we used in those days, unwanted sexual attention would pretty well describe the behavior of the guys who came to crash the party. They had, in fact, come with the explicit purpose of harassing us. Yet today, the notion of sexual harassment more likely would be applied to the mutually desirable relation between my women's studies teacher and the student who was her date to the dance.

When I think of that dance, I balk at the idea that teacher-student sex is synonymous with harassment. I remember the feminist student I was, what I wanted and what I didn't want, and I remember that it was precisely my sense of knowing what I did and didn't want that made me feel strong.

A year or so after that dance I began graduate school. My first semester there, feminist graduate students and faculty in the department recognized that I was a feminist and invited me to join a consciousness-raising group they were forming. It was in many ways a typical consciousness-raising group: In comparing our experiences we began to see them as not merely individual but as the shared experience of women. . . .

As I gather these experiences together—and place them in proximity to my seduction of my own teachers—I notice one consistency. In every instance, it was the student who made the first move; it was always the student who initiated sexual activity. This certainly runs counter to the cliché of the lecherous professor putting the moves on innocent young things. To be sure, I'm not trying to claim that teachers never make the first move; but that is not my experience. And I've had my share of experience, both as student and as teacher.

Although I no longer actually have sex with students, I still embrace such relations as principled. I resist the idea that what I did was wrong, and persist in seeing these liaisons as part of the wide range of sexual opportunities that I sampled as fully as possible in my younger days.

As someone who came of age during the sexual revolution, my teens and twenties were full of short-term serious romances and an even larger number of casual sexual encounters. This variety of experience was particularly good for me as a young intellectual woman, making me feel bold and forceful as well as desirable, helping me view the world as a place of diverse possibility. Especially for women pursuing the life of the mind, desire is a blessing rather than an insult. My desire gave me drive and energy; being an object of desire made me feel admired and wanted, worthy and lovable. Now long past my twenties, I am still convinced that desire is good and that when mutual desire makes itself felt, it is a very fine thing indeed.

Prohibitions against teacher-student relations seem based in a sense of sex as inherently bad. Sex for me is not some wholly separate, nasty, debased thing, but belongs more to the world of conversation and friendship, where people make contact with others who seem interesting, forceful, attractive. Because I value human connection above all else, I regard sex as a considerable good.

I think of my students primarily as people. As with people in general, I don't like some of them, I'm indifferent to many, and I find some of them especially admirable, congenial, or engaging. Although an awareness of our institutional roles definitely gave my affairs with students a certain pleasurable edge of transgression, I slept with students for essentially the same reasons I slept with other people—because they engaged me as human beings, because a spark of possibility lit between us.

It is ironic that relations between teachers and students have been banned as part of the fight against sexual harassment. We fight against sexual harassment precisely because it's dehumanizing, but the ban on consensual relations is dehumanizing too. Telling teachers and students that we must not engage each other sexually ultimately tells us that we must limit ourselves to the confines of some restricted professional transaction, that we *should not treat each other as human beings.*

Around 1990 I began to take loud and public exception to the new consensual-relations policies. I felt free to do so precisely because I hadn't been having sex with students since long before these policies came into existence. I thought I could risk opposing these policies because I was not in fact violating them.

This was, of course, before I found myself charged with sexual harassment. Two years after I started protesting these policies, the complaints against me were filed. A year after that, the university officially declared that I had violated its consensual-relations policy. Thus, I was found in violation of the very policy I had set about to protest.

I thought I was protesting a policy banning the sort of relations I used to have. I had not realized it was possible to apply the policy to the sorts of relations I still have with students.

Back in the days when I was sleeping with students, all the sex had taken place within a larger context of social and personal relations. For example, in that summer-school class where I started dating the grad student, there was another student, a female undergrad, whom I used to hang out with. She had great style, and I loved to go shopping for clothes with her. Or we'd go drinking and compare notes on the difficulties of dating men. The next year, while I rarely had sex with Scott, I often went uptown to a bar with him and his friends to play pinball. And my relation to Micki and Diane began as a friendship with a couple; at the time none of us expected the couple to break up. The drinking and talking, or going out on a weekend, was not unlike relations I had with other students.

I have such relations with students to this day, although now mainly with graduate students. I socialize with students in groups and singly: we might go out to dinner, play tennis, or see a movie. Or one of my graduate advisees will tell me about his love life while I thoroughly enjoy giving him advice. Some of my best friends are students. Even though I no longer have sex with students, my relations with students have not really changed at all.

Some of these personal relations remain pretty casual, but others get intense, complicated, and sticky. The intense relations involve students who take me very seriously as a teacher. These are students who want, in some way, to be intellectuals or academics like I am. And these are the students I most care about as a teacher.

It was indeed just such a relation that landed me in violation of the school's consensual-relations policy. When this graduate student took her first course from me, immediately after the second class meeting she came up and asked if we could talk. I told her to come to my office hours the next morning, but she didn't want to wait and pressed me to meet with her right then. Seeing how important it was to her, I relented and went with her to my office, despite the fact that it was 9:30 P.M. When we got there, she didn't even sit down but blurted out that she wanted me to be her advisor. She was jittery with excitement, and I was tickled to see someone who wanted that much to work with me. I immediately agreed to be her advisor; she was overjoyed and asked if we could go to the bar across the street to talk. Flattered by the ardor of her desire to work with me, I again agreed. And so began a relationship that involved not only working together in class and in my office, but going out for drinks and dinners, sometimes with other students or with her girlfriends, sometimes just the two of us.

Right from the start the relationship was not just professional, not even just social, but intensely personal and personally intense. She was, by her own admission, enamored of my work before she even met me. An ambitious woman with a flair for outrageous performance, she identified with me and thought I'd be the ideal teacher for her. I responded strongly to her desire for a career like mine. The relationship was charged with energy. And was, as such crucial relations often are, difficult. Because I believe that the most powerful educational experiences occur in an atmosphere of such intensity, I welcomed it, even though I often found it personally challenging.

I have had other teaching relationships that were as or more personal and intense. Although always tricky, they generally produce excellent results: I see the students consistently learn a lot, work really hard, and clearly benefit from working with me; I also learn a lot in such relationships and derive real satisfaction from seeing the difference I can make in the quality of their thinking and their work.

But, in this case, the relationship failed. Not because of its adventurous style but in the way so many teaching relations fall apart: More than once I told the student her work was not satisfactory; she did not accept my judgments and became increasingly suspicious and angry. And because so much passion had been invested in our relationship, the failure was particularly dramatic. The student felt let down, became outraged, and charged me with sexual harassment.

And because she did, the university had occasion to investigate my teaching practices. Although no evidence was found of the harassment the student claimed, the university looked at the pedagogical relation we had and decided it was against university rules.

As upsetting as it was to have someone I had worked so hard to help turn against me and accuse me of a loathsome crime, I am much more disturbed by the implications of the university's determination. Seeing a relation between a student enamored of a teacher's work, a student who wanted to be like that teacher, and the teacher who responded deeply to the student's desire to work with her, who wanted profoundly to help her do what she desired, the university deemed such a connection, passionate and involving so many personal hopes and dreams, an amorous relation.

And indeed it was.

In my formal response to the student's complaint, I used the psychoanalytic notion of "transference" to explain her relation to me. In psychoanalytic theory, transference is the human tendency to put people in the position our parents once held for us. It is a nearly universal response to people whose opinions of us have great authority, in particular doctors *and teachers*. Since our feelings about our parents include an especially powerful form of love, transference is undoubtedly an "amorous relation." But transference is also an inevitable part of any relationship we have to a teacher who really makes a difference.

In the official report on my case, the university recommends that in the future I should stop working with any student who has such a transference onto me. Which means that I would not work with any student who really believed I had something important to teach her. I would be forced to turn away precisely those students most eager to work with me, including those graduate students who come to the university where I teach expressly in order to work with me.

While I had vociferously opposed the consensual-relations policies before I was accused, I never dreamed how dangerous these policies could be. My case suggests the way the category of "amorous relations" can snowball. By moving from the restricted field of romantic love to the exceedingly wide field of relationships that are either social, personal, or involve intense feelings, what was originally a policy about sexual relations could become a policy restricting and chilling pedagogical relations.

At its most intense—and, I would argue, its most productive—the pedagogical relation between teacher and student is, in fact, a "consensual amorous relation." And if schools decide to prohibit not only sex but "amorous relations" between teacher and student, the "consensual amorous relation" that will be banned from our campuses might just be teaching itself.

PROFESSOR ACCUSED OF KISSING STUDENTS

. . . A group of women got up to dance together; my students invited me to join them. We all danced in a circle, reminding me of the women's group dancing of the early seventies. Although I had decided years ago that I was not a very good dancer and should stick to talking, in this context I was happy to participate in yet another reminder of the feminist pleasures of my student days.

When the dance was over, my advisee told me she was leaving. I had come to the bar with her and her friends, but I didn't want to leave yet. I found someone else who could give me a ride home and told my student I was staying. I wanted to prolong the conference day as much as possible, and I was going to stay at the bar as long as anyone from the conference was there.

She was leaving and I was staying; so we said good-bye. It had been our custom for some while to embrace upon parting. She had initiated this a few months earlier: She was dropping me off at my house and got out of her truck and asked if we could hug. Now we hugged and kissed whenever we said good-bye. But this time was different.

Our embrace would be witnessed by the assembled conference participants; it would be remembered the next day when she gave her paper about the erotics of our pedagogical relationship. The sense of an audience totally transformed our conventional gesture. In such a context, our customary, familiar embrace could not help but become a loaded performance.

We both were known to enjoy making spectacles of ourselves, and this opportunity for professional exhibitionism was bound to turn us on. We didn't say anything to each other, but somehow the usual good-bye peck suddenly became a real kiss.

I don't actually know who started it. I know it surprised me and seemed to occur simultaneously to both of us, as if spontaneously generated out of the moment. In any case, whichever of us actually initiated this torrid kiss, both of us were clearly into it.

It was a performance. By that, I do not mean that I wasn't really kissing her or that I didn't find it sexy. What I mean is that we didn't just happen to be seen kissing, but we kissed like that because we knew we were being watched. And it was precisely the knowledge of being watched that made it sexy.

I thought of the kiss as very much part of the conference, a sort of advance commentary on her paper the next day. I fancied that the kiss embodied a question about lesbian studies, trying to imagine "lesbian studies" not just as studies about lesbians or even studies by lesbians, but as a way of studying that is in itself somehow "lesbian," inbued with desire between women. To my mind, our student-teacher kiss enacted a fantasy of lesbian pedagogy: women together tasting from the forbidden tree of knowledge.

The kiss was brazen and public—and thus particularly appropriate for a conference distinguished by its intellectual and sexual daring. This was a performance tailor-made for the First Annual Graduate Student Gay and Lesbian Conference, whose title, after all, was "Flaunting It."

I thought I was back in 1971. Not that I thought I was a student again. But I thought I was back in a space where feminist professors and students, joined by a common pursuit of liberation, could play with our institutional roles rather than be limited by them.

I was wrong. I might have imagined it was 1971, but it was very much 1991. And the sight of a professor and a student kissing didn't signify sexy, new feminist pedagogical possibilities; it signified sexual harassment. It didn't matter that I was a woman; it didn't matter that I was a feminist; it didn't matter that we were at a conference exploring sexuality; it didn't matter that the student was obviously into this public display. All those connotations were obliterated by the fact that I was a professor and she a student.

I was, admittedly, trying to be outrageous. But I believed that I was in the company of other outrageous women, women who shared my ambition to flout conventional notions of propriety. I certainly did not think I was offending my student; I thought of her as a sort of partner in crime, likewise interested in being publicly appreciated as outrageous. Nothing she said or did that evening or for many months afterward suggested to me that she had any other relation to our joint performances.

But, a year and a half later, she charged me with sexual harassment. By then she no longer was my student, and we hadn't spoken in months. Her complaint alleged that she was upset by the kiss but had been too intimidated to tell me.

If she were upset, she showed no sign of it at the time. Whatever her real feelings might have been, those who witnessed the kiss saw her as a willing and even eager participant. And she was well aware of how it had looked. So aware that, when she decided to accuse me of harassment, she worried that the kiss would contradict her claim that I had subjected her to *unwanted* sexual advances.

She needn't have worried. In the climate of the nineties, our engagement in a *consensual* sexual relation (albeit one that lasted no more than a minute and didn't go below the neck) could actually function as "proof" of harassment. By the time she lodged her complaint, the question of whether her participation was willing or not didn't much matter. Professor/student sex had become more or less synonymous with sexual harassment.

On April 19, 1993, two years to the day after I kissed my advisee in a bar, the official student newspaper at our school ran the front-page banner headline: "Professor Accused of Kissing Students."

The article reports that an investigation was being conducted by the university affirmative-action office "into allegations that a female professor kissed two female students." According to the paper's informant (an unnamed faculty member in my department), "two female students have filed complaints about Jane Gallop, alleging that she kissed them."

The facts here are a tad confused. While there were indeed two complaints against me, I had kissed only one student. And that student didn't go to the affirmative-action office to complain that I'd kissed her. She went to claim that I tried to sleep with her and that, when she turned me down, I started rejecting her work. She filed her complaint in tandem with another student who made almost identical claims against me, even though I never kissed *her.* Both women charged me with classic quid pro quo sexual harassment.

The article, however never mentions sexual harassment. In the student newspaper version of things, the kiss looms so large that it is sufficient in and of itself to complain about. The article consults a paralegal from the university legal clinic who suggests that kissing "could be considered sexual contact" and that "if the students did not consent, the situations might be considered fourth-degree sexual assaults."

And if the students *had* consented? "Even if the two students did consent," the article goes on to say, "Gallop broke a university policy." The policy in question is quoted from the university's student handbook: "Consenting amorous or sexual relationships between instructor and student are *unacceptable.*"

This student newspaper account is almost comically ill-informed. The facts are muddled, the issue of sexual harassment is left out, and it looks like the affirmative-action office monitors not discrimination or even harassment but kissing. Yet, as silly as the article seemed, it was on to something.

At a moment when the investigator, the complainants, their supporters, my lawyer, and I were all focused on whether or not I was guilty of sexual harassment, the student newspaper completely ignored the entire question of harassment. Instead it focused exclusively on the kiss, treated it as if it were a sex act, and thus was led to the very policy that would ultimately determine the case.

At the time this article appeared, none of the principals in the case considered this policy applicable. But the investigation was still confidential, and the student reporter talked to no one directly involved—neither to the complainants, nor to the accused, nor to the investigator. He was ignorant of all our various complex and involved understandings and, perhaps *because* of his ignorance, he managed correctly to predict the official finding—eight months later—of "consenting amorous relationship."

The complainants were accusing me of serious crimes—sexual harassment, discrimination, and abuse of power—not of something as petty and ambiguous as a kiss. And even though I had kissed one student and not the other, they nevertheless insisted that I had treated them both the same. But the university begged to differ.

The official determination dismissed one complaint as improbable, while finding me at fault in the other. From the point of view of the university, one somewhat lengthy kiss made all the difference.

In its final determination, the university proved the silly, misinformed student newspaper version right. Although I had been accused of sexual harassment, the crime I was found guilty of was kissing students.

Nearly a year after the student newspaper article appeared, a local, left-leaning, countercultural weekly ran a wrap-up of the university investigation. Although this account only treats one of the complaints against me—the one by the student I *had* kissed—its coverage is otherwise thorough. Appearing after the investigation had been completed, this article was not hampered by the strictures meant to preserve confidentiality. The reporter had read the official determination and had interviewed both me and my accuser at length.

The article was written by the paper's news editor, who not only had been following the case for a year but had for several years been writing pieces exposing sexual harassment at the university. By dint of his muckraking, he had become a local expert on academic sex discrimination, harassment, and the doings of the affirmative-action office. With all this background, he produced a serious and well-informed account of the case.

Explicitly stating that "the case revolved around much more than the kiss," this article allots the kiss just one sentence. But that single sentence—while noting that the principals downplay the kiss—contends that the act is central to the case. Right next to the article, the weekly ran an eye-catching sidebar (boxed-in and shaded gray), devoted exclusively to the kiss.

Because the kiss is central, the paper features it. Because it is not supposed to be central, it is relegated to a sidebar. Incidental to the case proper, the case the complainants tried to make, the kiss is central to what the case nonetheless became. The flashy sidebar aptly represents the contradictory status of this kiss: tangential *and* prominent, both incidental and central.

The sidebar is signed with initials that match the article's byline. The local muckraker used a double strategy to cover the case. Not only did he produce two separate items to run side by side, but the two pieces present a striking contrast in tone.

The article proper is temperate, careful and balanced—perhaps even a bit too dry owing to its concentration on administrative procedure. On the other hand, the sidebar opens sensationally by quoting from the description of the kiss found in the student's complaint: "She mashed her lips against mine and shoved her tongue in my mouth."

Benefiting from the student's stylistic proclivity to pulp fiction, the sidebar portrays me as a literal as well as a figurative "masher." (A masher is "a man who attempts to force his amorous attentions upon a woman," my dictionary tells me.) And the reader is treated to a classic pulp kiss: a passive and innocent victim, an aggressor, violent verbs, images of forced penetration.

This is blatant sensationalism. It squeezes all the sex and violence it can out of what was, after all, just a kiss.

The sidebar infuriated me. It was excruciating to read this lurid description of myself, to think everyone in town was reading it. I fantasized turning public humiliation into superiority by getting up on my high-cultural horse, despising sensationalism and railing against exploitation. I imagined retaliating by unleashing a stock academic rant about the media, its pandering and lack of seriousness.

But, in this case, an attack on sensationalism was not going to work.

After all, it wasn't the media who made the kiss into a spectacle. That's what it was in the first place.

Sensationalism actually may be the most appropriate way to report the kiss, the best way to transmit its effect as provocative spectacle. The problem with the sidebar is not the sensationalism per se, but the way the flamboyant spectacle is split off from the serious treatment of the case. The sidebar literally takes the kiss out of context, isolating it from the larger story.

The article proper fulfills the journalist's responsibility to inform; the sidebar produces pleasure and excitement. While the split coverage implies that one effect has nothing to do with the other, the double coverage suggests they could really be linked.

People have been railing against sensationalism for at least as long as there have been newspapers. The fact that the complaint is as old as journalism itself suggests that it may not be possible or desirable to inform the public without also arousing sensations.

A journalist's responsibility is not unlike a professor's: both of us do research and transmit knowledge. To accuse a journalist of sensationalism is pretty much the equivalent of accusing a professor of sexualizing her teaching.

Sensationalism is not in and of itself bad journalism; it becomes bad precisely when sensation is split off from knowledge, when pleasure is procured at the expense of imparting knowledge. The same could be said about teaching. Sexy teaching is not in and of itself harassment. Sexual harassment occurs when sex is split off from teaching, when pleasure is procured at the expense of imparting knowledge.

Like the crusade to desexualize teaching, the attack on sensationalism involves fundamental assumptions about the relation between sex and knowledge. Both campaigns treat the incompatibility of sex and knowledge as a foregone conclusion: If it's sexy, it must not be knowledge.

Both campaigns are thus doomed to failure. It is no more possible to really teach without at times eliciting powerful and troubling sensations than it is to write powerfully without producing the same sort of sensations.

Teachers and writers might better serve the claims of knowledge if we were to resist not sex but the impulse to split off sex from knowledge.

When I said that graduate students were my sexual preference, when I kissed my advisee in a bar for all to see, I was making a spectacle of myself. And, at the same time, I was being a teacher.

The performance turned me on and was meant to turn my audience on, literally and figuratively. The spectacle was meant to shock and entertain, and to make people think.

I gave this book a tabloid title because I wanted, again, to make a spectacle of myself. When I told friends of the title, they worried that the book would be mistaken for sensationalism rather than a thoughtful consideration of important issues.

In fact, I'm hoping to produce a sensation. Not the hollow kind where sensation is achieved at the expense of thought. But the best kind, where knowledge and pleasure, sex and thought play off and enhance each other.

When I kissed my student at a conference, I was trying to produce just such a spectacle. But I failed to make myself understood.

By writing this book, I thought I'd give it another shot.

15

Reconciling Rapture, Representation, and Responsibility: An Argument against Per Se Bans on Attorney-Client Sex

Linda Fitts Mischler

INTRODUCTION

> A lawyer, like any other person, may in his private life be a cad or a king, an inconstant lover or a rock of stability, gracious or a grouch, but in his professional life he may not overstep the bounds and abuse his position of trust as counsel, confidante, champion and fiduciary.

These words make intuitive sense, but the line between personal life and professional life cannot always be drawn with precision, especially in the area of attorney-client sex. I argue in this article that the attorney has a personal "self" that is beyond the reach of professional regulation and that the indirect control of women effected by a per se ban on attorney-client sex

Linda Fitts Mischler gives a thoughtful account of the difficulties of regulating sexual encounters in professional-client relations. She argues against a "bright-line" test, emphasizing particularly the ways in which such a test might be detrimental to women. From "Reconciling Rapture, Representation, and Responsibility: An Argument against Per Se Bans on Attorney-Client Sex," *Georgetown Journal of Legal Ethics* 10:209–60 (1996). Copyright © 1996 by *Georgetown Journal of Legal Ethics*. Reprinted with permission of Georgetown University and *Georgetown Journal of Legal Ethics*.

is inappropriate. Rather than eclipse the personal self, the profession should undertake to nurture the responsible self in both attorney and client. . . .

Per se bans on attorney-client sex constitute an institutional control of sexuality that has its most egregious effect on women. While rules governing attorney-client sex appear to control male sexuality—by disciplining attorneys who engage the sexual relationships, the vast majority of whom are male—they indirectly control female sexuality by denying self-determination to female clients who desire a dual relationship with an attorney. The latter control is more repugnant because it is imposed rather than chosen. The attorney, as a member of the profession that enacted the prohibition, has in effect submitted to control of the sexual situation, while the female client is in a position of powerlessness. There is nothing new about this control of female sexuality, which is necessary to sustain a patriarchy dependent on institutionalized motherhood and heterosexuality.

The impact of attorney-client sex rules on clients cannot be ignored, and statistics show that the impact is felt almost exclusively by female clients. These rules strip women of sexual autonomy by denying them choice. The position of powerlessness is not rendered palatable by the fact that the woman may choose the intimate relationship by terminating the professional relationship. The crucial problem is depriving an adult of the ability to consent to a sexual relationship with a partner of her choosing.

Blanket prohibitions of sexual relations reek of paternalism and perpetuate stereotypes of female weakness and dependence:

> Indeed, by creating an absolute presumption of harm, the [rule creator] implicitly decides that a woman "will always be incapable of giving informed consent to a sexual relationship" once she comes under the domineering influence of a male professional. Moreover, such a presumption implies that women are simply incapable of dealing equally with men in the professional-client context.

Under the rules in California, Oregon, and New York, a woman may choose her lover as her lawyer, but not her lawyer as her lover. This distinction presumes that a professional relationship reduces a woman to a helpless waif and deprives her of the ability to think rationally.

Per se bans on attorney-client sex reflect deep-seated societal views toward women and sexuality generally. Western culture tends to interpret the world in hierarchical terms, a result, no doubt, of monotheism's emphasis on omnipotence and impotence. Within this "zero-sum" world view, males are socialized to be sexual aggressors and to exert power over females. Women are culturally defined as immature, dependent, passive, easily influenced, illogical, and unable to separate feelings from ideas. Sex between men and women, then, is typically seen not as an egalitarian, consensual meeting between two people for mutual benefit, but as a conquest, the use of one person's power to gain control over another, less powerful, person. "'[M]ale sexuality and violence in our culture seem to be inseparable.' . . . [R]ape represents an archetypical model of eroticism—the blending of sex and violence in one act."

Given this culturally presumed sexual hierarchy, it is perhaps not surprising that professional-client sex has been analogized to rape and parent-child incest. An abuse of power is assumed. When commentators discuss attorney-client sex, they almost always refer to the attorney placing his personal interests "above" those of the client. This hierarchical world view does not accommodate a view of attorney and client with sexual interests on a par, regardless of legal knowledge. According to this view, power in one area—professional expertise—renders the attorney powerful in all areas, including sexual potency. Consensual, egalitarian sex is beyond comprehension. It is not surprising that disciplinary rules prohibiting attorney-client sex are based on stereotypical concepts of men, women, and social power. "The presumptions about the differences between the sexes taken for granted in the culture are formalized as the rationales for *legal discrimination* between them."

The fallacy at the base of the per se bans on attorney-client sex is the concept of all sex as involving abuse of power, as in rape or incest. All sex is *not* rape. "The realization that rape is a crime of violence and has little to do with sexual gratification is just beginning to penetrate popular consciousness." Nor is attorney-client sex incest. This comparison takes the concept of female-client-as-child to its logical extreme. The client is presumed vulnerable, immature, in need of protection, and unable to make rational decisions. An adult client is *not* a child, and an attorney is *not* a parent. Indeed, an attorney may not ethically adopt a parental role in the conventional sense that involves surrogate decision making and substituted judgment.

The client-as-child analogy, which implies impaired decision-making ability, seems to be reserved for female clients.

16

✠

Exploited Consent

David Archard

Sexual relations between professionals—I have in mind here doctors, teachers, therapists, counselors, and even priests in a pastoral role—and their clients are rightly a matter of concern. Some codes of ethics expressly forbid such relations; others advise against, or stipulate conditions such as notification of the affair to a responsible other. One immediate and obvious reason for concern is that such sexual intimacy must compromise the professional nature of the relationship. This requires impartiality, objectivity, and independence. A teacher cannot be a fair-minded assessor of the work of a student with whom he has slept or is sleeping.

Such a distortion of the professional's role may also have adverse effects on third parties. Other patients will distrust and perhaps refuse to share con-

David Archard discusses the problem of the exploitation of consent in professional-patient relationships. He develops an account of how consent is problematic when it trades on inequality in the relationship. From David Archard, "Exploited Consent," *Journal of Social Philosophy* 25: 92-101 (1994). Copyright © 1994 by *Journal of Social Philosophy*. Reprinted with permission of Blackwell Publishers.

fidences with a doctor who they know to be sexually or romantically involved with a patient.

But let us imagine that these harmful consequences can be eliminated or at least significantly diminished. The professional does conscientiously strive to preserve his independent and fair-minded stance. He is successful in keeping his private emotions separated from his public role. He is also discrete, and relations with other clients are not corrupted. Let us further imagine that the relationship in question is consensual. Is it not now evident that the harms are insufficient to proscribe the relationship, especially given the familiar presumption in favor of freely chosen, self-regarding activity? Indeed, does it not demean the client and deny her autonomy not to accept that her consent should count?

One important reason for not answering these questions in the affirmative lies in challenging the assumption that such relationships can be truly consensual. I want to explore this line of argument by carefully distinguishing coerced, incapacitated, and manipulated consent from what I shall call exploited consent. It is the latter concept that I am chiefly interested in, and although I discuss it in the context of professional relations, I hope to show that it has a much wider application. . . .

Consent shall not count if it is incapacitated by ignorance or a serious failure of will. Someone does not consent if she does not know what she is consenting to. A patient who falsely believes that sexual intercourse with her doctor is a form of medical treatment does not truly consent to that intercourse. Nor shall consent count if the will of the person who gives her consent is, in some way, seriously impaired. By this I mean such things as being under the influence of alcohol or drugs, or suffering from a mental disorder.

The irrationality need not be permanent, nor amount to certifiable madness. It may encompass temporary but serious emotional instability, and can include, then, the case of the "highly vulnerable" or "desperately needy" woman who sleeps with her therapist. Or that of a woman, suffering severe grief at a family bereavement, who begins an affair with the priest who visits to console her. In none of these instances is there that clear sighted, voluntary undertaking of a course of action that should normally characterize consensual behavior.

By manipulated consent I mean any deliberate but morally questionable distortion of the conditions under which consent is given in order to make the giving of that consent more likely. This will include the intentional withholding of relevant information or deception, as well as attempts to make more pronounced that character trait of someone that disposes them to consent. Manipulation excludes persuasion, or any reasoned argument, which might convince the other to agree. Manipulation seeks not to argue for its end, but to exacerbate any weaknesses of will, emotions, or psychological irregularity that would secure consent. It is this that makes it morally suspect.

Interesting here is the concept of *seduction*. It has the literal sense of lead-ing astray. Yet he who persuades another to do wrong may be himself guilty of several distinct wrongs. He may be adjudged guilty as an accessory before the fact, counseling or commissioning another in the performance of wrong, and liable to the same condemnation as the actual wrongdoer. But he may also have manipulated the consent by, for instance, falsely representing its benefits, or trading on what he knows to be a pronounced weakness of will in respect of some course of action. However, it is worth keeping these two features of seduction separate. He who is seduced may be misled but also may be led into error.

To summarize so far: A client's consent to sexual relations with a profes-sional does not legitimate these relations if the consent is coerced, incapaci-tated, or manipulated. The professional is guilty of misconduct if he secures consent under these conditions. I also ruled out sexual harassment, and even consensual relations if they interfere with the impartial conduct of profes-sional affairs or damaged third parties. Now imagine a case that violates none of these excluding conditions. Is *it* not permissible and is not the con-sent here both freely given and valid?

It is at this point that I wish to introduce the notion of *exploited consent*. The gist of the idea is that such consent is only, and thus probably wrongly, given because of the unequal nature of the relationship between two peo-ple. More formally, A's consent to B's proposal is exploited if:

1. A's giving of consent is attributable, wholly or insignificant part, to the nature of the positions occupied by A and B within their relationship.

Put another way, and in explanation of these attribution of giving of consent:

1. A's consent would not be given to B if A and B did not occupy these positions.
2. As a consequence of their occupancy of these different positions, A and B are unequal in some significant respect(s).
3. Such inequality is necessary if the duties and functions of these posi-tions are successfully to be discharged.
4. The relationship that defines the positions occupied by A and B has a certain scope. Internal to, or defined by the terms of that re-lationship is an understanding of the range of activities appropri-ately covered by that relationship.
5. B appreciates, or can reasonably be expected to appreciate the truth of 1-4.

A pupil sleeps with her teacher or patient with her therapist because he is her teacher or therapist. She would be most unlikely to do so if he was not in this position. The relationship between professional and client is characterized by a fundamental inequality in a variety of respects: dependency, power, status, and expertise. She is dependent on his help; he is not on hers. He has a power significantly to affect her future, whereas she does not have the power to affect his future. It is important to recognize that here power is characterized as a capacity rather than its exercise or even disposition to exercise it in certain ways. His is a position with recognized social status and financial rewards; she most likely comes into the professional relationship without anything comparable. He has established and accredited skills to which she defers when she enters the professional relationship.

This inequality is necessary to or unavoidably follows from the conduct of the professional relationship. It might be attenuated in some of its respects but it cannot be in all. A doctor must be able to diagnose and prescribe for the well-being of someone who cannot. A teacher must be able to guide the learning of someone who is not, initially at least, able to do so for themselves.

Each professional relationship has its more or less well-defined scope. It is inappropriate, normally, for a doctor to advise a patient on the best make of car his patient should purchase. Or he would be unlikely to do so as a doctor. "Inappropriate" here need not have any moral connotations, any more than it would in the description of a chef's inclusion of his personal appearance in a recipe as "inappropriate." An understanding of this scope by both parties is important to the success of the relationship. It encourages a mutual trust that may nevertheless be more pronounced in the client. She knows what to expect from the professional and is confident in the relationship to the extent that this is confirmed by his actions.

The professional understands the scope of the relationship he enjoys with his client. He must also recognize that his client may consent to proposals he makes only or principally in virtue of the position he occupies within their relationship. Whether the explanation lies in a technical concept like "transference," or a common sense understanding of the crushes pupils can have on their teachers, he would be naive, self-deceiving, or self-serving if he attributed his influence on the other solely to his personal characteristics. If nothing else a well-publicized code of professional ethics serves to remind practitioners of the scope of their relationship to clients and its consequent responsibilities.

This then is exploited consent. The use of the term "exploited" is appropriate since it appeals to the core understanding of exploitation as one side taking unfair advantage of another. A more formal representation of exploitation sees it as defining any situation in which one party does better, and the other worse, than both would do in some alternative set of circumstances. Further, the difference between actuality and the conceivable alternative can be specified in terms of differential access to some set of resources. For a Marxist, capitalist exploitation arises insofar as the capitalist, but not the proletariat, has effective control over the means of production.

Is exploited consent exploitative in this sense? I have already argued that the professional would not receive the client's consent and the client would not give it if they did not occupy their respective positions in the professional relationship. It needs then to be shown that the giving of this consent benefits the professional but disadvantages the client. Are even consensual sexual relations in this context asymmetrical? I think that they can be shown to be.

The literature on sexuality within the context of work and professional organizations is very thin. If, however, one takes sexual relationships within the context of professional education, what studies there have been suggest that the vast majority of students who enter into affairs with their lecturers suffer as a consequence. They do not subsequently report that they were glad to have had the experience. Quite the contrary.

There is a ready explanation for this which derives from the inequality that characterizes the relationship. This is that, although a student may consent to an affair with her lecturer, her consent is not secured for the *terms* of its conduct. That is to say that the student has no control over how the sexual relationship, once entered into, is run. She is unlikely to be able to determine, for instance, how long it lasts, how regular the contact is, who initiates meetings, who knows about it, where it is conducted, what is ruled in or out as an appropriate expression of the relationship, and so on. This lack of control is directly related to the inequality between herself and the lecturer as professional. Put another way, if the two individuals did not occupy their respective positions within a professional relationship, and had a liaison, it is most unlikely that there would be the same inability on the part of one person to have a say in how the relationship was managed.

Is exploited consent wrong for being exploitative? Some forms of exploitation may be normal and not unjust insofar as differential advantage accrues to those whose better position in some context has arisen in the right kind of way. I have argued that an inequality characterizes the professional relationship. This is not unjustified inasmuch as occupancy of the superior position is merited on grounds of training, skill, experience, and qualification. That the professional enjoys benefits that the client cannot, need not be exploitative. Exploited consent *is* exploitation, however, because the activity to which the consent is given and which benefits the professional exceeds the scope of the professional relationship. As an exploitation of that relationship, what it is inappropriate, in a nonmoral sense, for that relationship to encompass, is morally inappropriate and unfair.

Moreover, exceeding the scope of the relationship is incompatible with its conduct in a further way. It undermines the very trust and confidence that, I suggested, arises from the relationship being managed within its own proper terms and thereby makes its future successful management more likely. Exploitation of a professional relationship is both wrong and destructive.

In the concluding section of this article I want to make several qualifying remarks that I hope will allow light to be shed beyond the strict terms of the professional relationship. The first of these concerns the question of why consent is forthcoming as a result of occupancy of a position within a professional relationship. I have given no explanations except to suggest that professionals would be ingenuous or indeed disingenuous to deny that there is *something* about being the client of a professional that disposes them to consent.

Any explanation must, it seems to me, satisfy a number of requirements. The first is to take sufficient account of the fact that it is overwhelmingly *male* professionals who enter into sexual relationships with *female* clients. The second is to take sufficient account of the inequalities that characterize the professional relationship without reducing the client to the status of a passive victim. The third is to be able adequately to distinguish the professional relationship from ordinary everyday relationships. Lying behind these requirements is a concern that the distinctive structures of male power be recognized without caricaturing women as always and everywhere its powerless prey.

I would suggest three characteristics of professional relationships that are relevant. The first is an ethos of intimacy, closeness, trust, openness, and confidence. The second is the relative dependence and vulnerability of the client. The third is the esteem, respect, and admiration that the client has for the professional. All of these dispose the client to be more open and receptive to the proposals of the professional. Anecdotal evidence suggests clients are flattered and boosted in their self-esteem by the attentions of professionals. The more these features are made apparent, the more the securing of consent to sexual intimacy can be seen as evidently exploitative.

The second set of qualifying remarks is directed to the question of whether exploitation occurs when a professional enters into a sexual relationship with someone who is not their client. Conditions (1) and (2) of my definition of exploited consent can be construed as applying. Although A and B are not in a professional relationship, A's consent to B's proposal may be attributable to A's being, and being perceived as, the occupier of a position that has a measure of prestige, power, and so on. A may sleep with B because he is *a* doctor or teacher, but not because he is *her* doctor or whatever. It is not uncommon to speak of somebody exploiting their position to their own advantage in just such a situation. Do politicians not aver that power is an aphrodisiac? If this is not seen as wrong, it is surely because there is nothing in our understanding of the everyday relationship between professional and nonprofessional that says sexual intimacy is inappropriate, that is outside its proper scope. This may be a self-serving intuition, but we must be careful not to condemn any consensual relation whose parties are not the equals of one another. If we do, we surely condemn too much.

The third set of remarks concerns the "innocent" uses of exploited consent. There are, it may be suggested, activities that a client performs for a professional that fall outside the scope of the professional relationship and consent to which is exploited under my definition, but whose performance does not seem to be obviously wrong. Consider, for example, a doctor who regularly requests and receives a lift home from a patient, or asks for, gets, and repays a loan from a patient, or has a patient baby-sit for him.

I think we would want to say the following: It is disturbing that a professional should use his position in this way even if it does not seriously compromise his professional relationship. If he is prepared to exploit his position to secure these benefits would he not be disposed to do so for more significant, and more obviously immoral purposes? We also recognize that there is an ascending scale of seriousness here. Securing a loan is worse than merely obtaining a lift home. Yet there is something especially serious about exploited consent in the case of sexual relations. This is surely because sexuality is an area in which it is particularly important to treat one another as ends, that is to take into account and respect a person's wishes and beliefs. We are acutely aware of the dangers of failing to do so, and to that extent regard full, knowing, and considered consent as a prerequisite or at least ideal requirement of intimacy.

17

Illustrative Policies

University policies on sexual harassment range from policies that track Title VII and Title IX quite narrowly, to policies that attempt to explain how legal requirements will be applied in the context of their own campuses, to policies with a broad sweep.

Reprinted here as examples of narrow policies that track federal law are those from the University of Florida and the University of Washington.

Somewhat more expansive are the policies from the University of Utah and Duke University, which attempt to capture the relationship between harassment policy and academic freedom.

Efforts to explain what is and is not permissible in the student-faculty pedagogical relationship are found in the policies from Harvard University and Wellesley College.

Finally, perhaps the most far-reaching policy has been developed and implemented by Antioch College for its Yellow Springs campus.

These policies are reprinted here as examples for discussion and policy formulation on campus. My aim was to select a variety so that readers would have illustrations of the type of policies that have been developed and adopted.

UNIVERSITY OF FLORIDA POLICY ON SEXUAL HARASSMENT

Sexual harassment is unwelcome conduct of a sexual nature. It constitutes a form of sex discrimination and is a form of employee misconduct that undermines the integrity of the University. All employees and students must be allowed to work in an environment free from unsolicited and unwelcome sexual overtures.

Sexual harassment does not refer to occasional compliments; it refers to behavior of a sexual nature that interferes with the work or education of its victims and their coworkers or fellow students.

Sexual harassment is a violation of both state and federal laws and of the rules and regulations of the University. Employees and students are responsible for their actions of sexual harassment. These actions may subject them to appropriate University disciplinary action up to and including dismissal or expulsion.

Further, any employee or student in a supervisory capacity who has knowledge of possible sexual harassment [and] who does not report the matter pursuant to the University's policy will be subject to disciplinary action up to and including dismissal or expulsion.

A supervisor may obtain knowledge of sexual harassment by direct observation, statements made by others (staff members), or by receipt of a complaint of sexual harassment (whether it be written or oral).

It is the intent of this policy to protect all members of the University community while trying to address and resolve the problem and eliminate any inappropriate behavior.

Please direct your questions or concerns about sexual harassment to the Affirmative Action Office at 392-6004.

UNIVERSITY OF WASHINGTON POLICY
ON SEXUAL HARASSMENT

Sex discrimination in the form of sexual harassment, defined as the use of one's authority or power, either explicitly or implicitly, to coerce another into unwanted sexual relations or to punish another for his or her refusal, or as the creation by a member of the University community of an intimidating, hostile, or offensive working or educational environment through verbal or physical conduct of a sexual nature, shall be a violation of the University's human rights policy. (University Handbook, Vol. IV, p. 44)

While most harassment involves men harassing women, either men or women can be harassed by members of the same or opposite sex. The University of Washington policy prohibits all forms of sexual harassment. The University will carry out a thorough investigation, protecting the rights of both the person complaining and the alleged harasser.

The University has been very successful in resolving sexual harassment complaints. If you believe you are being harassed, seek help the earlier the better. The University has designated special people to help you. Call the University Ombudsman and Ombudsman for Sexual Harassment at 543-0283 or 543-6028, or the University Complaint Investigation and Resolution Office at 616-2028.

DUKE UNIVERSITY HARASSMENT POLICY

This harassment policy applies to all persons who are enrolled or employed by Duke University. All such persons may use the accompanying grievance procedures in seeking resolution of harassment complaints involving other members of the Duke University community.*

Harassment of any kind is not acceptable at Duke University; it is inconsistent with the university's commitments to excellence and to respect for all individuals. Duke University is also committed to the free and vigorous discussion of ideas and issues, which the university believes will be protected by this policy. Pursuant to these commitments, and as a complement to Duke University's Equal Opportunity Policy, the following policy is adopted.

I. Duke University is committed to protecting the academic freedom and freedom of expression of all members of the university community. This policy against harassment shall be applied in a manner that protects the academic freedom and freedom of expression of all parties to a complaint. Academic freedom and freedom of expression include, but are not limited to, the expression of ideas, however controversial, in the classroom, in residence halls, and, in keeping with different responsibilities, in workplaces elsewhere in the university community.

II. Harassment at Duke University is defined as follows:

A. The creation of a hostile or intimidating environment, in which verbal or physical conduct, because of its severity and/or persistence, is likely to interfere significantly with an individual's work or education, or affect adversely an individual's living conditions.

This Harassment Policy replaces previous statements on harassment, sexual harassment in employment, and sexual harassment of students. Specifically it replaces Appendix W of the Faculty Notebook Policy IX.180 and Policy IX.190 in the Duke University Policy Manual, and the statement on Sexual Harassment of Students in the various school bulletins.

+Applicants for admission or employment who feel that they have been harassed by employees of Duke University and students and employees of Duke University who feel they have been harassed by persons doing business with the university should report their complaints to the Office of the University Vice-President and Vice-Provost.

B. Sexual coercion is a form of harassment with specific distinguishing characteristics. It consists of unwelcome sexual advances, requests for sexual favors, or other verbal or physical conduct of a sexual nature when:

1. submission to such conduct is made explicitly or implicitly a term or condition of an individual's employment or education; or
2. submission or rejection of such conduct is used as a basis for employment or educational decisions affecting an individual.

C. The conduct alleged to constitute harassment under this policy shall be evaluated from the perspective of a reasonable person similarly situated to the complainant and considering all the circumstances.

III. In considering a complaint under the Duke University Harassment Policy, the following understandings shall apply:

A. Harassment must be distinguished from behavior which, even though unpleasant or disconcerting, may be appropriate to the carrying out of certain instructional advisory or supervisory responsibilities.

B. In so far as Title VII (Equal Employment Opportunity) of the Civil Rights Act of 1964 is applicable (i.e., in complaints concerning carrying out of noninstructional workplace responsibilities), the university will use the definition of sexual harassment found in the Equal Employment Opportunity Commission (EEOC) Guidelines: "conduct of a sexual nature when such conduct has the purpose or effect of unreasonably interfering with an individual's work performance or creating an intimidating, hostile, or offensive working environment." The university will use new EEOC guidelines as they are promulgated. The community will be notified if such changes occur.

C. Instructional responsibilities require appropriate latitude for pedagogical decisions concerning the topics discussed and methods used to draw students into discussion and full participation.

D. In interactions of students and other members of the Duke community in social and living situations, the university believes it is generally more appropriate to encourage and nurture positive interactions and understanding between complainants and respondents rather than to invite charges of harassment for individual episodes of hostile, disrespectful, or intimidating speech.

IV. Individuals who believe that they have been harassed in violation of this policy should consult the Duke University Grievance Procedures for Claims of Harassment.

V. This Harassment Policy and the Grievance Procedures for Claims of Harassment are the only part of Duke University's effort to prevent harassment in our community. In addition to offering channels for making and resolving complaints, the university is also committed to programs of education to raise awareness concerning the nature of harassment and ways to prevent harassing behaviors.

Responding to Harassing Situations

A member of the Duke University community who believes that he or she has been harassed in violation of the Harassment Policy is encouraged to take action in any of the ways described here. Although none of the informal activities below are required before an individual may file a formal complaint, the Duke University Harassment Policy favors informal resolution of Harassment claims whenever such resolutions can be effected fairly.

UNIVERSITY OF UTAH SEXUAL HARASSMENT AND CONSENSUAL RELATIONSHIPS

Sexual harassment is defined as unwelcome sexual advances, requests for sexual favors, and other verbal or physical conduct of a sexual nature. Conduct alleged to be sexual harassment will be assessed by considering the totality of the particular circumstances in each case. Sexually related conduct may form the basis of a sexual harassment claim if a reasonable person would consider it sufficiently severe or pervasive to interfere with participation in the many opportunities at the University. These opportunities include education, employment, and involvement in the programs and activities on campus.

The free and open discussion of issues or theories relating to sexuality or gender in an academic or professional setting, when appropriate to subject matter, will be presumed not to constitute sexual harassment even if it offends or embarrasses an individual unless other factors are involved. Such factors include targeting the discussion to an individual or carrying out the discussion in terms that are both patently unnecessary and gratuitously offensive.

Romantic or sexual relationships between a faculty member and a student are generally unwise because of the power imbalance in the relationship. Even when both parties have consented to the development of such relationships, they can raise serious questions about the validity of such consent, conflicts of interest, and unfair treatment of others. Therefore, when the faculty member has any direct responsibility for evaluating the student's academic performance or professional future, a romantic or sexual relationship between faculty member and student, even a mutually consenting one, will be considered to constitute a violation of this policy unless the situation is remedied by reassigning responsibilities, etc.

Any faculty member who believes there is or has been an incident of sexual harassment should contact the cognizant academic chair or dean of the department or college within which the conduct occurred, the human resources department, the dean of student affairs, or the Office of Equal Opportunity and Affirmative Action (OEO/AA). The faculty member should also advise the informing individual of the option of an aggrieved party, to file a complaint with OEO/AA. Complaints regarding a possible violation of the sexual harassment/consensual relationship policy of the University may be filed in accordance with the options outlined in *PPM* 2-32.

The confidentiality of all parties involved in a sexual harassment complaint or concern shall be respected insofar as it does not interfere with the University's legal obligation to investigate allegations and to take corrective action or as otherwise provided by law.

HARVARD UNIVERSITY GUIDELINES

Sexual Harassment and Unprofessional Conduct: Guidelines in the Faculty of Arts and Sciences

The Faculty of Arts and Sciences [FAS] seeks to maintain a learning and work environment free from sexual harassment, including unprofessional conduct in faculty-student relationships and sexism in the classroom. These kinds of behavior are barriers to the educational, scholarly, and research purposes of the University.

Any member of the FAS community who believes that he or she has been sexually harassed, who has experienced problems involving unprofessional conduct, or who would like clarification or information on FAS complaint and resolution procedures is encouraged to speak with an appropriate officer of the Faculty. A list of officers is attached. There are specific procedures for the resolution of sexual harassment and unprofessional conduct problems. These cover situations involving individuals of different University status and individuals of the same University status. They range from informal counseling and mediation to formal procedures for disciplinary action. A written description of these procedures is available upon request from any of the officers listed.

(Please note that members of the Harvard Union of Clerical and Technical Workers [HUCTW] are covered by the sexual harassment policies agreed to in the collective bargaining agreement and described in the *Personnel Manual*. For union members these policies take precedence over the policies governing other members of the University community.)

Sexual Harassment

Sexual harassment is unacceptable because it interferes with a person's sense of dignity and well-being in the community. The determination of what constitutes sexual harassment will vary with the particular circumstances, but it may be described generally as unwanted sexual behavior, such as physical contact or verbal comments, jokes, questions, or suggestions. In the academic context, the fundamental element of sexual harassment is ordinarily the inappropriate personal attention by an instructor or other officer who is in a position to exercise professional power over another individual. This could involve an instructor who determines a student's grade or who can otherwise affect the student's academic performance or professional future; or a tenured professor whose evaluation of a junior colleague can affect the latter's professional life. Sexual harassment can also occur between persons of the same University status. An example would be persistent personal attention in the face of repeated rejection of such attention. Such behavior is unacceptable in a university. It seriously undermines the atmosphere of trust essential to the academic enterprise.

Unprofessional Conduct in Relationships between Individuals of Different University Status

Amorous relationships that might be appropriate in other circumstances always have inherent dangers when they occur between any teacher or officer of the University and any person for whom he or she has a professional responsibility (i.e., as teacher, advisor, evaluator, supervisor). Implicit in the idea of professionalism is the recognition by those in positions of authority that in their relationships with students or staff there is always an element of power. It is incumbent upon those with authority not to abuse, nor to seem to abuse, the power with which they are entrusted.

Officers and other members of the teaching staff should be aware that any romantic involvement with their students makes them liable for formal action against them. Even when both parties have consented at the outset to the development of such a relationship, it is the officer or instructor who, by virtue of his or her special responsibility and educational mission, will be held accountable for unprofessional behavior. Graduate student teaching fellows, tutors, and undergraduate course assistants may be less accustomed than faculty members to thinking of themselves as holding professional responsibilities. They may need to exercise special care in their relationships with students whom they instruct, evaluate, or otherwise supervise, recognizing that their students might view them as more powerful than they may perceive themselves to be.

Amorous relationships between members of the Faculty and students that occur outside the instructional context can also lead to difficulties. In a personal relationship between an officer and a student for whom the officer has no current professional responsibility, the officer should be sensitive to the constant possibility that he or she may unexpectedly be placed in a position of responsibility for the student's instruction or evaluation. This could involve being called upon to write a letter of recommendation or to serve on an admissions or selection committee involving the student. In addition, one should be aware that others may speculate that a specific power relationship exists even when there is none, giving rise to assumptions of inequitable academic or professional advantage for the student involved. Relationships between officers and students are always fundamentally asymmetric in nature.

Sexism in the Classroom

Sexism in the classroom usually involves conduct by members of the teaching staff that is discouraging or offensive especially, but not only, to women. Alienating messages may be subtle and even unintentional, but they nevertheless tend to compromise the learning experience of members of both sexes.

Some teaching practices are overtly hostile to women. For example, to show slides of nude women humorously or whimsically during an otherwise serious lecture is not only in poor taste, but is also demeaning to women.

Other alienating teaching practices may be simply thoughtless, and may even be the result of special efforts to be helpful to women students. For example, it is condescending to make a point of calling only upon women, in class on topics such as marriage and the family, imposing the assumption that only women have a natural interest in this area.

Consistent with principles of academic freedom, course content and teaching methods remain the province of individual faculty members. At the same time, faculty members should refrain from classroom behavior that focuses attention on sex characteristics in a context in which sex would otherwise be irrelevant.

NOTE: Anyone interested in arranging a training or discussion session concerning sexual harassment should call Janet Viggianni, 495-1560.

WELLESLEY COLLEGE GUIDELINES

I. Policy Against Sexual Harassment

A. General Policy Against Sexual Harassment and Definition

Sexual harassment is against the law and is explicitly prohibited by Title VII of the 1964 Civil Rights Act as well as by Massachusetts law. The standard reference, paraphrased in the 1981 Wellesley College policy statement, is the Equal Employment Opportunity Commission's (EEOC) "Policy Statement on Sexual Harassment" (1984). We have adopted a slightly edited version of the University of Minnesota's definition, which adapts EEOC language to the academic setting:

Definition of Sexual Harassment

¶1. Unwelcome sexual advances, requests for sexual favors, or other verbal or physical conduct of a sexual nature constitute sexual harassment when

¶2. submission to such conduct is made either explicitly or implicitly a term or condition of an individual's employment or academic advancement,

¶3. submission to or rejection of such conduct by an individual is used as the basis for employment decisions or academic decisions affecting such individual,

¶4. such conduct has the purpose or effect of unreasonably interfering with an individual's work or academic performance or creating an intimidating, hostile, or offensive working or academic environment.

B. Examples: What Does or Does Not Constitute Sexual Harassment

1. General Examples The kinds of behaviors which may constitute sexual harassment include, but are not limited to:

a. Insults of a sexual nature, including lewd, obscene, or sexually suggestive displays and remarks or conduct
b. Repeated unwanted touching, patting, or pinching
c. Repeated sexist remarks and sexist behavior
d. Repeated inappropriate social invitations or repeated unwanted requests for sexual favors
e. Repeated unwanted discussions of sexual matters
f. Requests or demands for sexual favors accompanied by implicit or explicit promised rewards or threatened punishment
g. Threatened, attempted, or completed physical sexual assault

Under these definitions, regardless of sexual preference or status, all members of the community may become harassers or victims of harassment: men, women, faculty members, students, Union personnel, staff members, and others associated with the college.

2. Vignettes: Sexual Harassment These behaviors may give rise to claims of sexual harassment under Wellesley College's "Policy Against Sexual Harassment," and, if the allegations were proven, may subject the harasser to disciplinary action:

a. Wendy is failing one of the courses required for her major. Her instructor offers to help her in the evening at home. In the course of the evening, the instructor makes it clear that granting sexual favors will improve Wendy's grade. [This constitutes sexual harassment under *Definition* ¶2 and under *General Examples*, section (f).]

b. Lisa, an instructor, is invited by one of her colleagues to share a hotel room when they attend a professional meeting. When she refuses, the colleague accuses her of being immature and expresses doubts about her ability to handle professional situations. [See *Definition*, especially ¶4 but also ¶2 and ¶3 depending upon the rank of the colleague; and *General Examples*, section (f). See also (d) and (e) if request is repeated.]

c. Judy is a work-study student in Food Services. Her coworkers regularly leave pornographic pictures where she will find them. She dreads going to work because of the situation. [See *Definition* ¶4; *General Examples*, section (a).]

d. Lee is an assistant professor. The department chair has been initiating conversations about sexual practices and has recently begun pressuring Lee for sex. When Lee refuses, the chair threatens to see to it that Lee is not promoted. [See ¶2; also ¶3-¶4; *General Examples*, section (e) and (f)]

e. Students in a seminar know that their professor is in a sexual relationship with one of their classmates. Although professor and student try to be discreet about their relationship, the other students notice the special attention their classmate receives. They feel this creates a hostile learning environment in the class. [See *Definition* ¶4.]

3. Vignettes: Not Sexual Harassment This set of cases shows clashes of beliefs or lifestyles but *not* instances of sexual harassment.

a. Fran teaches a course on "The Art and Sociology of the Nude" which includes slide presentations of naked women and men by both "straight" and "gay" artists. The pictures and their significance are discussed in class and written assignments are expected from the students. Two students who are offended by the pictures and upset about the assignments bring a complaint. The Affirmative Action officer explains to them that the course title and catalog description clearly explained the goals of the course and suggests that they drop the course if they find the materials difficult to deal with.

b. Jennifer elects a Grade III level course in literature and finds that one of the readings contains explicit descriptions of sadistic and scatological acts. She complains to her instructor that she is disgusted and offended by this material and cannot complete the written assignment on the topic. The instructor and the student discuss the situation and work out several solutions such as completing the assignment; completing a modified or alternative, assignment; or dropping the course.

c. Joan, a senior, is invited by her major professor to attend a professional meeting. Wondering whether this is a sexual advance, she asks what the housing arrangements will be. Sensing her concern, the instructor responds that in science departments students are often encouraged to take part in professional activities and that students are ordinarily housed separately from instructors. Joan expresses her preference for separate housing.

d. Linda and her classmates are invited to dinner at the home of their instructor, Professor Jones. Professor Jones introduces them to her partner, Ms. Smith. Afterwards, Linda complains to the Chair of the Department that her religious beliefs are offended by the relationship between Ms. Jones and Ms. Smith. She says that she is unable to concentrate in class and wants to bring a sexual harassment grievance against Professor Jones under the College's *Definition* ¶4 concerning atmosphere of the workplace. The Chair points out that Wellesley College has a policy committing it not to discriminate on the basis of sexual preference and that hers are not grounds for bringing a sexual harassment complaint against Professor Jones.

e. Jim is a new instructor at Wellesley College. A student in one of his classes repeatedly comments on his clothing and appearance and makes suggestive comments when she comes to his office hours. Jim discusses his discomfort with a colleague who refers him to the Affirmative Action Officer. The Officer suggests that he express his discomfort to the student and remind her of the College's "Guidelines Concerning Consensual Sexual Relations" (section II.B.2(a)). The Officer notes that if the behavior persists after that discussion, Jim could lodge a complaint. [See *Definition* ¶4.]

II. Guidelines Concerning Consensual Sexual Relations

A. General Guidelines

1. *Absence of Supervisory Relations* When there is no supervisory relation between students, or between faculty members, or between faculty and staff members, or between staff members—any recommendations by the College concerning sexual relations would constitute an intolerable invasion of privacy.

2. *Presence of Supervisory Relations* Even when there are supervisory relations, such as those between tenured and untenured members of the faculty, *no institutional mission* exists which would preempt individual rights to privacy.

a. Conflicts of Interest   Due to the presence of a conflict of interest, a supervisor (faculty or staff) who is sexually involved with an employee under her or his supervision shall not write a job performance review, recommend a salary increase, participate in reappointment, tenure, promotion, or merit increase decisions. An individual under review may also request the relevant Executive Officer to exclude a supervisor from participating in the review if the individual and the supervisor are, or have been, sexually involved. The Executive Officer shall notify the supervisor of the request and shall state the reason given.

b. Atmosphere of the Workplace   Individuals should exercise great care in such cases to make sure that the letter and spirit of EEOC guidelines are followed concerning the atmosphere of the work place (see *Definition of Sexual Harassment,* ¶4).

In particular, the parties to a sexual relationship should be aware that such relations often create general conflicts of interest and the fear from coworkers of unfair treatment when promotions are reviewed. The parties should also be aware that others in the workplace may be prompted to file complaints of conflict of interest or, under EEOC, of adverse effects to the workplace environment.

B. Sexual Relations between Faculty and Students under Their Supervision

When no supervisory relations are present, sexual intimacy can be detrimental to the ideal of a friendship-based mentoring environment. When such supervision is present, sexual relations between a faculty member and a student are clearly detrimental to the educational process and to promoting an environment where favoritism and the appearance of favoritism are absent.

Even when the initiator of the relationship is not the faculty member, if the relationship is severed or made public, any ensuing penalties will affect the faculty member whose institutional responsibility it is to deal in a professional manner with such situations when they are initiated.

In addition, because of the power differential (see "explicitly or *implicitly*" in ¶2 of the *Definition of Sexual Harassment*), if a student makes an allegation of sexual harassment, members of the faculty may find it difficult to prove that the relationship was fully consensual.

1. Absence of Supervisory Relations   Unlike relationships where no basic institutional interests are at stake, such as those between faculty members and administrative staff, relations between educators and students are informed by the goals of Wellesley College as an institution of higher education.

A basic feature of the mission of Wellesley College is to foster close intel-lectual relations among faculty members and students and to encourage mentoring on the part of the faculty. For this reason it is important that both students and faculty members seek to avoid otherwise perfectly licit sexual relations which may undermine the common educational goals defining our community and shaping the workplace.

Although close relationships between adults may engender sexual attrac-tion, both students and teachers are expected to maintain professional, non-sexual, relations with one another.

The present subsection cannot and should not be taken as proposing a rule to be enforced. Rather, it is an ideal of the community as it strives to-ward its educational goals. Clearly, individual exceptions will occur, but exceptions do not determine or undermine the general goals of an insti-tution.

2. *Presence of Supervisory Relations* When supervisory relations be-tween a student and a faculty member are present, sexual relations are un-conditionally unacceptable.

Definition of Supervisory Relations between Faculty and Students

a. Teacher/student relationship: With Grading and Recommendations
- the standard classroom situation where other students are involved
- the tutorial situation of 350s, 360s, 379s, or other independent work

b. Teacher/student relationship: With student majoring in Teacher's De-partment

The student, while not presently under a faculty member's direct supervi-sion, may later want or need to take a class with that faculty member, thus creating the situation described in the previous paragraph. [This is true of al-most any course taken at the College, but the issue becomes particularly grave in the case of majors being precluded from taking a class in their spe-cialization.]

- The faculty member may write recommendations or sit on commit-tees (e.g., Honors) (but also including interdepartmental committees like "Premed") where close relations create a conflict of interest for the faculty member and a fear of preferential treatment among other students.

c. Teacher/student relationship: With student a member of a group under Teacher's supervision
- Junior Year abroad programs (with grading and/or recommendations)
- Group activities during or between semesters (such as organized trips)

III. Complaints of Sexual Harassment

If any student, employee, or faculty member believes that he or she has been subjected to sexual harassment, that person has the right to seek resolution through any of those steps enumerated in Wellesley College's Equal Opportunity Grievance Procedures (which is incorporated in its entirety by reference into the body of this document). Specifically, that person may seek resolution through:

1. Informal Resolution

(a) Before and instead of initiating a written complaint, a complainant may utilize Wellesley College's informal resolution system to attempt to bring closure to the matter, and may consult: a) the Dean of the College, b) the Dean of Students, c) the Ombudsperson, d) the Head of House, e) members of the Cultural Advising Network, or f) the Dean of Religious Life.

(b) Use of the informal resolution process in no way precludes the complainant from using either the negotiated procedures, or the formal adjudicative procedures, which are part of our grievance process.

2. Negotiated Procedure

(a) By this procedure, the complainant formally requests ameliorative action on the part of the accused. If the accused agrees to participate, both parties work toward resolution with the help of a negotiator.

(b) Normally the negotiator will be the Director of AA/EEO. At the request of either party and with the agreement of both, the negotiator may be another member of the faculty or staff trained for this purpose.

(c) The complainant completes and signs a written statement through the Office of Equal Opportunity and Multi-cultural Policy which includes the names of the complainant and the accused, and the details of the conduct which is alleged to be discriminatory or harassment. The negotiator promptly forwards the report to the accused, provides the accused with a copy of the College's grievance policies and procedures, and requests participation in negotiations. The accused must reply within seven calendar days of receiving the notice.

3. Formal Grievance Procedure

(a) If the negotiated procedure fails to satisfy either party, the complainant or the accused may bring the matter to a Grievance Committee through a written complaint filed with the Director of AA/EEO. Linda Brothers is the Director of AMEEO, and is located in 232, Green Hall, x2240. The Grievance Committee is constituted from an elected Standing Panel.

(b) The Grievance Committee to hear a particular case shall be constituted from the membership of the staff member in all cases involving staff, and a union member in all cases involving the union. In cases involving faculty/staff/union combinations, the chair shall be chosen by lot.

(c) The Committee will determine the most appropriate manner to proceed with the case. Options include the examination of written evidence, a hearing, or further investigation, if needed.

When we receive any complaint of harassment we will promptly investigate the allegation in a fair and expeditious manner. We will proceed in such a way as to maintain confidentiality to the extent practicable under the circumstances. If it is determined that inappropriate conduct has occurred, we will act promptly to eliminate the offending conduct, and where appropriate we will also impose disciplinary action.

It is Wellesley College's goal to promote a learning environment and workplace which is free of sexual harassment. Sexual harassment in any form is unlawful and will not be tolerated by this organization. Further, any retaliation against an individual who has complained about sexual harassment or retaliation against individuals for cooperating with an investigation of a sexual harassment complaint is similarly unlawful and will not be tolerated.

IV. Disciplinary Action

If it is determined that inappropriate conduct has been committed by one of our employees, we will take such action as is appropriate under the circumstances. Such action may range from counseling to termination from employment, and may include such other forms of disciplinary action as we deem appropriate under the circumstances.

V. State and Federal Remedies

In addition to the above, if you believe you have been subjected to sexual harassment, you may file a formal complaint with either or both of the government agencies set forth below. Using our complaint process does not prohibit you from filing a complaint with these agencies.

1. The United States Equal Employment Opportunity Commission (EEOC)
   1. Congress Street - 10th Floor
   Boston, MA 02114
   (617) 565-3200

2. The Massachusetts Commission Against Discrimination (MCAD)
   Boston Office:
   One Ashburton Place - Rm 601
   Boston, MA 02108
   (617) 727-3990

   Springfield Office:
   424 Dwight Street, Rm 220
   Springfield, MA 01103
   (413) 739-2145

ANTIOCH COLLEGE GUIDELINES

Sexual Harassment College Policy

Antioch College deplores sexual harassment wherever it might occur between faculty and staff, faculty and students, staff and students, senior faculty and junior faculty, one student and another, or supervisor and employee. Any form of intimidation, abuse, or harassment based on gender or sexual preference is contrary to the ideals of Antioch College and may jeopardize a community member's ability to learn and function. Not only may sexual harassment produce negative educational and psychological consequences, it is often against the law.

Adopted by AdCil and ComCil, 1985

Definition of Sexual Harassment

Harassment on the basis of sex is a violation of section 703 of Title VII of the Civil Rights Act of 1964, and is defined as "unwelcome sexual advances, requests for sexual favors, and other verbal or physical conduct of a sexual nature."

Sexual harassment in the academic setting is behavior that emphasizes the gender or sexual identity of persons in a manner which prevents or impairs their emotional well-being, full enjoyment of educational or occupational benefits or opportunities. Such behavior may be especially harmful in any situation in which the imposition of unwanted sexual attention is accompanied by the promise of academic or employment rewards or the threat of reprisal.

Sexual harassment is defined to include, but may not be limited to, the following:

1. Verbal, physical, written, or pictorial communication relating to gender or to sexual preference which has the purpose or effect of unreasonable interference with an individual's performance or which creates a hostile, offensive, or intimidating atmosphere for the recipient.
2. Unwelcome and irrelevant comments, references, gestures, or other forms of personal attention which are inappropriate to the academic, employment, or residential setting—for example, the classroom, dormitory, or office—and which may reasonably be perceived as sexual overtures or denigration.
3. A request for sexual favors when submission to or rejection of such a request might be viewed as a basis for evaluative decisions affecting an individual's future.

4. Sexual assault: Threat or coercion of sexual relations; sexual contact which is not freely agreed to by both parties.

Community members should understand that many of the terms in the preceding definition are subject to interpretation. While overt forms of sexual harassment will usually be obvious, more subtle forms may be difficult to recognize. Perpetrators may not realize that their behavior is "unwelcome" or "inappropriate"; victims may be confused as to whether uncomfortable situations have actually been instances of sexual harassment.

If you feel that you have been the victim of sexual harassment, please do not ignore the situation or the offending person. Discuss the incident with someone you trust.

What to do . . .

Contact any member of

- the Sexual Offense Prevention and Survivors' Advocacy Program
- the Counseling Center
- the Dean of Students' Office
- the Sexual Harassment Committee
- the Campus Mediation Program

Concerns brought to these people will be held in the strictest confidence. These individuals will try to guide you through the best process for resolving your problem.

Possible actions on campus include:

- Confronting the offender yourself about what they did;
- Taking the offender to mediation through the campus mediation program;
- Having the Dean of Students or Associate Dean of Students talk with the offender;
- Taking the incident to the Sexual Harassment Committee or Community Standards Board, or if appropriate, to the Sexual Offense Hearing Board;
- If the offender is employed by the College or University, having the Dean of Students or Sexual Offense Program Director advise or assist you in an appropriate intervention.

Once campus remedies have been exhausted, you may want to contact an attorney about taking the matter to court. In certain cases, it may also be appropriate to contact the Equal Opportunity Employment Commission.

Sexual Harassment Committee

The Sexual Harassment Committee is primarily an educational committee. While it may mediate in sexual harassment cases, it does not adjudicate. The committee may be convened by a committee member, the director of the Sexual Offense Program, the Dean of Students, someone who feels offended, or someone, who has either offended or feels falsely accused.

Sexual Violence and Safety: Introduction to Policy

The statistics on the frequency of sexual violence on college campuses today are alarming. While we try to make Antioch a safe environment for everyone, we still have problems here. There is date and acquaintance rape, and stranger rape, and, while the majority of perpetrators are men and the majority of victims are women, there are also female perpetrators and male victims. There are also many students who have already experienced sexual violence before arriving at Antioch; healing from that experience may be an integral part of their personal, social, and academic lives while they are here.

Antioch has a Sexual Offense Prevention and Survivor's Advocacy Program which consists of an Advocate and trained Peer Advocates and Educators. They can talk with you confidentially about any questions or concerns you have, provide or arrange for counseling, and help you access resources about healing from sexual violence. They also provide advocacy for rape victims dealing with a hospital, police, the courts, and/or campus administrative procedures. The program is located on the second floor of Long Hall, next to Maples and above the infirmary. The telephone number is PBX 459 (767-6459). There is also a Rape Crisis Line at PBX 458 (767-6458) which you can call in an emergency. If you experience sexual harassment or assault on co-op, you can call us for support through 1-800-841-1314.

Antioch has two policies, a sexual harassment policy and a sexual offense policy, which have been designed to help deal with these problems when they occur on campus and/or when they involve an Antioch community member. Read these policies; you are held responsible for knowing them. Under the sexual offense policy:

- All sexual contact and conduct between any two people must be consensual;
- Consent must be obtained verbally before there is any sexual contact or conduct;
- If the level of sexual intimacy increases during an interaction (i.e., if two people move from kissing while fully clothed—which is one level—to undressing for direct physical contact, which is another level), the peo-

ple involved need to express that clear verbal consent before moving to that new level;

- If one person wants to *initiate* moving to a higher level of sexual intimacy in an interaction, *that person is responsible for getting the verbal consent of the other person(s) involved before moving to that level;*
- If you have had a particular level of sexual intimacy before with someone, you must still ask each and every time;
- If you have a sexually transmitted disease, you must disclose it to a potential sexual partner

Don't ever make any assumptions about consent; they can hurt someone and get you in trouble. Also, do not take silence as consent; it isn't. Consent must be clear and verbal (i.e., saying: yes, I want to kiss you also).

Special precautions are necessary if you, or the person with whom you would like to be sexual, are under the influence of alcohol, drugs, or prescribed medication. Extreme caution should always be used. Consent, even verbal consent, may not be meaningful. Taking advantage of someone who is "under the influence" is never acceptable behavior. If, for instance, you supply someone with alcohol and get her/him drunk so that person will consent to have sex with you (figuring you wouldn't get "as far" if that person were sober), then their consent may be meaningless and you may be charged under the sexual offense policy. If you are so drunk that you act with someone totally inappropriately (in a way maybe you wouldn't if you were sober), or if you are so drunk you don't hear "no," you may still be charged under the sexual offense policy.

If you have a hard time knowing or setting your own personal boundaries, or respecting other people's boundaries, you may have a harder time if alcohol or drugs are involved. For truly consensual sex, you and your partner(s) should be sober to be sexual.

Sexual harassment should be reported to the Advocate; depending on the wishes of the complainant, mediation may be attempted or the charge may be referred to the Hearing Board. Other forms of sexual offenses are also reported to the Advocate, and depending on the wishes of the victim/survivor may be referred for mediation or to the Hearing Board which hears cases of sexual offenses where the alleged offender is a student. If the accused violator is not a student, the case may be referred for follow-up to the appropriate person. In cases of rape and sexual assault, reporting to law enforcement authorities is also encouraged. Anonymous reports may also be made. Complaint forms are in a box outside the program offices in Long Hall, or you can make a report directly to the Advocate, either in person or at PBX 459. All reports are treated confidentially; every attempt is made to treat everyone involved fairly, and to honor the wishes of the victim regarding what is done (or not done).

If you are raped or sexually assaulted:

- Get somewhere safe.
- Contact a friend you trust, a hall advisor, or HAC.
- Contact a peer advocate or the Advocate directly, or through the Rape Crisis Line at PBX 458.
- You may also wish to notify the police.
- Do not bathe, change clothes, or otherwise clean up yet.

The peer advocate or Advocate will provide emotional support, help you to understand your thoughts and feelings at the time, explain your options to you, and support you in whatever actions you choose to make.

If you have been sexually harassed at a co-op site, tell your co-op advisor and the Advocate. You can call to report the harassment from out of town at 1-800-841-1314.

If you have been victimized sexually in the past and you would like some assistance in working on these issues, there is help available. See a counselor at the Counseling Center or contact the Advocate or a peer advocate. If it's appropriate for you to see a therapist off-campus, we will try to help you find someone suitable. There are also support groups available each term for men and women who are survivors of sexual abuse.

There are ways to help prevent sexual violence on campus. A few tips:

- *Always* lock your room door when you're going to undress, sleep, or if you're under the influence of a substance which might impair your ability to react quickly. It's a good idea to get in the habit of locking your door whenever you're inside.
- *Never* prop outside doors open—strangers can enter buildings, as well as friends.
- If you're walking or running on the bike path at times when you might be the only one around, take a friend.
- Learn self-defense.
- Know your sexual desires and boundaries and communicate them clearly to any (potential) sexual partner; "listen" to your boundaries and honor them. If you're not sure, say "no" rather than "yes" or "maybe."
- Ask what a (potential) sexual partner's desires and boundaries are; listen to and respect them.
- If someone violates a sexual boundary, confront him/her on it. That may mean telling them directly, or, as a first step, talking with your hall advisor or HAC, the Advocate or a peer advocate, a counselor, or the Dean of Students.

Sexual Offense Policy

All sexual contact and conduct on the Antioch College campus and/or occurring with an Antioch community member must be consensual.

When a sexual offense, as defined herein, is committed by a community member, such action will not be tolerated.

Antioch College provides and maintains educational programs for all community members, some aspects of which are required. The educational aspects of this policy are intended to prevent sexual offenses and ultimately to heighten community awareness.

In support of this policy and community safety, a support network exists that consists of the Sexual Offense Prevention and Survivors' Advocacy Program, an Advocate, Peer Advocates, and victim/survivor support groups through the Sexual Offense Prevention and Survivors' Advocacy Program and Counseling Services.

The Advocate (or other designated administrator) shall be responsible for initiation and coordination of measures required by this policy.

The implementation of this policy also utilizes established Antioch governance structures and adheres to contractual obligations.

Consent

1. For the purpose of this policy, "consent" shall be defined as follows: the act of willingly and verbally agreeing to engage in specific sexual contact or conduct.

2. If sexual contact and/or conduct is not mutually and simultaneously initiated, then the person who initiates sexual contact/conduct is responsible for getting the verbal consent of the other individual(s) involved.

3. Obtaining consent is an on-going process in any sexual interaction. Verbal consent should be obtained with each new level of physical and/or sexual contact/conduct in any given interaction, regardless of who initiates it. Asking "Do you want to have sex with me?' is not enough. The request for consent must be specific to each act.

4. The person with whom sexual contact/conduct is initiated is responsible to express verbally and/or physically her/his willingness or lack of willingness when reasonably possible.

5. If someone has initially consented but then stops consenting during a sexual interaction, she/he should communicate withdrawal verbally and/or through physical resistance. The other individual(s) must stop immediately.

6. To knowingly take advantage of someone who is under the influence of alcohol, drugs, and/or prescribed medication is not acceptable behavior in the Antioch community.

7. If someone verbally agrees to engage in specific contact or conduct, but it is not of her/his own free will due to any of the circumstances stated in (a) through (d) below, then the person initiating shall be considered in violation of this policy if:

    a) the person submitting is under the influence of alcohol or other substances supplied to her/him by the person initiating:

    b) the person submitting is incapacitated by alcohol, drugs, and/or prescribed medication;

    c) the person submitting is asleep or unconscious;

    d) the person initiating has forced, threatened, coerced, or intimidated the other individual(s) into engaging sexual contact and/or sexual conduct.

Offenses Defined

The following sexual contact/conduct are prohibited under Antioch College's Sexual Offense Policy and, in addition to possible criminal prosecution, may result in sanctions up to and including expulsion or termination of employment.

Rape: Nonconsensual penetration, however slight, of the vagina or anus; nonconsensual fellation or cunnilingus.

Sexual Assault: Nonconsensual sexual conduct exclusive of vaginal and anal penetration, fellatio and cunnilingus. This includes, but is not limited to, attempted nonconsensual penetration, fellatio, or cunnilingus; the respondent coercing or forcing the primary witness to engage in nonconsensual sexual contact with the respondent or another.

Sexual Imposition: Nonconsensual sexual contact. "Sexual contact" includes the touching of thighs, genitals, buttocks, the pubic region, or the breast/chest area.

Insistent and/or Persistent Sexual Harassment: Any insistent and/or persistent emotional, verbal, or mental intimidation or abuse found to be sexually threatening or offensive. This includes, but is not limited to, unwelcome and irrelevant comments, references, gestures, or other forms of personal attention which are inappropriate and which may be perceived as persistent sexual overtones or denigration.

Nondisclosure of a Known Positive HIV Status: Failure to inform one's sexual partner of one's known positive HIV status prior to engaging in high-risk sexual conduct.

Nondisclosure of a Known Sexually Transmitted Disease: Failure to inform one's sexual partner of one's known infection with a sexually transmitted disease (other than HIV) prior to engaging in high-risk sexual conduct.

Procedures

1. To maintain the safety of all community members, community members who are suspected of violating this policy should be made aware of the concern about their behavior. Sometimes people are not aware that their behavior is sexually offensive, threatening, or hurtful. Educating them about the effects of their behavior may cause them to change their behavior.

If someone suspects that a violation of this Sexual Offense Policy may have occurred, she/he should contact a member of the Sexual Offense Prevention and Survivors' Advocacy Program or the Dean of Students.

It is strongly encouraged that suspected violations be reported, and that they be reported as soon as is reasonable after a suspected violation has occurred. Where criminal misconduct is involved, reporting the misconduct to the local law enforcement agency is also strongly encouraged.

Any discussion of a suspected violation with a member of the Sexual Offense Prevention and Survivors' Advocacy Program or the Dean of Students will be treated as confidential.

2. When a suspected violation of this policy is reported, the person who receives the report with the Sexual Offense Prevention and Survivors' Advocacy Program or the Dean of Students office will explain to the person reporting all of her/his options (such as mediation, the Hearing Board, and criminal prosecution) which are appropriate to the suspected offense.

3. If the person reporting a suspected policy violation wishes to arrange for mediation, then the Advocate, the Dean of Students, or a staff member of the Sexual Offense Prevention and Survivors' Advocacy program shall arrange for mediation consistent with the mediation guidelines used by the Sexual Offense Prevention and Survivors' Advocacy Program.

   a) If the Dean of Students arranges mediation, the Dean shall notify the Advocate of the mediation session.
   b) A written agreement with educational and/or behavioral requirements may be part of the outcome of a mediation session. Copies of this agreement shall be given to the parties involved, the Advocate, and the Dean of Students.
   c) Should a student persist in sexually threatening or offensive behavior after mediation has been attempted, the Sexual Harassment Committee or the Advocate should refer the case to the Hearing Board.
   d) If a satisfactory conclusion is not reached through mediation, or if the mediation agreement is not adhered to by any of its participants, then the case may be referred to the Hearing Board.

4. In the event that an action taken by the Dean of Students regarding a sexual offense is appealed, the appeal shall be made to the Hearing Board.

5. If the primary witness wishes the Hearing Board to make a finding regarding an alleged policy violation, the primary witness must file a written complaint with the Advocate. The Advocate shall inform the primary witness of her/his rights regarding procedure and appeal under this policy.

6. When a written complaint is filed, if the respondent is an employee, the Advocate shall inform the President or the President's designee of the reported violation of the Sexual Offense Policy. The matter will be promptly investigated by the appropriate administrator or other supervisor with the assistance of the Advocate. If whatever review process appropriate to the employee results in a determination that the policy has been violated, then the remedy should be commensurate with the seriousness of the violation, and procedures specified in College and University policies should be followed.

7. When an official report is filed, if the respondent is a student, then the following procedures shall be followed:

a) The Advocate shall notify the Dean of Students, or another senior College official, who shall have the respondent report to the Dean of Students' office within a reasonable period of time, not to exceed the next business day the College is open that the respondent is on campus. When the respondent reports, the respondent will then be informed by the Advocate and/or the Dean of Students of the report of the sexual offense, the policy violation which is being alleged, and her/his rights regarding procedure and appeal. The respondent will be given an opportunity to present her/his side of the story at that time. If the respondent does not report as directed, then implementation of this policy shall proceed.

b) Based on the information available, the Advocate, or the Dean of Students in the Advocate's absence, will determine whether there is reasonable cause to believe that a policy violation may have occurred.

c) In the event that the respondent is situated on campus, if (1) there is reasonable cause to believe that a policy violation may have occurred, and (2) there is reasonable cause to believe that the respondent may pose a threat or danger to the safety of the community, the Hearing Board will be convened as soon as possible, preferably within 24 hours from the time of the report to the Advocate to determine whether the respondent shall be removed from campus until the conclusion of the Hearing process. If the Hearing Board cannot be convened within 24 hours but there is reasonable cause as stated in (1) and (2) above, the Dean of Students, or the Advocate in the Dean of Students' absence, can act to remove the respondent from campus.

If the respondent is living on-campus and is temporarily banned from campus, the College will help arrange housing if the respondent is unable to locate any on her/his own.

If the respondent is taking classes on campus and is temporarily banned from attending classes, the College will help provide alternative instruction.

The emergency removal of the respondent from campus shall not constitute a determination that the respondent has violated this policy.

d) The Hearing Board will then convene for a Hearing, to hear the case. Consistent with this policy, the Hearing Board will take into account the primary witness's story, the respondent's story, witnesses, the past history of the respondent, and other relevant evidence, and will determine whether or not a policy violation has occurred and which aspect of the policy has been violated.

e) The Hearing shall take place as soon thereafter as is reasonable, no longer than seven days from the date of filing or the notification of the respondent, whichever is later, unless the Advocate determines that reasonable cause exists for convening the meeting at a later, still reasonable time, in which event the Advocate shall so notify the Chair of the Hearing Board.

f) If the primary witness chooses, she/he may have a representative at all hearings of the Hearing Board and/or through any appeals process. The primary witnesses advocate is to provide advocacy and emotional support for the primary witness. When appropriate, if the primary witness chooses, the Advocate or a Peer Advocate may act as the primary witness's representative at all hearings of the Hearing Board and/or through any appeals process. The primary witness may also choose to have someone outside the Sexual Offense Prevention and Survivors' Advocacy Program serve as her/his representative. Choosing a representative from within the Antioch community is encouraged.

g) If the respondent chooses, she/he may have a representative at all hearings of the Hearing Board and/or through any appeals process. The respondent's advocate is to provide advocacy and emotional support for the respondent. When appropriate, if the respondent chooses, the respondent may select an advocate from the list maintained by the Dean of Students' office of administrators and tenured faculty who have agreed to serve in this role. This advocate may act as the respondent's representative at all hearings of the Hearing Board and/or through any appeals process.

The respondent may also choose to have someone outside this lisst serve as her/his representative. Choosing a representative from within the Antioch community is encouraged.

8. The Hearing Board and any appellate body which hears a case under this policy shall administer its proceedings according to these fundamental assumptions:

a) There will be no reference to the past consensual, nonviolent sexual contact and/or conduct of either the primary witness or the respondent.

b) No physical evidence of a sexual offense is necessary to determine that one has occurred, nor is a visit to the hospital or the administration of a rape kit required. The primary witness shall be supported by the Advocate in whatever decisions she/he makes, and be informed of legal procedures regarding physical evidence.

c) The fact that a respondent was under the influence of drugs or alcohol or mental dysfunction at the time of the sexual offense will not excuse or justify the commission of any sexual offense as defined herein, and shall not be used as a defense.

9. This policy is intended to deal with sexual offenses which occurred in the Antioch community, and/or with an Antioch community member, on or after February 7, 1991. Sexual offenses which occurred prior to that date were still a violation of community standards, and should be addressed through the policies and governance structures which were in effect at the time of the offense.

The Hearing Board

1. The Hearing Board's duties are:
   a) to hear all sides of the story;
   b) to investigate as appropriate;
   c) to determine if a violation of this policy has occurred;
   d) to develop, in consultation with the Dean of Students and the Advocate, an appropriate remedy in cases where mandatory remedies are not prescribed in this policy;
   e) to prepare a written report setting forth its findings which it distributes to the parties involved and the Dean of Students.

2. The Hearing Board will consist of three community representatives as voting members and the Dean of Students as an ex-officio member.

3. By the end of each Spring quarter, nine representatives will be chosen to form a Hearing Board pool to begin serving at the beginning of the next academic year (Fall quarter) for the duration of that academic year: three each from the categories of students, faculty, and administrators/staff members.

   a) The nine members of the Hearing Board pool shall be appointed by ADCIL from the following recommended candidates:
      1) Six students recommended by COMCIL;
      2) Six faculty members recommended by the Dean of Faculty and FEC;
      3) Six administrators/staff members who shall be recommended by the President of the College.
   b) At least five members of the Hearing Board pool shall be women.
   c) Three of the representatives shall be appointed by ADCIL to serve each quarter as a Hearing Board. One Hearing Board member must

be from each of the three categories listed above, and at least one member must be a person of color.

For every case which is heard, at least one Hearing Board member must be the same sex as the primary witness, and at least one Hearing Board member must be the same sex as the respondent.

d) One member of the Hearing Board shall be designated by ADCIL to serve as Chair. The Chair shall preside for all Hearing Board meetings that quarter, and shall make the necessary physical arrangements to convene the Hearing Board (i.e., contact Hearing Board members, notify all parties involved of date, time, place, etc.)

e) The six representatives who are not serving in a particular quarter shall be alternates in case an active members is not available or has a conflict of interest.

f) If an active member of the Hearing Board has a conflict of interest in the case, that member is responsible to report the conflict as soon as possible. ADCIL shall be responsible to determine if the conflict requires replacing the member, with an alternate chosen by ADCIL to immediately take her/his place. If convening ADCIL for this purpose would serve to delay the Hearing Board process, then the President shall make a determination regarding conflict and, if necessary, appoint an alternate.

4. All members of the Hearing Board pool shall receive training by the Advocate and the College attorney regarding this policy and pertinent legal issues.

5. The Hearing Board is expected to follow the procedures outlined in Appendix D. Any procedures not covered in this policy, including Appendix D, shall be determined according to the discretion of the Hearing Board.

Remedies

1. When a policy violation by a student is found by the Hearing Board, the Hearing Board shall also determine a remedy which is commensurate with the offense, except in those cases where mandatory remedies are prescribed in this policy.

When a remedy is not prescribed, the Hearing Board shall determine the remedy in consultation with the Dean of Students and the Advocate, and shall include an educational and/or rehabilitation component as part of the remedy.

2. *For Rape:* In the event that the Hearing Board determines that the violation of rape has occurred, as defined under this policy, then the respondent must be expelled immediately.

3. *For Sexual Assault:* In the event that the Hearing Board determines that the violation of sexual assault has occurred, as defined under this policy, then the respondent must; a) be suspended immediately for a period of no less than six months; b) successfully complete a treatment program for

sexual offenders approved by the Director of Counseling Services before returning to campus; and c) upon return to campus, be subject to mandatory class and co-op scheduling so that the respondent and primary witness avoid, to the greatest extent possible, all contact, unless the primary witness agrees otherwise.

In the event that the Hearing Board determines that a second violation of sexual assault has occurred, with the same respondent, then the respondent must be expelled immediately.

4. *For Sexual Imposition:* In the event that the Hearing Board determines that the violation of sexual imposition, has occurred as defined under this policy, then the recommended remedy is that the respondent: a) be suspended immediately for a period of no less than three months; b) successfully complete a treatment program for sexual offenders approved by the Director of Counseling Services before returning to campus; and c) upon return to campus, be subject to mandatory class and co-op scheduling so that the respondent and primary witness avoid, to the greatest extent possible, all contact, unless the primary witness agrees otherwise.

In the event that the Hearing Board determines that a second violation of sexual imposition has occurred, with the same respondent, then the recommended remedy is that the respondent: a) be suspended immediately for a period of no less than six months; b) successfully complete a treatment program for sexual offenders approved by the Director of Counseling Services before returning to campus; and c) upon return to campus, be subject to mandatory class and co-op scheduling so that the respondent and primary witness avoid, to the greatest extent possible, all contact, unless the primary witness agrees otherwise.

In the event that the Hearing Board determines that a third violation of sexual imposition has occurred, with the same respondent, then the respondent must be expelled immediately.

5. *For Insistent and/or Persistent Sexual Harassment:* In the event that the Hearing Board determines that the violation of insistent and/or persistent sexual harassment has occurred as defined under this policy, then the recommended mended remedy is that the respondent: a) be suspended immediately for a period of no less than six months; b) successfully complete a treatment program for sexual offenders approved by the Director of Counseling Services before returning to campus; and c) upon return to campus, be subject to mandatory class and co-op scheduling so that the respondent and primary witness avoid, to the greatest extent possible, all contact, unless the primary witness agrees otherwise.

In the event that the Hearing Board determines that a second violation of insistent and/or persistent sexual harassment has occurred, with the same respondent, then the respondent must be expelled immediately.

6. *For Nondisclosure of a Known Positive HIV Status:* In the event that the Hearing Board determines that there has been nondisclosure of a known

positive HIV status, as defined under this policy, then the recommended remedy is that the respondent be expelled immediately.

7. *For Nondisclosure of a Known Sexually Transmitted Disease:* In the event that the Hearing Board determines at there has been nondisclosure of a known sexually transmitted disease, as defined under this policy, then the recommended remedy is that the respondent be suspended immediately for a period of no less than three months.

In the event that the Hearing Board determines that there has been a second failure to disclose one's known sexually transmitted disease, as defined under this policy, then the recommended remedy is that the respondent be suspended immediately for a period of no less than six months.

In the event that the Hearing Board determines that there has been a third failure to disclose one's known sexually transmitted disease, as defined under this policy, then the recommended remedy is that the respondent be expelled immediately.

8. In all cases, *a second offense* under this policy, regardless of category, must receive a more severe consequence than did the first offense if the second offense occurred after the Hearing Board's first finding of a respondent's violation of this policy.

9. The remedy for *a third offense* of this policy, regardless of category, must be expulsion, if the third offense occurred after the Hearing Board's first or second finding of a respondent's violation of this policy.

10. It is the responsibility of the Dean of Students to ensure that the Hearing Board's remedies are carried out.

The Appeals Process

1. In the event that the respondent or primary witness is not satisfied with the decision of the Hearing Board, then she/he shall have the right to appeal the Hearing Board's decision within seventy-two hours of receiving that decision.

2. In the event of an appeal, the College shall secure the services of a hearing review officer with experience in conducting arbitrations or administrative agency or other informal hearings. A hearing review officer, who is not a current member of the Antioch College community, shall be selected by ADCIL in consultation with the Advocate for the purpose of handling such appeals.

3. The hearing review officer shall review the record(s) and/or written report(s) of the Hearing, any briefs or other written materials supplied to her/him by any of the involved parties, and meet with any of the involved parties which she/he determines appropriate, to determine if there was fundamental fairness in the Hearing process.

The hearing review officer's analysis shall include a determination of whether the respondent was fully apprised of the charges against her/him; that the appealing party had a full and fair opportunity to tell her/his side of the story; and whether there was any malfeasance by the Hearing Board. The hearing review officer will present her/his finding and recommendation for action, if any, to the President of the College.

Confidentiality

1. All of the proceedings of the Hearing Board, and all testimony given, shall be kept confidential.

2. For the duration of the Hearing process and any appeals process, the primary witness, the respondent, and any witnesses coming forward shall have the right to determine when and if their names are publicly released. No one shall make a public release of a name not their own while the process is under way. Any public breach of confidentiality may constitute a violation of community standards and be presented to the Community Standards Board for debate.

   a) The name of the primary witness shall not be considered public knowledge until such time that the primary witness releases her/his name publicly.

   b) The name of the respondent shall not be considered public knowledge until such time that the respondent releases her/his name publicly, unless the respondent is found in violation of the policy, at which time the release of the respondent's name may be included with the release of the Hearing Board's findings. The name of the respondent will be released with the Hearing Board's findings if a violation is found and the remedy includes the suspension or expulsion of the respondent.

   c) The names of any witnesses who testify to the Hearing Board shall not be released publicly until such time that each witness chooses to release her/his own name publicly.

Notes

CHAPTER 1: SEXUAL HARASSMENT

1. F. J. Till, *Sexual Harassment: A Report on the Sexual Harassment of Students*. Report of the National Advisory Council on Women's Educational Programs. Washington, D.C.: U.S. Department of Education, 1980.

2. Quoted in Elizabeth Keller, "Consensual Amorous Relationships between Faculty and Students:The Constitutional Right to Privacy," *Journal of College and University Law* 15:21–42 (1988), p. 22.

3. *Silva v. University of New Hampshire*, 888 F. Supp. 293 (D.N.H.1994).

4. Perry Parks, "Professor Loses His Job in a War Over Words," *Norfolk Virginian-Pilot,* March 20, 1994, p. B1.

5. Andrienne Drell, "Bible Scholar Sues to Fight Taint of Sex Harassment," *Chicago Sun Times,* March 25, 1994, p. 5.

6. Courtney Leatherman, "Fighting Back," *The Chronicle of Higher Education,* March 16, 1994, p. A17.

7. Robin Wilson, "A 'Fractured' Department," *Chronicle of Higher Education,* January 13, 1995, p. A15.

8. Catharine MacKinnon, *Only Words.* Cambridge, MA: Harvard University Press, 1993, p. 56.

9. Ibid., p. 51.

10. Courtney Leatherman, "Colleges Seek New Ways to Deal with Sexual Harassment as Victims on Campuses Are Reluctant to File Complaints," *Chronicle of Higher Education*, December 4, 1991, p. A26.

11. Robin Wilson, "Harassment Charges at Cornell U," *Chronicle of Higher Education*, February 10, 1995, p. A15.

12. G. Walker, L. Erickson, and L. Woolsey, "Sexual Harassment: Ethical Research and Clinical Implications in the Academic Setting," *International Journal of Women's Studies* 8:424–33 (1985).

13. 29 C.F.R. § 1604.11. Further policy guidance can be found in EEOC Policy Guidance No. N-915-050, "Current Issues of Sexual Harassment" (March 19, 1991).

14. See EEOC, "Policy Guidance on Current Issues of Sexual Harassment," No. N-915,050 (issued 3/19/90), available at <www.eeoc.gov/docs/currentisues.html>

15. The H.H.S. regulations are at 45 C.F.R. part 86 and the Department of Education regulations are at 34 C.F.R. part 106. They are identical except for the reference to the relevant department. In the spring of 1997, the Office of Civil Rights of the Department of Education issued a "Sexual Harassment Guidance Document," Federal Register 62: 12034-51 (March 13, 1997). For a proposal for Title IX regulations based on the Title VII regulations, see Carrie N. Baker, "Comment: Proposed Title IX Guidelines on Sex-Based Harassment of Students," *Emory Law Journal* 43:271–324 (1994).

16. Catharine MacKinnon. *Sexual Harassment of Working Women*. New Haven, CT: Yale University Press, 1979 (selection reprinted in chapter 8.)

17. Anita Superson, "A Feminist Definition of Sexual Harassment," *Journal of Social Philosophy* 24:46–64 (1993). (selection reprinted in chapter 12.)

18. Martha Chamallas, "Jeans Jew's Case: Resisting Sexual Harassment in the Academy," *Yale Journal of Law and Feminism* 6:71–90 (1994).

19. See chapter 12, this volume, p. 179.

20. Edmund Wall, ed., *Sexual Harassment: Confrontations and Decisions*. Buffalo, NY: Prometheus Books, 1992, p. 13.

21. Stephanie Riger, "Gender Dilemmas in Sexual Harassment Policies and Procedures," *American Psychologist* 46:497–505 (1991).

22. Douglas D. Baker, David E. Taerpstra, and Bob D. Cutler, "Perceptions of Sexual Harassment: A Reexamination of Gender Differences," *Journal of Psychology* 124:409–16 (1990).

23. See, for example, Carolyn Grose, "Same-Sex Sexual Harassment: Subverting the Heterosexist Paradigm of Title VII," *Yale Journal of Law and Feminism* 7:375–98 (1995).

24. For a discussion of this ambiguity of cultural norms (what women see as problematic or threatening, men see as innocent), see "Note: Sexual Harassment Claims of Abusive Work Environment under Title VII," *Harvard Law Review* 97:1449–67 (1984).

25. Helen Longino, *Science as Social Knowledge*. Princeton, NJ: Princeton University Press, 1990; Sandra Harding and Merril Hintikka, *Discovering Reality: Feminist Perspectives on Epistemology, Metaphysics, Methodology, and Philosophy of Science*. Dordrecht, Holland: D. Reidel, 1983.

26. U.S. Merit Systems Protection Board, *Sexual Harassment in the Federal Workplace: Is It a Problem?* Washington, D.C.: Government Printing Office, 1981.

27. U.S. Merit Systems Protection Board, *Sexual Harassment in the Federal Government: An Update*. Washington, D.C.: Government Printing Office, 1988.

28. Eric L. Dey, Jessie S. Korn, and Linda J. Sax, "Betrayed by the Academy: The Sexual Harassment of Women College Faculty," *Journal of Higher Education* 67:149–74 (1996).

29. Jeffery Selingo, "Students Engage in Behavior Posing Serious Health Risks, CDC Study Finds," *The Chronicle of Higher Education*, September 5, 1997, p. A66.

30. B. Dzeich and L. Weiner, *The Lecherous Professor*. Boston: Beacon Press, 2d ed. 1990 (selection reprinted in chapter 9). Robert O. Riggs, Patricia H. Murrell, and Joanne C. Cutting, *Sexual Harassment in Higher Education: From Conflict to Community* (ASHE-ERIC Higher Education Report No. 2). Washington, D.C.: The George Washington University School of Education and Human Development, 1993; Kathy Hotelling, "Sexual Harassment: A Problem Shielded by Silence," *Journal of Counseling & Development* 69:467–501 (1991).

31. Robert O. Riggs, Patricia H. Murrell, and Joanne C. Cutting, *Sexual Harassment in Higher Education: From Conflict to Community* (1993 ASHE-ERIC Higher Education Report No. 2). Washington, D.C.: The George Washington University, School of Education and Human Development, 1993.

32. Stephanie Riger, "Gender Dilemmas in Sexual Harassment Policies and Procedures," *American Psychologist* 46:497–505 (1991).

33. Mollie L. Jaschik-Herman and Alene Fisk, "Women's Perceptions and Labeling of Sexual Harassment in Academia Before and After the Hill-Thomas Hearings," *Sex Roles: A Journal of Research* 33:439–47 (1995).

34. Anne Lawton, "The Emperor's New Clothes: How the Academy Deals with Sexual Harassment," *Yale Journal of Law and Feminism* 11:75–154 (1999).

CHAPTER 2: THE ROLES OF EDUCATION, EXPRESSION, AND FREEDOM

1. But perhaps the warning was not so odd; Nat Hentoff reports that a Penn State University faculty member requested removal of a print of Goya's Naked Maja from a classroom, on the basis that the print was sexual harassment. Eugene Volokh, "What Speech Does 'Hostile Work Environment' Harassment Law Restrict?" *Georgetown Law Journal* 85:627–47 (1997), p. 642.

2. Writing in 1968, Jacques Barzun, then provost of Columbia University, described the post-war explosion of teaching and research and the strains this explosion had, in his judgment, brought to American higher education. Barzun noted, somewhat pessimistically, that the university had lost its traditional monopoly on teaching and research, to among other institutions big business (for research) and the media (for teaching). Concomitantly, Barzun regretted, the university had become "a residual institution . . . the last outpost of help, like the government of a welfare state. . . . [E]very new skill or item of knowledge developed within the academy creates a new claim by the community. Knowledge is power and its possessor owes the public a prompt application, or at least diffusion through the training of others." Jacques Barzun, *The American University*, 2d ed. Chicago: University of Chicago Press, 1993.

3. *Statistical Abstract of the United States*, 1996, p. 602.

4. Charles J. Sykes, *Profscam: Professors and the Demise of Higher Education*. New York: Kampmann & Co., 1988.

5. National Center for Education Statistics, "Enrollment in Higher Education: Fall 1995." NCES 97–440, May 1997.

6. John Stuart Mill, *On Liberty*, Ch. 1 (many editions).

7. John Dewey, *Democracy and Education*. New York: Macmillan, 1936, p. 3.

8. Ibid., p. 96.

9. Ibid., p. 99.

10. Amy Gutmann, *Democratic Education*. Princeton, NJ: Princeton University Press, 1987, p. 44.

11. Ibid., p. 45.

12. Ibid., p. 173.

13. For an extensive survey of the private and social rates of return of higher education, together with levels of government support, see Larry Leslie and Paul Brinkman, *The Economic Value of Higher Education*. New York: Macmillan Publishing Co., 1988.

14. For example, Julius Getman, *In the Company of Scholars: The Struggle for the Soul of Higher Education*. Austin: University of Texas Press, 1992.

15. This point is made by Michael McDonald, in the panel discussion published by the *Harvard Journal of Law & Public Policy* 18:475–99 (1995).

16. Herbert I. London, "Introduction," in Jacques Barzun, *The American University*, 2d ed. Chicago: University of Chicago Press, 1993, p. xii. ("There is, indeed, a college for everyone. But few ask if there should be a college for everyone. With standards reduced to the lowest common denominator, universities have vitiated the pursuit of excellence.")

17. Andrew Koppelman describes these two conceptions of what he calls the "antidiscrimination project" in *Antidiscrimination Law and Social Equality*. New Haven, CT: Yale University Press, 1996.

18. The conservative view has been articulated most recently by defenders of the canon, such as Allan Bloom. Thus Bloom wrote: higher education "is intended . . . to preserve the treasury of great deeds, great men, and great thoughts." *The Closing of the American Mind*. New York: Simon & Schuster, 1987, p. 249.

19. Arthur Schlesinger, for example, in a critique of multiculturalism, celebrates "the old American ideal of assimilation," an ideal in which cultures of origin were deliberately left behind and, arguably, a new ideal fashioned from supercession of the old. Arthur Schlesinger, *The Disuniting of America: Reflections on a Multicultural Society*. New York: Norton, 1991, revised ed. 1998.

20. Issues raised by this and other examples of cultural preservation are discussed in Amy Gutmann, ed., *Multiculturalism*. Princeton, NJ: Princeton University Press, 1994.

21. *Grove City College v. Bell*, 465 U.S. 555 (1984).

22. William Galston, *Liberal Purposes: Goods, Virtues, and Diversity in the Liberal State*. Cambridge: Cambridge University Press, 1991.

23. Karl Marx, *The German Ideology*, ed. R. Pascal. New York: International Publishers, 1947.

24. Noam Chomsky, *American Power and the New Mandarins.* New York: Pantheon Books, 1969.

25. Robert Paul Wolff, *The Ideal of the University.* Boston: Beacon Press, 1969.

26. William Spanos, *The End of Education; Towards Posthumanism.* Minneapolis: University of Minnesota Press, 1993.

27. Stanley Fish, *There's No Such Thing as Free Speech, and It's a Good Thing, Too.* New York: Oxford University Press, 1994, p. 34.

28. Richard Ohmann, "On PC and Related Matters," in Jeffrey Williams, ed., *PC Wars: Politics and Theory in the Academy.* New York: Routledge, 1995, pp. 11–21.

29. Amy Gutmann, ed., *Multiculturalism,* Princeton: Princeton University Press, 1994, pp. 18–19.

30. Mari J. Matsuda, "Public Response to Racist Speech: Considering the Victim's Story" in Matsuda et al., eds., *Words that Wound.* Boulder, CO: Westview Press, 1993, p. 44.

31. Charles R. Lawrence III, "If He Hollers Let Him Go," in Matsuda et al., *Words that Wound,* p. 53.

32. Andrew Altman, "Liberalism and Campus Hate Speech: A Philosophical Examination," *Ethics* 103:302–17 (1993).

33. *Konigsberg v. State Bar of California,* 366 U.S. 36, 60–61 (1961) (Black, J., dissenting).

34. *Konigsberg v. State Bar of California,* 366 U.S. 36, 49–51 (1961).

35. Kent Greenawalt, *Fighting Words.* Princeton, NJ: Princeton University Press (1995).

36. *Chaplinsky v. New Hampshire,* 315 U.S. 568, 571–72 (1942).

37. Kent Greenawalt, *Fighting Words.* Princeton: Princeton University Press, 1995, pp. 52–53.

38. Andrew Altman, "Liberalism and Campus Hate Speech." A Philosophical Examination," *Ethics* 103:302–17, 1993.

39. Catharine MacKinnon, *Only Words.* Cambridge, MA: Harvard University Press, 1993.

40. Frederick Schauer, *Free Speech: A Philosophical Enquiry.* Cambridge, MA: Cambridge University Press, 1982, p. 94.

41. Ibid., pp. 97–98.

42. *R.A.V. v. City of St. Paul,* 505 U.S. (1992).

43. Frederick Schauer, *Free Speech: A Philosophical Enquiry.* Cambridge, MA: Cambridge University Press, 1982, Ch. 9.

44. Charles R. Lawrence III, "If He Hollers Let Him Go," in *Words that Wound,* ed. Mari J. Matsuda, Charles R. Lawrence III, Richard Delgado, and Kimberlé Williams Crenshaw. Boulder, CO: Westview Press, 1993, p. 59.

45. Ibid. p. 62.

46. Catharine MacKinnon, *Only Words.* Cambridge: Harvard University Press, 1993, pp. 30–31.

47. Kent Greenawalt, *Fighting Words.* Princeton: Princeton University Press, 1995, p. 48.

48. Stanley Fish, *There's No Such Thing as Free Speech, and It's a Good Thing, Too.* New York: Oxford University Press, 1994, p. 102.

49. Willmore Kendall, "The Open Society and Its Fallacies," *American Political Science Review* 54:972–79 (1960).

50. John Stuart Mill, *On Liberty*, many editions. This confusion is fostered by the analogy often attributed to Mill and liberalism between the development of knowledge and a marketplace of ideas. The analogy suggests that ideas, like goods, compete for customers; some are highly successful in gaining adherents, some are fashionable for a time, and others are utterly ignored. Successful goods in the marketplace are better in the sense that they are preferred by more customers and thus are more profitable; preferences are taken as a given, and there are no further questions about whether they are rational or wise. The idea in the marketplace analogy that success among ideas is like triumph among consumer preferences reflects skepticism about the possibility of any nonrelativistic account of truth. There appears to be no historical basis for attributing the marketplace view to Mill; indeed, his argument for freedom of expression assumes that there is truth to be found. The origin of the link may have been Justice Oliver Wendell Holmes. It is unfortunate that the AAUP is among the groups that has explicitly adopted the marketplace lingo.

51. "As mankind improve, the number of doctrines which are no longer disputed or doubted will be constantly on the increase: and the well-being of mankind may almost be measured by the number and gravity of the truths which have reached the point of being uncontested." John Stuart Mill, *On Liberty*, Spitz ed., p. 42.

52. This confusion between educational leveling and the importance of diversity is central to today's heated controversies over "multiculturalism." Proponents defend the importance of learning about different cultures, both because of the intrinsic interest of the cultures and for the light they shed on the traditional canon. Opponents argue that multiculturalism is curricular leveling: that teaching Alice Walker's *The Color Purple* alongside Shakespeare is like teaching creationism alongside evolutionary theory. The example is not accidental; Stanley Fish traces to its source the false rumor that Walker's novel is taught more frequently than Shakespeare. Stanley Fish, *There's No Such Thing as Free Speech . . . and It's a Good Thing too.* Oxford: Oxford University Press, 1994, pp. 94–96.

53. That we should tolerate most the speech we hate is a traditional refrain of the American Civil Liberties Union. This view of tolerance is examined in Gene LaMarche, ed., *Speech & Equality: Do We Really Have to Choose?* New York: New York University Press, 1996.

54. The fascinating history of conflict in the United States between Christian fundamentalists and those they call "secular humanists" reflects just this concern. This is detailed in Nomi Maya Stolzenberg, "'He Drew a Circle that Shut Me Out': Assimilation, Indoctrination, and the Paradox of a Liberal Education," *Harvard Law Review* 106:581–667 (1993).

55. Danny Scoccia, "Can Liberals Support a Ban on Violent Pornography?" *Ethics* 106:776–99 (1996).

56. Fred Schauer, *Free Speech: A Philosophical Enquiry.* New York: Cambridge University Press, 1982.

57. Judith Jarvis Thomson, *The Realm of Rights.* Cambridge, MA: Harvard University Press, 1989, p. 249. A similar point is made by Jonathan Rauch, *Kindly Inquisitors: The New Attacks on Free Thought.* Chicago: University of Chicago Press, 1993. Rauch criticizes kindness as a basis for restricting hurtful speech.

58. Schauer, p. 652.

59. For an example of such criticism, see Jonathan Rauch, *Kindly Inquisitors: The New Attacks on Free Thought.* Chicago: The University of Chicago Press, 1993. Rauch argues that the liberal give and take of ideas is not "nice"—and sometimes not even humane—but that it is crucial to long-term commitments to truth and dignity.

60. Joel Feinberg, *The Moral Limits of the Criminal Law*, vol. 1 (*Harm to Others*). New York: Oxford University Press, 1984, p. 36.

61. Joel Feinberg, *The Moral Limits of the Criminal Law*, vol. 2 (*Offense to Others*). New York: Oxford University Press, 1985, pp. 1–5.

62. Ibid., vol. 1, p. 188.

63. Matsuda, pp. 20–21. The story is from *Crichton v. Firestone Steel Products Co.*, 1984 Michigan Civil Rights Commission, Case Digest 13, pp. 17–18.

64. Catharine MacKinnon, *Only Words.* Cambridge: Harvard University Press, 1993, p. 53. The description is from *Robinson v. Jacksonville Shipyards, Inc.*, 760 F. Supp. 1486 (M.D. Fla. 1991).

65. I owe this point to Vicki Schultz. See her "Reconceptualizing Sexual Harassment," *Yale Law Journal* 107:1683–1805 (1998).

66. This proposal is made by Richard Delgado, "Words that Wound: A Tort Action for Racial Insults, Epithets, and Name Calling," in Matsuda, et al., pp. 89–110.

67. An example is Jonathan Rauch, *Kindly Inquisitors.* Chicago: University of Chicago Press, 1993.

68. Kimberlé Crenshaw, "Beyond Racism and Misogyny: Black Feminism and 2 Live Crew," in Matsuda et al., p. 131.

69. Matsuda et al., p. 36.

70. The historical summary in this paragraph is based on Walter P. Metzger, "Origins of the Association: An Anniversary Address," *AAUP Bulletin* (Summer 1965):229-37.

71. "1940 Statement of Principles on Academic Freedom and Tenure," in *AAUP Policy Documents & Reports.* Washington, D.C.: AAUP, 1990, p. 3.

72. "Recommended Institutional Regulations on Academic Freedom and Tenure," in *AAUP Policy Documents & Reports.* Washington, D.C.: AAUP, 1990, p. 21.

73. "1940 Statement of Principles on Academic Freedom and Tenure," p. 3.

74. *Silva v. University of New Hampshire*, 888 F. Supp. 293 (D.N.H. 1994).

75. "Recommended Institutional Regulations on Academic Freedom and Tenure," p. 26.

76. "1940 Statement of Principles on Academic Freedom and Tenure," p. 3.

77. Ibid., p. 4.

78. "Committee A Statement on Extramural Utterances," *AAUP Policy Documents & Reports.* Washington, D.C.: AAUP, 1990, p. 32.

79. "Academic Freedom and Artistic Expression," *AAUP Policy Documents & Reports.* Washington, D.C.: AAUP, 1990, pp. 35–36.

80. "Faculty Appointment and Family Relationship," *AAUP Policy Documents & Reports.* Washington, D.C.: AAUP, 1990, p. 116.

81. "On Discrimination," *AAUP Policy Documents & Reports.* Washington, D.C.: AAUP, 1990, p. 87.

82. "On Processing Complaints of Discrimination on the Basis of Sex," *AAUP Policy Documents & Reports.* Washington, D.C.: AAUP, 1990, pp. 88–95.

83. "Affirmative Action in Higher Education: A Report by the Council Committee on Discrimination," *AAUP Policy Documents & Reports*. Washington, D.C. AAUP, 1990 pp. 96-104.

84. "Sexual Harassment: Suggested Policy and Procedures for Handling Complaints," in *AAUP Policy Documents & Reports*. Washington, D.C.: AAUP, 1990.

85. "1940 Statement of Principles on Academic Freedom and Tenure," p. 3.

86. "1940 Statement of Principles on Academic Freedom and Tenure with 1970 Interpretive Comments," p. 6.

87. See, for example, Samuel Walker, *Hate Speech: The History of an American Controversy*. Lincoln: University of Nebraska Press, 1994, p. 148.

88. Michael W. McConnell, "Academic Freedom in Religious Colleges and Universities," *Law and Contemporary Problems* 53:303–24 (1990), p. 304.

89. Bloom, *The Closing of the American Mind*, p. 98.

90. Stanley Fish, *There's No Such thing as Free Speech, and It's a Good Thing Too*. Oxford: Oxford University Press, 1994, p. 107.

91. Ibid., p. 34.

92. Samuel Walker, *Hate Speech: The History of an American Controversy*. Lincoln: University of Nebraska Press, 1994, p. 133.

93. Ibid., p. 145.

94. 721 F. Supp. 852 (E.D. Mich. 1989).

CHAPTER 3: SEXUAL HARASSMENT IN THE LAW

1. *Cohen v. San Bernardino Valley College*, 883 F. Supp. 1407 (C.D. Cal. 1995). This description of the case also is based on the briefs filed with the Court of Appeals and a telephone conversation with Susan Boyle, one of the lawyers involved.

2. *Cohen v. San Bernardino Valley College*, 883 F. Supp. 1407 (C.D. Cal. 1995), quoting J. Peter Byrne, "Academic Freedom: A Special Concern of the First Amendment," *Yale Law Journal* 99:251–340, p. 253 (1989).

3. *Cohen v. San Bernardino Valley College*, 92 F.2d 968 (9th Cir. 1996).

4. Civil Rights Act of 1964, Title VII, 42 U.S.C. § 2000e (1998).

5. Before 1972, state governments were not included as "employers" under Title VII, and the Fourteenth Amendment's guarantee of equal protection was the chief basis for raising employment discrimination claims against state agencies. In 1972, Title VII was amended to include state agencies as employers, but the Fourteenth Amendment continued to play a role in employment discrimination claims against state governments. State universities and colleges are state agencies, and so they are subject to both Title VII and the Fourteenth Amendment. As the law has developed since 1972, Title VII and Fourteenth Amendment standards have been treated as largely the same, but the possibility of divergence remains. Any differences between the two will be translated into differences between the legal treatment of state universities and colleges private institutions, to which the Fourteenth Amendment does not apply.

6. *Gebser v. Lago Vista Independent School District*, 424 U.S. 274 (1998).

7. *Davis v. Monroe County Board of Education*, 526 U.S. 629 (1999).

8. This is, to be sure, only a matter of statutory interpretation and there have been calls for Congress to amend Title IX so that it explicitly parallels Title VII. The limits

of congressional power under the Commerce and Spending Clauses may differ, however, and so achieving this result may be constitutionally problematic.

9. 413 F. Supp. 654 (D.D.C 1976).

10. Currently at 29 C.F.R 1604.11 (1995); originally published in 45 F.R. 74677 (1990).

11. 477 U.S. 57 (1986).

12. 477 U.S. at 76.

13. Jane L. Dolkart, "Hostile Environment Harassment: Equality, Objectivity, and the Shaping of Legal Standards," *Emory Law Journal* 43:151 (1994).

14. E.g., *Rabidue v. Osceola Refining Co.*, 805 F.2d 611 (6th Cir. 1986), cert. denied, 481 U.S. 1041 (1987).

15. *Ellison v. Brady,* 924 F.2d 872 (9th Cir. 1991).

16. A major early case of this type is *Burns v. McGregor Electronic Industries, Inc.,* 989 F.2d 959 (8th Cir. 1982).

17. *Harris v. Forklift Systems, Inc.,* 510 U.S. 17 (1993).

18. *Oncale v. Sundowner Offshore Services, Inc.,* 1998 U.S. LEXIS 1599 *10 (March 4, 1998).

19. *Burlington Industries, Inc. v. Ellerth,* 1998 U.S. LEXIS 4217 *22 (June 26, 1998).

20. 42 U.S.C. 2000e.

21. *Faragher v. City of Boca Raton,* 1998 U.S. LEXIS 4216 *17 (June 26, 1998).

22. *Burlington Industries, Inc. v. Ellerth,* 1998 US. LEXIS 4217 *39 (June 26, 1998). See also *Faragher v. City of Boca Raton,* 1998 US. LEXIS 4216 (June 26, 1998).

23. 20 U.S.C. 1681(a).

24. However, the definition of "program" under Title IX has ebbed and flowed. The ebb was *Grove City College v. Bell,* 465 U.S. 555 (1984), after which Congress amended Title IX.

25. 42 U.S.C. §1983.

26. *Cannon v. U. of Chicago,* 441 U.S. 677 (1979).

27. *Franklin v. Gwinnett County Public Schools,* 503 U.S. 60 (1992).

28. Title VII requires that claims be brought within 300 days.

29. I compiled these data on the basis of a date-limited LEXIS search for "college or university" and "sexual harassment." Because sexual harassment law is largely federal, nearly all of the reported decisions were in federal courts. Many of the cases involved several reported decisions, including dispositions of preliminary motions, rulings on motions for summary judgment, or rulings on appeal. I counted a case as a "win" if the plaintiff's lawsuit was ongoing at the time of the last ruling; thus a plaintiff who had survived a motion to dismiss on the pleadings was counted as "winning," even though the case had not gone to trial.

30. 524 U.S. 274 (1998).

31. *Gebser v. Lago Vista Independent School District,* 524 U.S. 274, 290 (1998).

32. 524 U.S. 274, 283 (1998).

33. 524 U.S. 274, 285 (1998).

34. 524 U.S. 274, 286 (1998).

35. 524 U.S. 274, 301 (Stevens, J., dissenting).

36. 526 U.S. 629 (1999).

37. 526 U.S. 629,—, 119 S.Ct. 1661, 1671 (1999).

38. 526 U.S. 629,—, 119 S.Ct. 1661, 1678 (Kennedy, J., dissenting)

39. Linda Greenhouse, "The Supreme Court: the Overview; Sex Harassment in Class Is Ruled Schools' Liability," *New York Times*, p. A1 (May 25, 1999).

40. Department of Education, Office of Civil Rights, *Sexual Harassment Guidance: Harassment of Students by School Employees, Other Students, or Third Parties*, 62 Federal Register 12038–50 (March 13, 1997).

41. 62 Federal Register 12040.

42. *Gebser v. Lago Vista Independent School District*, 524 U.S. 274, 294 (1998).

43. *Klemencic v. Ohio State University*, 111 F.3d 131 (6th Cir. 1997).

44. *Kadiki v. Virginia Commonwealth University*, 892 F. Supp. 745 (E.D. Va. 1995).

45. 62 Federal Register 12041 (March 13, 1997).

46. For example, *McClellan v. Board of Regents of the State University and Community College System of Tennessee*, 921 S.W.2d 684 (Tenn. 1996).

47. *Brzonkala v. Virginia Polytechnic and State University*, 935 F. Supp. 772 (W.D. Va. 1996). Another example is *Slaughter v. Waubonsee Community College*, 1995 U.S. Dist. LEXIS 14236 (N.D. Ill., 1995), in which the court ruled that a single incident that did not involve physical threat or humiliation could not as a matter of law establish a claim of hostile environment.

48. For example, *Seamons v. Snow*, 864 F. Supp. 1111 (D. Utah 1994); *Doe v. Petaluma City School District*, 1995 U.S. App. LEXIS 10476 (9th Cir. 1995).

49. There are problems with the doctrine even in employment law. For example, Mane Hajdin argues that unwelcomeness cannot be a workable criterion for delineating sexual harassment in employment law because it creates an infinite regress. To ascertain whether a comment or an advance is welcome, the actor has to ask, but then the actor has to ask whether the asking is welcome, and so on. "Sexual Harassment in the Law: The Demarcation Problem," *Journal of Social Philosophy* 25:102-22 (1994). This account misunderstands the welcomeness standard, however, which is really a requirement of reasonableness: Was it reasonable, in the situation, for the actor to believe the comment or the advance was welcome? If so, there is no need to ask. See Andrew Altman, "Making Sense of Sexual Harassment Law," *Philosophy and Public Affairs* 25:36–63 (1996). Significant issues remain, however, about the reasonableness requirement: From whose perspective is reasonableness to be assessed? Under what circumstances is it reasonable to assume welcomeness, and under what circumstances is it not? Who bears the burden of proving an assumption of welcomeness was unreasonable?

50. See, for example, *Reed v. Shepard*, 939 F.2d 484 (7th Cir. 1991). For criticism of the "unwelcomeness" requirement as an unjustified burden on the victim, in both employment and education, see Joan S. Weiner, "Note: Understanding Unwelcomeness in Sexual Harassment Law: Its History and a Proposal for Reform," *Notre Dame Law Review* 72:621–53 (1997).

51. Guidance, Federal Register 62, p. 12040 (March 13, 1997).

52. Weiner, p. 643.

53. *Kinman v. Omaha Public School District*, 94 F.3d 463 (8th Cir. 1996).

54. *Boucher v. University of Pittsburgh*, 713 F. Supp. 139 (W.D. Pa. 1989). On the other hand, there are several reported settlements of complaints brought by undergraduates who had sexual relationships with professors.

55. For a discussion of these issues, see "Comment: Proposed Title IX Guidelines on Sex-Based Harassment of Students," *Emory Law Journal* 43:271 (1994).

56. A particularly good discussion of this issue is Gillian K. Hadfield, "Rational Women: A Test for Sex-Based Harassment," *California Law Review* 83:1151–89 (1995).

57. 924 F.2d 872, 879 (9th Cir. 1991) ("We adopt the perspective of a reasonable woman primarily because we believe that a sex-blind reasonable person standard tends to be male-biased and tends to systematically ignore the experiences of women.")

58. Guidance, n. 44.

59. *Oncale v. Sundowner Offshore Services, Inc.*, 524 U.S. 75 (1998).

60. *Kinman v. Omaha Public School District*, 94 F.3d 463 (8th Cir. 1996).

61. It is worth noting that this is a liberal conclusion. Radical feminists might argue that same-sex behavior is not sexual harassment unless it can be brought within the model of oppression of women by men. Some same-sex harassment may fit this model, if it is a manifestation of male or malelike power, but some will not.

62. Anne Lawton, "The Emperor's New Clothes: How the Academy Deals with Sexual Harassment," *Yale Journal of Law and Feminism* 11:75–154 (1999).

63. For example, diaries, medical records, and academic records have been discoverable in sexual harassment suits. See, for example, *Topol v. University of Pennsylvania*, 160 F.R.D. 476 (E.D. Pa. 1995); *Mann v. University of Cincinnati*, 864 F. Supp. 44 (S.D. Ohio 1994) *Bougher v. University of Pittsburgh*, 713 F. Supp. 139 (W.D. Pa. 1989).

64. For example, *Tonkovich v. Kansas Board of Regents*, 1996 U.S. Dist. LEXIS 18323 (D. Kan. 1996); *Levenstein v. Board of Trustees of the University of Illinois*, 1997 U.S. Dist. LEXIS 619 (N.D. Ill. 1997). On the other side, critics contend that suppressing information about sexual harassment makes it easy for a harasser to slip into a position at another institution. Courtney Leatherman, "Some Colleges Hush Up Charges to Get Rid of Problem Professors," *The Chronicle of Higher Education*, December 6, 1996, p. A14

65. For example, *McDaniels v. Flick*, 59 F.3d 446 (3d Cir. 1995); *Starishevsky v. Hofstra University*, 612 N.Y.S.2d 764 (Supreme Court of New York, Suffolk County, 1994).

66. *Robinson v. Jacksonville Shipyards*, 760 F. Supp. 1486 (M.D. Fla. 1991) is the only case squarely deciding the issue, and it involved pornography at the workplace.

67. Commentators defending the speech side include Kingsley Browne, "Title VII as Censorship: Hostile-Environment Harassment and the First Amendment," *Ohio State Law Journal* 52:481 (1991); John A. Powell, "Worlds Apart: Reconciling Freedom of Speech and Equality," *Kentucky Law Journal* 85:9–95; Nadine Strossen, "Regulating Workplace Sexual Harassment and Upholding the First Amendment—Avoiding a Collision," *Villanova Law Review* 37:757–85 (1992); and Eugene Volokh, "Comment: Freedom of Speech and Workplace Harassment," *UCLA Law Review* 39:1791–1872 (1992).

68. Eugene Volokh, "What Speech Does 'Hostile Work Environment' Harassment Law Restrict?" *Georgetown Law Journal* 85:627–48 (1997).

69. *Dube v. The State University of New York*, 900 F.2d 587 (2d Cir. 1990).

70. *Pickering v. Board of Education*, 391 U.S. 563 (1968); *Connick v. Myers*, 461 U.S. 138 (1983).

71. *Dambrot v. Central Michigan University*, 55 F.3d 1177, 1187–88, 1190 (6th Cir. 1995).

72. *Levin v. Harleston*, 966 F.2d 85 (2d Cir. 1992).

73. *Jeffries v. Harleston*, 21 F.3d 1238 (2d Cir. 1994), vacated and remanded 115 S.Ct. 502 (1994).

74. *Johnson v. Lincoln University*, 776 F.2d 443, 452 (3d Cir. 1985).

75. *Burnham v. Ianni*, 1997 U.S. App. LEXIS 17343 (8th Cir, July 11, 1997).

76. See, for example, *Scallet v. Rosenblum,* 1997 U.S.App. LEXIS 1465 (1997).

77. For example, "U. of New Hampshire Professor Wins Big," *The Chronicle of Higher Education*, December 14, 1994, p. A19; *Silva v. University of New Hampshire*, 888 F. Supp. 293 (DNH 1994).

CHAPTER 4: SEXUAL HARASSMENT AS A MORAL WRONG

1. Jeffrey Selingo, "Students Engage in Behavior Posing Serious Health Risks, CDC Study Finds," *The Chronicle of Higher Education*, September 5, 1997, p. A66.

2. Susan Estrich, *Real Rape.* Cambridge, MA: Harvard University Press, 1987.

3. See Leslie Francis, ed., *Date Rape: Law, Philosophy and Feminism.* State College: Penn State University Press, 1996; Lois Pineau, "Date Rape," *Law and Philosophy* 8:217 (1989); Stephen Schulhofer, "Taking Sexual Autonomy Seriously: Rape Law and Beyond," *Law and Philosophy* 11:35–91 (1992).

4. See, for example, the California decision recognizing a spouse's cause of action for loss of consortium, *Rodriguez v. Bethlehem Steel Corp.*, 525 P.2d 669 (Cal. 1974).

5. Standard works on the causes of rape include Menachim Amir, *Patterns in Forcible Rape* (Chicago: University of Chicago Press, 1971), which argues that rape is a crime of violence rather than a crime of sex; and Larry Baron and Murray Straus, *Four Theories of Rape in American Society* (New Haven, CT): Yale University Press, 1989, which argues that gender inequality and social disorganization, as well as a subculture of violence, are correlated with increased rape rates.

6. *Brzonkala v. Virginia Polytechnic and State University,* 935 F. Supp. 772 (W.D. Va. 1996). Brzonkala's case has had an impressive subsequent history. She brought her original complaint under both Title IX and the federal Violence Against Women Act. The district court denied her Title IX claim of disparate treatment by VPI, and the court of appeals agreed. The district court denied her Title IX claim of hostile environment; the Fourth Circuit remanded the hostile environment claim with instructions to reconsider the claim in light of the Supreme Court's decision in the *Davis* case about institutional liability for peer harassment. Brzonkala's claim under the Violence Against Women Act prompted the court of appeals to hold that statute unconstitutional, *Brzonkala v. Virginia Polytechnic and State Univ.*, 169 F.3d 820 (4th Cir. 1999). The U.S. Supreme Court agreed. United States v. Morrison, 120 S. Ct. 1740 (2000).

7. Michael Bayles, "Coercive Offers and Public Benefits," *The Personalist* 55:139–44 (1974).

8. Vicki Schultz, "Reconceptualizing Sexual Harassment," *Yale Law Journal* 107:1683–1807 (1998), argues that sexual harassment in employment should be understood as excluding women from traditionally male jobs.

9. Michael Bayles, "Coercive Offers and Public Benefits," *The Personalist* 55:139–44 (1974), p. 142.

10. An example is John Hughes and Larry May, "Sexual Harassment," *Social Theory and Practice* 6:249–80 (1980).

11. Nancy Tuana, "Sexual Harassment: Offers and Coercion," *Journal of Social Philosophy* 19:30–42 (1988).

12. John Hughes and Larry May, "Sexual Harassment," *Social Theory and Practice* 6:249–80 (1980).

13. For a fuller examination of this position, see Leslie Francis, ed., *Date Rape: Law, Philosophy and Feminism.* State College, PA: Penn State University Press, 1996.

14. Katie Roiphe defends this view in *The Morning After: Sex, Fear, and Feminism on Campus* (Boston: Little, Brown & Co., 1993). Objecting to what she sees as the paternalism in many views of date rape, Roiphe writes: "All competent female college students are compromised by the association of gullibility, low self-esteem, and the inability to assert ourselves with our position in relation to men. We should not be pressured and intimidated by words like 'I'll break up with you if you don't'—and anyone who is intimidated should be recognized as the exception, not the rule. Allowing verbal coercion to constitute rape is a sign of tolerance toward the ultrafeminine stance of passivity. . . . Whether or not we feel pressured, regardless of our level of self-esteem, the responsibility for our actions is still our own" (p. 68).

15. Susan Estrich, *Real Rape*, supra note 2.

16. *Gebser v. Lago Vista Independent School District*, 524 U.S. 275 (1998).

17. *Davis v. Monroe County Board of Education*, 526 U.S. 629 (1999).

18. John Hughes and Larry May, "Sexual Harassment," *Social Theory and Practice* 6:249–80 (1980).

19. Courtney Leatherman, "Some Colleges Hush Up Charges to Get Rid of Problem Professors," *The Chronicle of Higher Education*, December 6, 1996, p. A14.

20. American Bar Association Model Rules of Professional Conduct, Rule 5.1.

21. American Bar Association Model Rules of Professional Conduct, Rule 8.3.

CHAPTER 5: THE WRONGS OF SEXUAL HARASSMENT

1. Andrew Altman develops an account of sexual harassment law as protecting employment opportunities generally and the opportunities of disadvantaged groups in particular. Based on this account, he argues that the unwelcomeness requirement in sexual harassment law should be understood as part of a reasonableness standard. Andrew Altman, "Making Sense of Sexual Harassment Law," *Philosophy and Public Affairs* 25:36–63 (1996). Altman's view does permit the possibility that an overture would be deemed intrusive by the recipient, as violating her personal space, but not be judged to be sexual harassment because it was reasonable. This conclusion seems justifiable for an area of sexual harassment policy that is an aspect of a theory of distributive justice, here protecting equality of opportunity within the context of ordinary social interchange. It might not be justifiable for an area where the predominant value is protecting the autonomy of the recipient, as in actual sexual intimacy. See the discussion of the Antioch policy in chapter 7.

2. Ellen Frankel Paul argues for the use of tort remedies in some seductive situations. Her individualistic rights perspective is that sexual harassment is a harm to an individual, akin to the invasion of privacy or the infliction of emotional distress. Her

view is that sexual harassment should not be viewed as a form of sex discrimination against women; she rejects Catharine MacKinnon's argument that sexual harassment is a manifestation of the exercise of power by men over women. Instead, she prefers the EEOC definition, which includes "unwelcome sexual advances, requests for sexual favors, and other verbal or physical conduct of a sexual nature which . . . has the purpose or effect of unreasonably interfering with an individual's work performance or creating an intimidating, hostile, or offensive working environment" as better capturing the harms to individuals in harassment. She would allow tort recovery only when a reasonable person would regard the conduct of the seducer as extreme or outrageous and when the victim suffered economic detriment or extreme emotional distress as a result. She regards as an advantage of this view that it will deflect responsibility from employers and universities unless they knew or should have known of the offending conduct. Ellen Frankel Paul, "Sexual Harassment as Sex Discrimination: A Defective Paradigm," *Yale Law and Policy Review* 8:333–65 (1990). The position defended here is that Paul's individualism takes no account of the detrimental impact of unwanted sexual advances and of the ways in which institutions can help to avoid or mitigate those effects.

3. Vicki Schultz argues that workplace harassment should not be limited to sexuality; it should be seen as efforts to exclude from the workplace based on sex. Thus she groups together sexist remarks—"dumb broad"—with sexually charged remarks—"I bet I arouse you." One of her concerns is that legal doctrines that require plaintiffs to show that harassment was sexually based function to divide and conquer the case of a plaintiff who has met with a pattern of harassment, only some of which was sexually based.

4. This point is made by Robert L. Holmes, "Sexual Harassment and the University," *Monist* 97:499–518 (1996) (reprinted in part II ch. 13).

5. Sam Howe Verhovek, "Texas Law Professor Prompts a Furor over Race Comments," *New York Times*, September 16, 1997, p. A28.

6. Texas's race-based affirmative action program was held unconstitutional in a recent highly publicized federal appellate decision, *Hopwood v. Texas*, 84 F. 3d 720 (5th Cir. 1996). As a result, like California, Texas has suffered from the perception that it is a problematic choice for minority students.

7. Dormitory rooms are a relatively central part of students' lives. They're unavoidable for a student who wants to sleep. They are perhaps the only private space students have—and offer limited privacy at that. I would argue that they are next in importance after classes and the library in enabling students to experience the educational opportunities a university provides. Proposals have been made to consider other university spaces as central in the same way as dormitories or classrooms, such as the Internet. See Evelyn Oldenkamp, "Pornography, the Internet, and Student-to-Student Sexual Harassment: A Dilemma Resolved with Title VII and Title IX," *Duke Journal of Gender Law and Policy* 4:159–80 (1997).

8. Rule 4.4.

9. The resolution reads in pertinent part: "The American Bar Association . . . condemns the manifestation by lawyers in the course of their professional activities, by words or conduct, of bias or prejudice against clients, opposing parties and their counsel, other litigants, witnesses, judges and court personnel, jurors and others, based upon race, sex, religion, national origin, disability, age, sexual orientation or

socio-economic status, unless such words or conduct are otherwise permissible as legitimate advocacy on behalf of a client or a cause." The resolution was adopted in lieu of a disciplinary rule that would have made such conduct disciplinable, largely because of concerns that enforcing it would be subject to challenges under the First Amendment. Stephen Gillers and Roy D. Simon, Jr. *Regulation of Lawyers: Statutes and Standards.* Boston: Little, Brown & Co., 1997.

10. Ronald Dworkin defends a right to equal respect and concern in many of his writings. See especially *Taking Rights Seriously.* Cambridge, MA: Harvard University Press, 1977.

11. A good example of such intersectionality scholarship is the work of Kimberlé Crenshaw. See, for example, "Mapping the Margins: Intersectionality, Identity Politics, and Violence Against Women of Color," *Stanford Law Review* 43:1241–99 (1991).

CHAPTER 6: CONSENSUAL SEX ON CAMPUS

1. For a discussion of how the constitutional right to privacy applies to regulation of consensual amorous relationships in public colleges and universities, see Elizabeth Keller, "Consensual Amorous Relationship between Faculty and Students: The Constitutional Right to Privacy," *Journal of College and University Law* 15:21–42 (1988).

2. John Rawls, *A Theory of Justice.* Cambridge, MA: Harvard University Press, 1971, especially section 53.

3. Several state bar associations prohibit any sexual relationships between a lawyer and a client that did not predate the lawyer-client relationship; see Minnesota Rule 1.8(k), Oregon DR 5-110, West Virginia Rule 1.8(g), Wisconsin Rule 1.8(k). Florida establishes a rebuttable presumption that sexual relationships with a client are exploitative and subject the lawyer to discipline, Florida Rule 4–8.4(I). California, the first state to address sexual relationships between lawyers and clients, prohibits coercive relationships or relationships that compromise the quality of legal services. California Rule 3-120.

4. For a particularly good account of autonomy and informed consent in medicine, see Allen Buchanan and Dan W. Brock, *Deciding for Others: The Ethics of Surrogate Decisionmaking.* Cambridge and New York: Cambridge University Press, 1989.

5. See, for example, Susan Sherwin, *No Longer Patient: Feminist Ethics and Health Care.* Philadelphia: Temple University Press, 1992.

6. For a discussion of the concept of a total institution, see Erving Goffman, *Asylums: Essays on the Social Situation of Mental Patients and Other Inmates.* Garden City, NY: Anchor Books, 1961.

CHAPTER 7: SEXUAL HARASSMENT POLICIES AND PROCEDURES

1. Billie Wright Dziech and Linda Weiner, *The Lecherous Professor,* 2d ed. Urbana: University of Illinois Press, 1990. See Part II, Chapter 9.

2. An excellent study of the economics of deterrence in the criminal law is Neal Kumar Katyal, "Deterrence's Difficulty," *Michigan Law Review* 95:2385–2475 (1997).

3. For a good study arguing that insurance and alcohol prices had a deterrent effect on binge drinking and driving under the influence but criminal sanctions did not, see Frank A. Sloan, Bridget A. Reilly, and Christoph Schenzler, "Effects of Tort Liability and Insurance on Heavy Drinking and Drinking and Driving," *Journal of Law and Economics* 38:49–77 (1995). According to the authors of this study, the only criminal law variable that had a significant effect on rates of driving under the influence was deployment of police.

4. See Anne Lawton, "The Emperor's New Clothes: How the Academy Deals with Sexual Harassment," *Yale Journal of Law and Feminism* 11:75–154 (1999).

5. For a good discussion of the differences between disciplinary and diversionary programs for lawyers, see Mark E. Hopkins, "Note: Open Attorney Discipline: New Jersey Supreme Court's Decision to Make Attorney Disciplinary Procedures Public—What it Means to Attorneys and to the Public," *Rutgers Law Journal* 27:757–92 (1996). For a discussion of diversionary programs for physicians, see R.P. Schwartz, R. K. White, D. R. McDuff, and J. L. Johnson, "Four Years Experience of a Hospital's Impaired Physician Committee," *Journal of Addiction and Disability* 14:13–21 (1995).

6. There is considerable controversy about whether the data show high rates of recidivism among sexual offenders. See Stephen J. Morse, "Symposium: Blame and Danger: An Essay on Preventive Detention," *Boston University Law Review* 76:113–45 (1996).

7. Larry May and Edward Soule, "Sexual Harassment as a Rape or Battery," in Keith Burgess-Jackson, ed., *A Most Detestable Crime: New Philosophical Essays on Rape*. Oxford: Oxford University Press, 1999.

8. Mary P. Rowe, "Dealing with Sexual Harassment," *Harvard Business Review* 59: 42–46 (1981).

9. The classic discussion of perfect, imperfect, and pure procedural justice is found in John Rawls, *A Theory of Justice*. Cambridge, MA: Harvard University Press, 1971, pp. 83–90.

10. Hunter R. Rawlings III, "President's Statement on Sexual Harassment," Cornell University Policy Library—Policy 6.4 (July 8, 1996).

11. May and Soule, "Sexual Harassment as a Rape or Battery."

12. For an argument that grievance procedures erroneously treat sexual harassment as a problem of individual behavior, rather than as a problem of campus inequality, see Frances Hoffman, "Sexual Harassment in Academia: Feminist Theory and Institutional Practice," *Harvard Educational Review* 56:105–21 (1986).

13. Susan Estrich, *Real Rape*. Cambridge, MA: Harvard University Press, 1989.

14. For a summary of these changes, see Leslie Francis, "Rape (including date rape)," *Encyclopedia of Applied Ethics,* ed. Ruth Chadwick. San Diego, CA: Academic Press, 1998.

15. The University of Pennsylvania, for example, offers a formal committee hearing only in cases of suspension or dismissal. *Handbook for Faculty and Academic Administrators,* VI.D. Sexual Harassment Policy, c.1 (November 7, 1995).

16. Owen Fiss, "Comment: Against Settlement," *Yale Law Journal* 93:1073–89 (1984).

17. For a defense of the position, see Anne Lawton, "The Emperor's New Clothes: How the Academy Deals with Sexual Harassment," *Yale Journal of Law and Feminism* 11:75–154 (1999).

18. In *Topol v. Trustees of the University of Pennsylvania,* the trial court admitted into evidence a diary maintained by the complainant detailing her relationship with the accused. 160 F.R.D. 476 (E.D. Pa. 1995).

19. *Mann V. University of Cincinnati,* 1997 U.S. App. LEXIS 12482 (6th Cir. 1997). The appellate court upheld an order of sanctions against the university's attorney for obtaining the records without adequate notice to the plaintiff.

20. Courtney Leatherman, "Some Colleges Hush Up Charges to Get Rid of Problem Professors," *Chronicle of Higher Education,* December 6, 1996, p. A14.

21. University of Pennsylvania, Handbook for Faculty and Academic Administrators, VI.D. Sexual Harassment Policy f (November 7, 1995).

22. Ellen Frankel Paul, "Sexual Harassment as Sex Discrimination: A Defective Paradigm," *Yale Law and Policy Review,* 8:333–65 (1990) (selection reprinted in part II, ch. 11).

23. Diana Tietjens Meyers, "Rights in Collision: A Non-Punitive, Compensatory Remedy for Abusive Speech," *Law and Philosophy* 14:203–43 (1995).

Selected Bibliography

Abrams, Kathryn, "The New Jurisprudence of Sexual Harassment," *Cornell Law Review* 83:1169–1230 (1998).

———, "Postscript, Spring 1998: A Response to Professors Bernstein and Franke," *Cornell Law Review* 83:1257–68 (1998).

Adams, Michelle, "Knowing Your Place: Theorizing Sexual Harassment at Home," *Arizona Law Review* 40:17–71 (1998).

Altman, Andrew, "Making Sense of Sexual Harassment Law," *Philosophy and Public Affairs* 25:36–64 (1996).

Archard, David, "Exploited Consent," *Journal of Social Philosophy* 25:92–101 (1994).

Barr, Paula A., "Perceptions of Sexual Harassment," *Sociological Inquiry* 63:460–70 (1993).

Bayles, Michael, "Coercive Offers and Public Benefits," *Personalist* 55:139–44 (1974).

Benditt, Theodore, "Threats and Offers," *Personalist* 58:382–84 (1977).

Bernays, Anne. *Professor Romeo.* New York: Weidenfeld & Nicholson, 1989.

Bernstein, Anita, "Treating Sexual Harassment with Respect," *Harvard Law Review* 111:445–527 (1997).

———, "An Old Jurisprudence: Respect in Retrospect," *Cornell Law Review* 83:1231–44 (1998).

————, "Law, Culture, and Harassment," *University of Pennsylvania Law Review* 142:1227–1311 (1994).

Biebel, John H., "I Thought She Said Yes: Sexual Assault in England and America," *Suffolk Transnational Law Review* 19:153–83 (1995).

Blumenthal, Jeremy A., "The Reasonable Woman Standard: A Meta-Analytic Review of Gender Differences in Perceptions of Sexual Harassment," *Law and Human Behavior* 22:33–57 (1998).

Bowman, Cynthia Grant, "Street Harassment and the Informal Ghettoization of Women," *Harvard Law Review* 106:517–639 (1993).

Burgess-Jackson, Keith. *Rape: A Philosophical Investigation.* Dartmouth, England: Aldershot Press, 1996.

Cahn, Naomi R., "Symposium—The Looseness of Legal Language: The Reasonable Woman Standard in Theory and in Practice," *Cornell Law Review* 77:1398–1446 (1992).

Campbell, Bebe Moore. *Brothers and Sisters.* New York: Putnam's, 1994.

Carpenter, Dale, "Same-Sex Sexual Harassment Under Title VII," *South Texas Law Review* 37:699–726 (1996).

Chamallas, Martha, "Feminist Constructions of Objectivity: Multiple Perspectives on Sexual and Racial Harassment Litigation," *Texas Journal of Women and the Law* 1:95–142 (1992).

————, "Essay, Writing About Sexual Harassment: A Guide to the Literature," *UCLA Women's Law Journal* 4:37–58 (1993).

Cheng, Edward S., "Boys Being Boys and Girls Being Girls—Student to Student Sexual Harassment from the Courtroom to the Classroom," *UCLA Woman's Law Journal* 7:263–321 (1997).

Cho, Sumi K., "Converging Stereotypes in Racialized Sexual Harassment: When the Model Minority Meets Suzie Wong," *Journal of Gender, Race & Justice* 1:177–211 (1997).

Clougherty, Lydia A., "Feminist Legal Methods and the First Amendment Defense to Sexual Harassment Liability," *Nebraska Law Review* 75:1–26 (1996).

Crichton, Michael. *Disclosure.* New York: Alfred A. Knopf, 1994.

Crocker, Phyllis L., "Annotated Bibliography on Sexual Harassment in Education," *Women's Rights Law Reporter* 7:91–106 (1982).

Davis, Nancy (Ann), "Sexual Harassment in the University," in Steven M. Cahn, ed., *Moral Responsibility and the University.* Philadelphia: Temple University Press, 1990, pp. 150–76.

Dey, Eric L., Jessica S. Korn, and Linda J. Sax, "Betrayed by the Academy: The Sexual Harassment of Women College Faculty," *Journal of Higher Education* 676:149–74 (1996).

Dodds, Susan M., Lucy Frost, Robert Pargetter, and Elizabeth W. Prior, "Sexual Harassment," *Social Theory and Practice* 14:111–30 (1988).

Dolkart, Jane, "Hostile Environment Harassment: Equality, Objectivity and the Shaping of Legal Standards," *Emory Law Journal* 43:151–244 (1994).

Dziech, Billie, and Linda Weiner. *The Lecherous Professor,* 2d ed. Urbana: University of Illinois Press, 1990.

Ehrenreich, Nancy S., "Pluralist Myths and Powerless Men: The Ideology of Reasonableness in Sexual Harassment Law," *Yale Law Journal* 99:1177-1234 (1990).

Ellis, Judy Trent, "Sexual Harassment and Race: A Legal Analysis of Discrimination," *Journal of Legislation* 8:20–45 (1981).

Eskridge, William N., "The Many Faces of Sexual Consent," *William and Mary Law Review* 37:47–67 (1995).

Estlund, Cynthia L., "Freedom of Expression in the Workplace and the Problem of Discriminatory Harassment," *Texas Law Review* 75:687–777 (1997).

Estrich, Susan, "Sex at Work," *Stanford Law Review* 43:813–61 (1991).

Fitzgerald, Louise F., Sandra L. Shullman, Nancy Bailey, Margaret Richards, Janice Swecker; Yael Gold; Margaret Richards; and Lauren Weitzman, "The Incidence and Dimensions of Sexual Harassment in the Workplace," *Journal of Vocational Behavior* 32:152–75 (1988).

———, Lauren M. Weitzman, Yael Gold, and Mimi Ormerod, "Academic Harassment: Sex and Denial in Scholarly Garb," *Psychology of Women Quarterly* 12:329–40 (1988).

Francis, Leslie P., ed. *Date Rape: Feminism, Philosophy and the Law.* State College, PA: Penn State University Press, 1996.

Franke, Katherine M., "What's Wrong with Sexual Harassment?" *Stanford Law Review* 49:691–772 (1997).

———, "Gender, Sex, Agency and Discrimination: A Reply to Professor Abrams," *Cornell Law Review* 83:1245-56 (1998).

Frankel Paul, Ellen, "Sexual Harassment as Sex Discrimination: A Defective Paradigm," *Yale Law & Policy Review* 8:333–65 (1990).

Gallop, Jane. *Feminist Accused of Sexual Harassment.* Durham, NC: Duke University Press, 1997.

Gervasio, Amy Herstein, and Katy Ruckdeschel, "College Students' Judgments of Verbal Sexual Harassment," *Journal of Applied Social Psychology* 22:190-211 (1992).

Grauerholz, Elizabeth, "Sexual Harassment of Women Professors by Students: Exploring the Dynamics of Power, Authority, and Gender in a University Setting," *Sex Roles* 21:789-801 (1989).

Hager, Mark, "Harassment as a Tort: Why Title VII Hostile Environment Liability Should Be Curtailed," *Connecticut Law Review* 30:375–439 (1998).

Held, Virginia, "Coercion and Coercive Offers," in J. Roland Pennock and John Chapman, eds., *Coercion, Nomos XIV.* Chicago: Aldine and Atherton, 1972, pp. 49–62.

Hajdin, Mane, "Sexual Harassment in the Law: The Demarcation Problem," *Journal of Social Philosophy* 25:102–22 (1994).

Hoffmann, Frances L., "Sexual Harassment in Academia: Feminist Theory and Institutional Practice," *Harvard Educational Review* 56:105–21 (1986).

Holmes, Robert L., "Sexual Harassment and the University," *The Monist* 79:499–518 (1996).

Hotelling, Kathy, "Sexual Harassment: A Problem Shielded by Silence," *Journal of Counseling & Development* 69:497–501 (1991).

Hughes, John C., and Larry May, "Sexual Harassment," *Social Theory and Practice* 6:249–80 (1980).

Keller, Elizabeth, "Consensual Amorous Relationships between Faculty and Students: The Constitutional Right to Privacy," *Journal of College and University Law* 15:21–42 (1988).

Komaromy, Mieriam, Andrew B. Bindman, Richard J. Haber, and Merle A. Sande, "Sexual Harassment in Medical Training," *New England Journal of Medicine* 328:322–26 (1993).

Larsen, Jane, "Women Understand So Little, They Call My Good Nature 'Deceit': A Feminist Rethinking of Seduction," *Columbia Law Review* 93:374–472 (1992).

Lawton, Anne, "The Emperor's New Clothes: How the Academy Deals with Sexual Harassment," *Yale Journal of Law and Feminism* 11:75–154 (1999).

Leatherman, Courtney, "Some Colleges Hush Up Charges to Get Rid of Problem Professors," *Chronicle of Higher Education,* December 6, 1996, p. A14.

———, "Ex-Student Sues Professor at U. of Pennsylvania for Sexual Harassment," *Chronicle of Higher Education,* April 13, 1994, p. A16.

———, "Fighting Back: Professors Accused of Sexual Harassment Say Their Rights Have Been Breached," *Chronicle of Higher Education,* March 16, 1994, p. A17.

———, "Ohio State Retracts Job Offer to Scholar Accused of Harassment," *Chronicle of Higher Education,* January 10, 1997, p. A11.

Levy, Yael, "Attorneys, Clients, and Sex: Conflicting Interests in the California Rule," *Georgetown Journal of Legal Ethics* 5:649-73 (1992).

Lindemann, Barbara, and David Kadue, *Sexual Harassment in Employment Law.* Washington, D.C.: Bureau of National Affairs, 1992.

MacKinnon, Catharine. *Sexual Harassment of Working Women.* New Haven, CT: Yale University Press, 1978.

Marks, Michelle A., and Eileen S. Nelson, "Sexual Harassment on Campus: Effects of Professor Gender on Perception of Sexually Harassing Behaviors," *Sex Roles* 28: 207–17 (1993).

Martin, Jane Roland, "Bound for the Promised Land: The Gendered Character of Higher Education," *Duke Journal of Gender Law & Policy* 4:3–26 (1997).

Matsuda, Mari J., Charles R. Lawrence III, Richard Delgado, and Kimberle Williams Crenshaw. *Words That Wound: Critical Race Theory, Assaultive Speech, and the First Amendment.* Boulder, CO: Westview Press, 1993.

May, Larry, "Vicarious Agency and Corporate Responsibility," *Philosophical Studies* 43:69–82 (1983).

———, and Edward Soule, "Sexual Harassment as Rape or Battery," in Keith Burgess-Jackson, ed., *A Most Detestable Crime: New Philosophical Essays on Rape.* Oxford: Oxford University Press, 1999.

Mazer, Donald B., and Elizabeth F. Percival, "Students' Experiences of Sexual Harassment at a Small University," *Sex Roles* 20:1–22 (1989).

McKinney, Kathleen, "Sexual Harassment of University Faculty by Colleagues and Students," *Sex Roles* 23:421–38 (1990).

Minson, J. P., "Social Theory and Legal Argument: Catharine MacKinnon on Sexual Harassment," *International Journal of the Sociology of Law* 19:355–78 (1991).

Mischler, Linda Fitts, "Reconciling Rapture, Representation, and Responsibility: An Argument Against Per Se Bans on Attorney-Client Sex," *Georgetown Journal of Legal Ethics* 10:209–69 (1996).

Morris, Celia. *Bearing Witness: Sexual Harassment and Beyond—Everywoman's Story.* Boston: Little, Brown, 1994.

Morrison, Toni, ed. *Race-ing Justice, En-gendering Power: Essays on Anita Hill, Clarence Thomas, and the Construction of Social Reality.* New York: Pantheon Books, 1992.

Nozick, Robert, "Coercion," in Morganbesser, Suppes, and White, eds., *Philosophy, Science and Method*. New York: St. Martin's, 1969.

Oldenkamp, Evelyn, "Pornography, the Internet, and Student to Student Sexual Harassment: A Dilemma Resolved with Title Vll and Title IX," *Duke Journal of Gender Law & Policy* 4:159–79 (1997).

Ontiveros, Maria L., "Fictionalizing Harassment—Disclosing the Truth," *Michigan Law Review* 93:1373–1400 (1995).

Ore-Aguilar, Gaby, "Sexual Harassment and Human Rights in Latin America," *Fordham Law Review* 66:631–46 (1997).

Patai, Daphne. *Heterophobia: Sexual Harassment and the Future of Feminism*. New York: Rowman & Littlefield, 1998.

Pichaske, David R., "When Students Make Sexual Advances," *Chronicle of Higher Education*, February 24, 1995, p. B1.

Riger, Stephanie, "Gender Dilemmas in Sexual Harassment Policies and Procedures," *American Psychologist* 46:497-505 (1991).

Riggs, Robert O., Patricia H. Murrell, and JoAnn C. Cutting. *Sexual Harassment in Higher Education: From Conflict to Community*. Washington, D.C.: George Washington University, ASHE-ERIC Higher Education Report No. 2, 1993.

Robertson, Claire, Constance E. Dyer, and D'Ann Cambell, "Campus Harassment: Sexual Harassment Policies and Procedures at Institutions of Higher Learning," *Signs: Journal of Women in Culture and Society* 13:792–812 (1988).

Roiphe, Katie. *The Morning After: Sex, Fear and Feminism on Campus*. Boston: Little, Brown, 1993.

Rosen, Jeffrey, "In Defense of Gender-Blindness," *The New Republic*, June 29, 1998, pp. 25–35.

Rubin, Linda J., and Sherry B. Borgers, "Sexual Harassment in Universities during the 1980s," *Sex Roles* 23:397–411 (1990).

Sandler, Bernice R., Carolyn S. Bratt, and Robert J. Shoop. *Sexual Harassment on Campus: A Guide for Administrators, Faculty, and Students*. Boston: Allyn & Bacon, 1997.

—— and Roberta M. Hall. *Out of the Classroom: A Chilly Campus Climate for Women?* Washington, D.C.: Project on the Status and Education of Women, Association of American Colleges, 1984.

Schneider, Beth E., "Graduate Women, Sexual Harassment, and University Policy," *Journal of Higher Education* 58:46–65 (1987).

Schultz, Vicki, "Reconceptualizing Sexual Harassment," *Yale Law Journal* 107:1683-1805 (1998).

Sterba, James P., "Feminist Justice and Sexual Harassment," *Journal of Social Philosophy* 27:103-22 (1996).

Stevens, Robert, "Coercive Offers," *Australasian Journal of Philosophy* 66:83–95 (1988).

Storrow, Richard F., "Same-Sex Sexual Harassment Claims After *Oncale*: Defining the Boundaries of Actionable Conduct," *American University Law Review* 47:677–745 (1998).

Summers, Russel J., and Karin Myklebust, "The Influence of a History of Romance on Judgments and Responses to a Complaint of Sexual Harassment," *Sex Roles* 27:345–57 (1992).

Superson, Anita M., "A Feminist Definition of Sexual Harassment," *Journal of Social Philosophy* 24:46–64 (1993).

Thompson, Deborah, M. "'The Woman in the Street': Reclaiming the Public Space from Sexual Harassment," *Yale Journal of Law and Feminism* 6:313–81 (1994).

Toobin, Jeffrey, "The Trouble with Sex: Why the Law of Sexual Harassment Has Never Worked," *The New Yorker,* February 9, 1998, at 48.

Tuana, Nancy, "Sexual Harassment in Academe: Issues of Power and Coercion," *College Teaching* 33:53–63 (1983).

———, "Sexual Harassment: Offers and Coercion," *Journal of Social Philosophy* 19:30–42 (1988).

Volokh, Eugene, "What Speech Does 'Hostile Work Environment' Harassment Law Restrict?" *Georgetown Law Journal* 85:627-48 (1996).

Waldo, Craig R., Jennifer L. Berdahl, and Louise F. Fitzgerald, "Are Men Sexually Harassed? If So, by Whom?" *Law and Human Behavior* 22:59–79 (1998).

Wilson, Robin, "Harassment Charges at Cornell U.," *Chronicle of Higher Education,* February 10, 1995, p. A13.

———, "A 'Fractured' Department," *Chronicle of Higher Education,* January 13, 1995, p. A13.

Young, Sherry, "Getting to Yes: The Case against Banning Consensual Relationships in Higher Education," *American University Journal of Gender & the Law* 4:269–302 (1996).

Zimmerman, David, "Coercive Wage Offers," *Philosophy and Public Affairs* 10:121–45 (1981).

SELECTED LEGAL CASES

Alexander v. Yale University, 631 F.2d 178 (2d Cir. 1980), on appeal from 549 F. Supp. 1 (D. Conn 1977).

Bougher v. University of Pittsburgh, 713 F. Supp. 139 (W.D. Pa. 1989).

Burlington Industries, Inc., v. Ellerth, 524 U.S. 742 (1998).

Cohen v. San Bernardino Valley College, 92 F. 2d 968 (9th Cir. 1996), on appeal from 883 F. Supp. 1407 (S.D. Cal. 1995).

Davis v. Monroe County Board of Education, 526 U.S. 629 (1999).

Faragher v. City of Boca Raton, 524 U.S. 775 (1998).

Gebser v. Lago Vista Independent School District, 524 U.S. 274 (1998).

Harris v. Forklift Systems, Inc., 510 U.S. 17 (1993).

Jew v. University of Iowa, 398 N.W.2d 861 (Iowa, 1987).

Karibian v. Columbia University, 14 F.2d 773 (2d Cir.), cert. denied, 512 U.S. 1213 (1994).

Lipsett v. University of Puerto Rico, 864 F.2d 881 (1st Cir. 1988).

Mann v. University of Cincinnati, 1997 U.S. App. LEXIS 12482 (6th Cir., May 27, 1997).

Meritor Savings Bank v. Vinson, 477 U.S. 57 (1986).

Moire v. Temple University School of Medicine, 613 F. Supp. 1360 (E.D. Pa. 1985).

Oncale v. Sundowner Offshore Services, Inc., 523 U.S. 75 (1998).

Silva v. University of New Hampshire, 888 F. Supp. 293 (D.N.H. 1994).

Topol v. Trustees of the University of Pennsylvania, 160 F.R.D. 476 (E.D. Pa. 1995).

United States v. Morrison, 120 S. Ct. 1740 (2000), upholding *Brzonkala v. Virginia Polytechinc and State University,* 169 F.3d 820 (4th Cir. 1999).

Yusuf v. Vassar College, 35 F.3d 709 (2d Cir. 1994)

Index

AAUP. *See* American Association of University Professors

Academe, 124

academic freedom, 19–45; and roles of university, 38–45

academy: Barzun on, 251n2; Bennis on, 153; capability of dealing with sexual harassment, 155; and equality of opportunity, 23–24; knowledge values of, 21–23; and perpetuation of ideology, 27–28; responsibilities of, 81–83, 188–89; roles of, 20–28, 38–45; sexual harassment and, 183–90; and transmission of culture, 24–27; typical environment of, 67–69, 86

accommodation, 97–98

accused: confidentiality for, 121–24; personal experience of, 191–208

accuser, confidentiality for, 121–24

action, versus speech, 29–32

affirmative action, 23, 262n6

agency, and harassment responsibility, 51, 55–57

alternative dispute resolution, 120–21

Altman, Andrew, 30, 261n1

American Association of University Professors (AAUP), 38, 124

American Bar Association, 95, 263n9

American Civil Liberties Union, 92

American Heritage Dictionary, 180

American Philosophical Association, 26

Amir, Menachim, 260n5

Antioch College, sexual harassment policy, 234–48

appeals process, Antioch College on, 247–48

Archard, David, 212–18

arts, AAUP and, 40–41
Association of American Law Schools,
    26
attorney-client sex, 209–11
Austin, J. L., 30–31
autonomy, 101–2, 109

Baron, Larry, 260n5
Barth, John, 146–47
Bartky, Sandra, 181
Barzun, Jacques, 251n2
Bayles, Michael, 76–78, 158
Bennis, Warren, 153
biology, arguments from, 133, 143–45
bisexual harassment, 167–68
Black, Hugo, 29
Black's Law Dictionary, 180
Bloom, Allan, 43, 252n18
Bork, Robert, 167
Brigham Young University, 26
bright-line test, case against, 209–11
Brown, Nancy, 169
Brown v. Board of Education, 32
*Brzonkala v. Virginia Polytechnic and
    State University*, 260n6
bystanders, responsibilities of, 83–85

California State University at Chico, 6
campus setting: bystander
    responsibilities in, 83–85; consensual
    sex in, 99–112; significance of, 79–85
canon debate, 27
Chaplisky case, 29–30
Chicago Theological Seminary, 5–6
Chomsky, Noam, 27
City of Los Angeles v. Manhart, 135
City University of New York, 40, 65
cognitive capacity, and consent, 110–11
Cohen, Dean, 46–48
College of the Albemarle, 5
communitarianism, 25, 33, 43
confidante, harasser as, 150–51
confidentiality: Department of
    Education on, 62–63; in sexual
    harassment policies, 121–24, 248
conflict of interest, 105, 107–8
consensual sex, 8, 99–112; bribery and,

9; Department of Education on, 61;
    and educational quality, 103–6;
    MacKinnon on, 141; permissive
    policy on, case for, 101–3; versus
    sexual harassment, 168–70, 188,
    195–99, 209–11; Wellesley College
    on, 101, 229–31
consent: Antioch College on, 239–40;
    exploited, 212–18; feminism on, 198;
    impaired, 108–11
conservatism: on freedom of
    expression, 42–43; on role of
    academy, 24–27
Constitution, and sexual harassment
    law, 63–66
Cornell University, 6–8, 119
counselor-helper, harasser as, 150
counselors, 121
Crenshaw, Kimberlé, 37
Crichton, Michael, 13
culture: academy and, 24–28;
    institutional, 119

date rape, 9, 79–81, 261n14
*Davis v. Monroe County Board of
    Education*, 57–58
decision-making capacity: and consent,
    110–11; of women, 210
democracy, education and, 22
Department of Education Sexual
    Harassment Guidance Document,
    58–66
deterrence, policies and, 115–17
Dewey, John, 22, 39
differences approach, 134–36
discipline, policies and, 124–25
discrimination, concepts of, 134–35
diversity, 33, 254n52
Dodds, Susan, 169
dominance: and sexual harassment, 6–7,
    12–13, 175–82.
See also power
dormitories: guests in, 93–94, 107;
    significance of, 262n7
Duke University, sexual harassment
    policy, 221–24
Dziech, Billie, 115, 146–56

education: Bennis on, 153; effects of, 33–34; on harassment, as remedy, 125; quality of, consensual sex and, 103–6; sexuality and, 105, 191–208. *See also* academic freedom; academy

EEOC. *See* Equal Employment Opportunity Commission

Ellison v. Brady, 61–62

Emerson, Thomas I., 129–31

emotional distress, 171

environment, 119

Equal Employment Opportunity Commission (EEOC), 11, 49, 233; *Guidelines*, 180

equality of opportunity: AAUP and, 39–42; academy and, 23–24; consensual sex and, 106–8

equality, sexual harassment paradigms and, 164–74, 209–11

Estrich, Susan, 80–81

ethics. *See* wrongs

evaluation, consensual sex and, 105, 107–8, 212

evidence, problems of, 119–20

exploited consent, 212–18

expression: freedom of, 28–38, 42–43; protection of, justifications for, 32–38

fairness, 118–21

Feinberg, Joel, 34–36

female/male harassment, 12–13, 179–80

feminism: of accused, 191–208; on consent, 198; on sexual harassment definitions, 175–82

fighting words, 29–30

First Amendment, and sexual harassment law, 63–66

Fish, Stanley, 28, 32, 44, 254n52

Fiss, Owen, 120

Fourteenth Amendment, 53, 135–36

freedom of association, and consensual sex policies, 101

freedom of expression, 28–38; conservatism on, 42–43

Gallop, Jane, 73–74, 105, 191–208

Galston, William, 26

Gebser v. Lago Vista Independent School District, 55–57

gender harassment, 5–7; prevalence of, 16; sexism as, 91–93; sexuality as, 93–97; wrongs of, 90–97

generalized sexism, 5–7

Gilbert v. General Electric, 135

Graglia, Lou, 92

Great Books movement, 27

Greenawalt, Ken, 30, 32

group injury, sexual harassment as, 166

Grove City College, 26

Gutmann, Amy, 22–23, 28

Hajdin, Mane, 258n49

harassers: characteristics of, 146–56; roles of, 150–51

harassment, versus sexual harassment, 185

Harlan, J. M., 29

harm, 34–36

Harris v. Forklift Systems, 50

Harvard University, sexual harassment policy, 224–26

hate speech, 30, 37; regulation of, in academia, 44–45

Held, Virginia, 158

Hentoff, Nat, 251n1

Hill, Anita, 12, 16, 181

Holmes, Robert L., 183–90

homosexuality: discrimination and, 26; and harassment, 14, 50; and pedagogy, 204

hostile environment harassment, 11, 47, 49; Department of Education on, 59; MacKinnon on, 140; standards for, 50

Hughes, John, 78–79, 82, 169, 177

humanity, 133–34

Hyde, Henry, 42

hypersensitivity, 35, 97–98, 106, 181

ideal theory, 102–3

ideology, perpetuation of, academy and, 27–28

illocutionary force, 30–31

immunity, 54

impaired consent, 108–11

inequality approach, 134–36, 164–74, 209–11
informal mediation, 115, 120–21
institutional culture, 119; Harvard University on, 226
intellectual seducer, harasser as, 151

Jeffries, Leonard, 40, 65
Jew, Jean, 12

Kennedy, Anthony M., 57
knowledge values of academy, 21–23; AAUP and, 39–42; and sexual harassment policies, 155

law: on rape, 119–20; on sexual harassment, 46–66, 133–34
Lawrence, Charles, 28, 32
Levin, professor, 65
liberalism: on freedom of expression, 32–34; on role of academy, 21–24
linked offers, 9. *See also* sexual bribery

MacKinnon, Catharine A., 7, 11–12, 129–45; on expression, 37; on female/male harassment, 13; and freedom of expression, 31; Paul on, 164–66; on tort remedies, 170
males, definitions of harassment, 13
Mamet, David, 13
Mann v. University of Chicago, 265n18
Mapplethorpe, Robert, 6
marital rape, 74
Massachusetts Commission Against Discrimination, 233
Matsuda, Mari, 28, 36–37
May, Larry, 78–79, 82, 169, 177
McConnell, Michael, 42–43
Mead, Margaret, 153–54
medical ethics, versus academic ethics, 109–11
medical records, confidentiality of, 124
Meritor Savings Bank v. Vinson, 49, 180
Merit Systems Protection Board, 15
Meyers, Diana, 125
Mill, John Stuart, 21–23, 32–34, 254n50–254n51

Mischler, Linda Fitts, 102, 209–11
miscommunication: and seductive behavior, 88–89; versus sexual harassment, 185–86, 188
multiculturalism, 28, 33, 252n19, 254n52
Murillo, Anita, 46–48

National Advisory Council on Women's Educational Programs, 5
New York State Division of Human Rights, 138
non-disclosure of HIV/STD, 240–41
nondiscrimination, 22–23
nonrepression, 22–23

O'Connor, Sandra Day, 57
offense, 35–36
opportunist, harasser as, 151
opportunity. *See* equality of opportunity

partial compliance theory, 102–3
paternalism: blanket prohibitions and, 210, 261n14; opposition to, 102
Paul, Ellen Frankel, 125, 164–74, 262n2
peer harassment, 188
Pennsylvania State University, 251n1
perlocutionary force, 30–31
perspective, Department of Education on, 61–62
pervasiveness, 10–11
Pickering test, 64
Plato, *Symposium,* 105
pornography, MacKinnon on, 31
power: in academy, 187–88; and consent, 108–11; and harassment, 11–12, 175–82; MacKinnon on, 143; and sexual harassment procedures, 118–19. *See also* dominance
preferences, and consent, 109–10
prevention, policies and, 115–17
privacy: and consensual sex policies, 101; sexual harassment procedures and, 123–24, 183–90
private harasser, 149–50
professionalism, 103–4
professionals, regulations on sex with clients, 38, 209–18

psychological damage, 35
public concern, 65
public harasser, 148–49
punishment, policies and, 115–17, 124–25

quid pro quo harassment, 11, 49; MacKinnon on, 140

Rabidue v. Osceola Refining Co., 170
race, and harassment, 12, 139
radicals: on freedom of expression, 44–45; on role of academy, 27–28
rape, 9; definition of, 240; law on, 119–20; marital, 74
Rauch, Jonathan, 254n57, 255n59
Rawls, John, 102–3
reasonable comparability, 135
reasonable person standard, 14, 50, 171–72
reasonable woman standard, 61–62
Redbook, 138
religious institutions, 26, 43
remedies, 124–25; Antioch College on, 245–47; *See also* tort remedies.
repression, cultural reproduction as, 27–28
respect, 95–96
Riger, Stephanie, 14
Robinson v. Jacksonville Shipyards, 259n66
Roiphe, Katie, 261n14
role morality, 38; in campus setting, 83–85, 95–96
Rowe, Mary, 117

same-sex harassment, 14, 50; Department of Education on, 62
San Bernardino Valley College, 46
Schauer, Frederick, 31–32
Schlesinger, Arthur, 252n19
Schultz, Vicki, 262n3
seductive behavior, 7–8; prevalence of, 16; sexism and, 89–90; wrongs of, 87–90
sensationalism, 207–8
sex discrimination, 135–36, 164–74

sexism, 6; definition of, 5; as gender harassment, 91–93; Harvard University on, 226; and seductive behavior, 89–90; versus sexual harassment, 186–87
sexist speech, 7
sex object treatment, wrongs of, 177–78
sex-plus, 166–67
sex stereotyping, 178–79
sexual assault, 9–10; characteristics of, 69–70; definition of, 240; prevalence of, 16; wrongs of, 69–71
sexual bribery, 8–9, 157–63; versus consensual sex, 168–70; prevalence of, 16; versus threats, 75–79, 140–42; wrongs of, 75–79, 158–59
sexual coercion, 9, 157–63; analysis of, 159–60; Duke University on, 222; prevalence of, 16; wrongs of, 73–74. *See also* sexual bribery; sexual threats
sexual desire, in males versus females, 178–79
sexual harassment: and academy, 183–90; cases of, 142–45; conceptualizing, 4–15; versus consensual sex, 168–70, 195–99, 209–11; epidemiology of, 15–16; epistemology of, 14–15; examples of, 227–28; experience of, 137–42; images of, 146–56; issues in, 3–18; law on, 46–66, 133–34; as moral wrong, 67–85; myths regarding, 179; power and, 11–12; prevalence of, 133, 137; sex discrimination as, 135–36, 164–74; social nature of, 176–80; types of, 117; underreporting of, 138–39; warning signs of, 147–48; in work environment (*see* work harassment); wrongs of, 184
sexual harassment complaints, records of, 122–23
sexual harassment definitions, 4–5, 12, 172, 183–84; Antioch College on, 234–35; Department of Education on, 59–60; Duke University on, 221;

feminism on, 175–82; subjective
    versus objective, 180–82, 186;
    Wellesley College on, 227
sexual harassment policies and
    procedures, 44–45, 113–26; AAUP
    on, 41–42; on consensual sex, 101,
    103–4; consultative strategies for, 94,
    107; court challenges to, 47–48;
    Department of Education on, 62–63;
    examples of, 219–48; goals of,
    114–17; recommendations for,
    151–53, 189–90
sexual imposition, definition of, 240
sexuality: in academy, 68; definition of,
    5; and education, 105, 191–208;
    emphasis on, and sexual harassment,
    148; as gender harassment, 6–7,
    93–97
sexual offers. *See* sexual bribery
sexual speech, 7
sexual threats: versus bribery, 75–79,
    140–42, 157–63; prevalence of, 16;
    wrongs of, 71–75. *See also* sexual
    coercion
sexual violence, prevention of, 238
shield cases, 55
Simmel, George, 134
situation-altering utterances, 30
social context, of sexual harassment,
    133, 135–36, 176–80
Spanos, William, 27
speech: versus action, 29–32;
    classification of, 29–32, 34–35; harm
    by, 36–37
Stanford University, 44
Stevens, John Paul, 56
Straus, Murray, 260n5
substance abuse policies, 116–17
Superson, Anita M., 12–13, 175–82
Supreme Court: on freedom of
    expression, 29, 45; on Title IX, 55–58
Swift, Jonathan, 46
sword cases, 55

taboos, 153–55
Talmud, 5–6
targeted sexism, 5–7

Thomas, Clarence, 16, 181
Thomson, Judith Jarvis, 35
Title VII, Civil Rights Act, 11, 17, 25–26,
    48–52, 135–36
Title IX, Civil Rights Act, 11, 17, 26, 48,
    52–66
Tong, Rosemarie, 180
*Topol v. Trustees of the University of
    Pennsylvania,* 265n17
tort remedies, 125, 170–73, 262n2;
    criticism of, 179–81
transference, 215
trust, in campus setting, 81, 187–90
Tuana, Nancy, 78, 157–63
2 Live Crew, 6

uniqueness, 133–34
University of California: at Berkeley,
    158; sexual harassment policies and
    procedures, 44–45
University of Florida, sexual harassment
    policy, 220–21
University of Iowa, 12; sexual
    harassment policy, 103–4, 117
University of Michigan, 45
University of Michigan in Ann Arbor, 71
University of Nebraska, 6
University of New Hampshire, 5
University of Pennsylvania, 265n15
University of Texas, 92
unwelcomeness, 8, 49, 258n49;
    academy and, 183–90; Department
    of Education on, 60–61

vicarious liability for sexual harassment,
    51, 55–57; Department of Education
    on, 58–59
victims: blaming, 181; Paul on, 166, 173;
    speech and, 30; stereotyping women
    as, 179
Vinson, Mechelle, 49

Walker, Alice, 254n52
weak imperatives, 30
Weiner, Linda, 115, 146–56
Wellesley College, sexual harassment
    policy, 101, 226–33

Williams v. Saxbe, 49

Wolff, Robert Paul, 27

womanhood, 133–34

women, sexual harassment paradigms and, 164–74, 209–11

work harassment, 37, 262n3; examples of, 132–33; law on, 48–52; MacKinnon on, 129–45

Working Women United Institute, 137–38

wrongs: of gender harassment, 90–97; of seductive behavior, 87–90; of sexual assault, 69–71; of sexual bribery, 75–79; of sexual coercion, 73–74; of sexual harassment, 67–85, 184; of sexual threats, 71–75

About the Author

Leslie P. Francis is a professor of law, a professor of philosophy, and a member of the Division of Medical Ethics in the Department of Internal Medicine at the University of Utah. She received her Ph.D. in philosophy from the University of Michigan in 1974 and her J.D. from the University of Utah in 1981. She was a law clerk to Judge Abner Mikva of the United States Court of Appeals for the District of Columbia Circuit in 1981–82.

Francis specializes in ethics, bioethics, philosophy of law, health law, and legal ethics. She is the author of several articles on issues in philosophy of law, health care, and professional ethics. She is currently a member of the American Law Institute (elected 1986) of the American Bar Association's Commission on the Legal Problems of the Elderly, and she was recently appointed to a four-year term on the Medicare Coverage Advisory Committee (HCFA), on which she serves as a member of the executive committee and as vice-chair of the subcommittee on drugs, biologics, and therapeutics.